The Company We Kept

Percy Muir with a customer.

THE COMPANY WE KEPT

by Barbara Kaye
(Mrs. Percy Muir)

Barbara Kaye

WERNER SHAW LTD
26 CHARING CROSS ROAD, LONDON
in collaboration with
ELKIN MATHEWS
BLAKENEY, HOLT, NORFOLK
1986

ISBN 0 907961 04 5

Printed and bound in Great Britain
for the joint publishers, Werner
Shaw Limited, 26 Charing Cross Road
(Suite 34), London WC2H 0DH, and
Elkin Mathews, Blakeney, Holt,
Norfolk NR25 7NL, by A. Wheaton & Co.,
Ltd., Hennock Road, Exeter, Devon.
Typeset in Janson by Alacrity
Phototypesetters, Banwell Castle,
Weston-super-Mare, Avon. Jacket
design by Alan Downs.

TO THE
3RD GENERATION

HARRIET
SARA
THOMAS
MARTHA
JAMES
and
TANYA

Contents

Contents (contd.)

List of Illustrations

Spring 1938

CHAPTER ONE

After a rapid tour through our part of the house the removal man came to a halt in the hall, reflected for a moment, then said briskly: 'That'll cost yer four pun' ten. 'Nother ten bob for the rockery.'

'All right,' Percy said, 'you can have the job.'

The removal man was also our local greengrocer with a small family business in Circus Road, just round the corner. We had asked him to quote a price for moving us to the Essex village some thirty miles from London where we had bought a house. We were getting the job done on the cheap because we were going to do all the packing ourselves, not that Percy would have allowed anyone else to handle the several tea-chests of books we were taking with us, even had we been able to afford it.

The year was 1938. We were both convinced that war with Germany was not far off so we were getting out of London, with our year-old daughter, while the going was good. After months of house-hunting we had found a pair of farm workers' cottages in the process of conversion into a four-bedroomed house. It was a speculative venture by a local estate agent with an eye for picturesque properties to be converted cheaply for the growing commuter market. It stood on the edge of the village between a dreary looking farmhouse and a splendid old timbered barn.

The village straggled along the main road for more than two miles. Public services had not yet come to the part where we were to live, but the agent had assured us confidently that they would all soon be available. There was a well in the garden which he guaranteed would never run dry, and in any case we would have main water in a matter of weeks.

The conversion was far from complete when we first saw the property. Oak beams had been exposed to catch the eye of people like us, looking for old world charm. Frameless windows gaped, laths like bleached bones showed in places where the crumbling old plaster had

1

fallen away. Where there had once been a couple of cottage gardens there was only a trampled, rubbish-strewn plot. And yet it was already beginning to look like the house it must once have been before it was down-graded into old farm cottages. A pair of dormer windows looked down from the steeply pitched red-tiled roof. The tiles were at least two hundred years old and hung on the rafters with wooden pegs. At one end of the long, low frontage a wing containing the kitchen and a bedroom above extended slightly forward to break the line and was topped with a wide gable, like a coolie's hat.

Unfinished as it was it had a battered charm. Like a pretty but slovenly woman it needed smartening up. Basically it looked right to us and we bought it. Or rather the building society did.

For the previous three years we had been living in a three-storied late Victorian semi-detached villa in St. John's Wood. There was a miniscule garden in front and a walled-in strip at the back shaded by an unproductive pear tree which had been planted, though heaven knows why, by D.H. Lawrence. There Percy with a new-born enthusiasm for alpines, had built a rock garden from which he was loath to part.

Number five Acacia Road was a house with literary associations. Bram Stoker the author of *Dracula* had once lived there and during the first world war it had been, for a short time, the home of Katherine Mansfield and Middleton Murry. The D.H. Lawrences had briefly shared it with the Murrys and S.S. Kotelianski — Kot to his friends — had joined them and stayed on after the Murrys left.

Kot was a Russian Jew. He had fled to England from Kiev during the abortive uprising of 1905, joined a group of literary ex-patriates in London and managed to earn a precarious living doing translation work. During this time he met D.H. Lawrence and became one of his most devoted disciples.

When the Murrys left Number Five Kot arranged for the Farbmans, Russian friends of his, to take over the lease and take him on as their lodger. It was an arrangement that lasted some twenty years until Farbman died and his widow and daughter decided to move to a smaller house.

Faced with the almost unbearable prospect of leaving Number Five or, alternatively, of taking over a lease he could not afford, Kot decided the lesser evil was to find someone to replace the Farbmans. He disliked the idea but it was preferable to being forced to move out.

Percy and I were at that time living in a rather dismal little flat just off St. John's Wood High Street and one evening when Percy was on his way home from work he ran into Kot, whom he had known for a number of years. They had first met when Kot came to Dulau's, the antiquarian bookshop in Bond Street where Percy was then working. He had brought with him a set of *Signature*; the short-lived periodical that the Murrys and Lawrence brought out while they were at Acacia Road. By then the three issues had become a collector's item and Kot, who had also been involved in the venture, had saved a few sets from the wreck. Percy had bought the set and from then on Kot would call at Dulau's from time to time, when he needed money, with books to sell, or sometimes just for a chat. Through an introduction from Kot, Percy was able to make a trip to Russia in 1928 in the hope (which was eventually frustrated) of buying some of the treasures in famous private libraries taken over by the Communists.

Kot clutched at Percy like the proverbial straw. The outcome of this chance meeting was an invitation for us both to tea at Number Five, with a view to us taking the lease off his hands. As far as Kot was concerned Percy was a man he could talk to and a man who had always treated him fairly when he had something to sell; they were not close friends, but that was just as well. We would keep to our part of the house and Kot to his. Kot had not then met me. That he should have been willing to share a house with a young woman he didn't know and knew nothing about is a measure of how desperate he must have been, for he was already a confirmed bachelor, obsessively tidy and set in his ways. Either that or he deliberately refused to contemplate the problems that might arise.

As for me, I blithely assumed that we would all get on together splendidly. A house with a garden in a leafy residential road was bound to be an improvement on our dark and pokey flat; if it meant taking on an elderly Russian as a lodger the prospect wasn't going to deter me, or even worry me. I was young, happy to be living in London with Percy (we had been together less than two years) and of an optimistic temperament. I was also intrigued by the literary associations, for my own ambition was to be a writer.

Kot's habits were frugal; his way of life to me, at least, was spartan. He enjoyed entertaining his friends to tea, but only in ones and twos. Invited into his sparsely furnished living room, one sat at a scrubbed-top kitchen table on a cushionless windsor chair. The floor was covered with polished brown lino and, in winter, the heat was from a small gas fire. The tea would be weak, the tea service a dainty pink and white porcelain and there would be a plate of sweet biscuits, but no cake. Kot was nearing sixty when we went to live at Number Five, heavily built and sallow skinned with a mop of grizzled black hair. Deep lines ran from his large nose to his long upper lip; his eyes were dark and expressive under thick brows. Although he could laugh with gusto, his mouth more often turned down in gloom, or disgust, and his habitual expression was sombre.

Women took to him; far more women than men came to visit him. His manner with them was warm and welcoming, but authoritative; if it was occasionally playful, it was a dignified, leonine playfulness. As Percy wrote a stream of women were in regular attendance on Kot. In our day they included the Dowager Lady Glenavy, Marjorie Wells H.G.'s daughter-in-law, the poet Ruth Pitter and the pretty widow of Mark Gertler, the artist. They would be invited, individually, to tea and, as Kot would say, to gossip.

I was rather overawed by Kot when we went to see the house. As he took us through the rooms we were left in no doubt as to his intention to retain the two best ones, on the ground floor. We were offered the two on the floor bove, two little attics on the second floor and a below-stairs room with a french window opening on to stone steps leading up to the back garden. This room had once, briefly, served as the editorial office for the short-lived *Signature*. When we had stripped off the navy blue paint it made a tolerable dining-room. The old-fashioned semi-basement kitchen, the small scullery and the bathroom on the half-landing were all to be shared.

Kot was courteous to me but addressed himself to Percy. No doubt I seemed to him young and flighty and he assumed the decision was to be Percy's. But had I not liked the idea of sharing a house with Kot, Percy would never have attempted to make me change my mind.

The lease was transferred to us the following month. The rent was £350 a year and it was agreed that Kot should pay us £2 a week for his rooms. We moved in and everyone was happy, or so we thought. If Kot had begun to have misgivings he kept them to himself.

At first all went well. I had a job and delegated our responsibility for the cleaning of the shared parts of the house to a char, a cheerful little cockney woman. Kot had said from the start that he always cleaned his rooms himself. As I was out all day we only met in the evening when Kot came into the kitchen to cook his evening meal.

It was his invariable habit to fry a piece of steak for his supper, which he ate with one slice of bread, but no vegetables. More often than not his appearance in our shared kitchen promptly at seven o'clock coincided with my own preparations for Percy's and my evening meal. I would have saucepans bubbling on the gas cooker, meat roasting or sizzling under the grill, pastry ready to be popped into the oven, when Kot appeared, nostrils distended in disgust.

With his piece of steak in one hand, his frying pan in the other he would advance on the gas cooker, as of right.

'*Ten* minutes, Ba-ba-ra,' he would say, his voice deep with gloom. 'Only *ten* minutes.'

I never dared to ask him to wait, even for a couple of minutes. I would shift my saucepans to make room for his frying pan and retreat, hovering in the background until his steak was done. As he cooked it his glance would travel over my clutter of mixing basins, pastry board and spilled flour on our shared kitchen table and he would sigh heavily.

'When Mrs *Farbman* did her cooking the kitchen was like a *laboratory*,' he told me reprovingly, one evening. My offer to cook his steak had already been turned down firmly. I knew I had been measured against Mrs Farbman and found wanting.

As the days went by the atmosphere in the kitchen became increasingly charged. Finally, one evening when Percy came home from work Kot intercepted him in the hall.

'May I have a word with you, Muir?'

I was told later what had been decided. Kot was to have the kitchen all to himself and I was to have the small, chilly scullery. It seemed that sharing with me had reduced him to such a state of nerves that he couldn't bear it any longer. As a sop he offered to let me have the gas cooker moved into the scullery and he would manage with a couple of rings.

'I had to agree,' Percy told me apologetically. 'He was in such a state about the kitchen. He said he couldn't go on any longer ...'

Kot was good at getting his own way. Percy might be legally the leaseholder, but Number Five was still Kot's house.

After that, our below-stairs contact was confined to Kot's need to wash up his evening meal at the communal sink in my kitchen-cum-scullery.

'Just *two* minutes,' he would say, moving to the sink. And I would stand aside while he carefully washed a plate, knife and fork, cup and saucer and frying pan.

We also shared a telephone. In those days when local calls were the same price during the twenty-four hours, Kot's calls would be almost always matutinal, protracted and usually in Russian.

'Da, da,' I would hear him say, from the hall, in his deep, gravelly voice. Or, more often and decidedly: 'Niet!' These were the only Russian words I ever made out. Although we paid the rent Kot's attitude to the telephone was as proprietorial as it was to the kitchen. Because it stood in the front hall, close to his sitting room, when it rang he usually reached it first.

'It is for me, I think,' he would say, picking up the receiver as I came dashing down the stairs at the sound of the bell.

The Farbmans had left some pieces of unwanted furniture in the rooms we took over, mostly of poor quality. They included a double bed with a cheap oak head and foot board, a broken spring and a lumpy mattress. We wasted no time in getting a junk man to collect this, along with some other bits and pieces.

Disturbed by a noise on the stairs Kot emerged from his sitting room and standing in the doorway watched, long-faced, as the bed was unceremoniously carried away.

When it had gone he said to me sorrowfully: 'That was Katherine Mansfield's bed.' From the way he spoke we might have desecrated her tomb. I explained, apologetically, that we hadn't known. Not that we would have kept it if we had. Shaking his head at such unfeeling behaviour Kot had gone back into his room in silence. I realised that we had wounded him, however unintentionally, and felt guilty.

Poor Kot. He had been deeply in love with Katherine Mansfield; he had kept her letters to him, refusing generous offers for them, hard up though he was. To him it was unforgivable that Middleton Murry should have made money out of the publication of Katherine's correspondence. Kot's dislike of Murry was so great that he could not bring himself to utter his name, referring to him either as 'that blighter,' or as 'Smerdyaskov' a character in *The Brothers Karasamov*.

When, usually about once a month, he invited us to take tea with him he would use the occasion to hold forth against Murry.

'Did you see, Muir? That blighter has written another book?' Many years later Percy was to buy Middleton Murry's books from his widow and third wife. By then there was practically nothing by Katherine Mansfield left.

Kot told me once that D. H. Lawrence had taught him that a man should be able to do his own washing and ironing. This lesson had been taken to heart and once a week he would take possession of the bathroom and remain in occupation for most of the morning, soaking his clothes and household washing in the bath. Subsequently the garden would be half hidden behind a long clothes line, tied at one end to D. H. Lawrence's pear tree (perhaps that had been why he had planted it) and hung with a sheet and pillow slip, towels, shirts and pyjamas.

Mostly we went along with Kot's quirks, though occasionally not all the way. There was the problem of his aversion to the smell of hot mutton or lamb fat. Neither Percy nor I were prepared to forgo our joints of roast lamb, or our mutton chops, but in an attempt to prevent this smell from percolating through to Kot's rooms I would cook with the door into the passage closed and the windows open. This seldom worked.

'Ba-ba-ra, you are cooking *mutton*,' he would say appearing in the doorway accusingly, nostrils distended in disgust. 'The *smell* of it comes all through the house.'

'I'm sorry, Kot. It's nearly cooked now. Look, I'll keep the back door open.'

It was never any good trying to appease him. He would shake his head reproachfully, don his black cloak and broad-brimmed black hat and stomp gloomily out of the house, as if I'd deliberately driven him into the night. Sometimes it would be raining and I'd feel it was all my fault.

Kot had few men friends; the only one who visited him regularly while we were at Number Five was James Stephens, the Irish poet and author. He was a little gnome of a man with a beguiling Irish voice. He would call in the evening, coming invariably on a bus from King's Cross. According to Kot, wherever he was staying in London he would have to come to Acacia Road via King's Cross Station because that was the only route he could manage to remember.

I would sometimes open the door to James Stephens and try to keep him talking for a few minutes, for I had long delighted in his books, but Kot would appear all too quickly and whisk Stephens away into his sitting room. Kot never invited us to meet his friends, nor did they meet other friends of his at Number Five. He liked to keep people in separate compartments; or perhaps it was that he wanted their exclusive attention. When Percy and I were invited to tea once a month the talk would be almost entirely of books and writers, for Kot liked to hear from Percy which modern authors were being collected. As a reader for the Cresset Press this was, naturally, of interest to him.

While we were living at Number Five he was working on a translation of the plays and short stories of Tchekhov for the Everyman Edition. Occasionally, stuck for an elusive word, he would appeal to me for help. Standing in the hall manuscript in hand, he would call up the stairs: 'Ba-ba-ra!' Never would he come into our sitting room.

Towards the end of our three years in Acacia Road Kot had a minor heart attack and began to slow up and grow more melancholy. While not complaining in so many words he would sometimes press his hand dramatically over his heart, especially if he met me rushing up the stairs when he was descending them from the bathroom.

When I became pregnant and after a time gave up my job Kot and I saw more of each other. We would stand chatting in the hall, or on the half-landing by the bathroom door when he was soaking his laundry in the bath and I was waiting for the chance to go in, the bathroom being also the lavatory. When in a good mood he enjoyed a chat; an unfailing topic of conversation was the behaviour of the orthodox Jewish family next door, 'the mad ones' as Kot called them. The family consisted of a shrivelled, ill-tempered old woman and her three daughters, one of whom was clearly off her head and in the habit of letting out blood-curdling screams.

The eldest, a harmless simple-minded creature, would sometimes come to our door asking if we would change florins or half-crowns into shillings for their gas meter. Kot was always kind and helpful to her, believing her to be ill-treated by a cruel mother.

During my pregnancy I had wondered rather uneasily if Kot would be able to put up with a baby in the house. I need not have worried. When I came home from the maternity home with my fair-haired, blue eyed little daughter Kot was instantly captivated, calling her 'the little princess'.

After the birth of my daughter I tried to snatch an hour or so each day at my typewriter. We were saving to buy a house and writing was a way of making a little pin money. A friend who was editing the Woman's Page of a Sunday newspaper paid me to do some 'ghosting' for her and Dennis Wheatley, out of the kindness of his heart, gave me some of his typing to do. I was also typing articles for Percy.

From my window overlooking the back garden, as I sat at the typewriter, I would see Kot walk softly across the lawn to the pram in the shade of the pear tree. He would stand, gazing down at the baby; if she was awake he would croon to her or dangle some trinket to amuse her. For all his easily aroused ire against bureaucrats, decryers of the genius of D.H. Lawrence and literary Johnny-come-latelys, Kot was a gentle, tender-hearted man.

We had warned him that we were planning to move to the country and when, early in 1938, we found a house we could afford and told him so, he said little. There were still two years of the lease to run. He said he wished it to be assigned to him when we left, although the rent was more than he could afford. We gave him plenty of time to find someone to take our place, but he said that he preferred to live alone. Perhaps he believed that it would not be for long, for he was increasingly gloomy and preoccupied with his health.

When the day came for us to leave Kot remained behind closed doors while the greengrocer and his mate tramped up and down the stairs carrying out our belongings, including Katherine Mansfield's wash-stand, to the van. I knew Kot was hating the commotion. His gloomy silence those last few days had told us he considered that we were deserting him. Worse still, we were taking away his 'little princess'.

After we had seen the van drive away and had stowed our personal

Kot and Barbara with Helen at 5 Acacia Road in 1937.

luggage into the car, along with Helen in her Karricot, he came out of his sitting room to see us off. Beside Helen on the back seat was my black tom cat, mewing miserably from his basket. That was certainly one member of our family Kot wouldn't miss. He had always disliked it, complaining, not without truth, that it made the house smell.

'Good-bye Kot,' we said. 'We'll come and visit you soon.'

He bade us good-bye heavily, though with a tender smile for Helen. As we drove away I looked back and saw him still standing on the top of the steps, looking like an Old Testament prophet, his hand raised in farewell.

Would he miss us? Perhaps, but he hadn't said he would.

For our part we were eager to be on our way. We were to have a house of our own at last — and all to ourselves. At least, that was what we thought then.

CHAPTER TWO

The first time I saw Percy he was with Francis Meynell. I was playing tennis when they came into my view strolling along a path overlooking the court, two tall, good-looking men in flannels, deep in conversation. They paused briefly to watch the game, but it didn't hold their interest and they strolled on out of sight. My own interest was aroused; I was sure I hadn't seen them before and I asked my partner who they were.

Francis Meynell, I learnt, had come over from Toppesfield a few miles away to play in a village cricket match. Percy Muir, said my partner, rented a cottage at Great Bardfield and usually came from London for the week-ends. His wife was fond of tennis and they would sometimes come to the Hall for a game.

The name Meynell meant nothing to me then, nor would I have been any the wiser had I been told he owned The Nonesuch Press, for at that time my ignorance of fine printing and limited editions was total. But the name Muir had cropped up several times since my solicitor husband and I had been coming to Little Bardfield Hall where a rather raffish set would gather at week-ends for tennis or squash, drinking, philandering and bathing in the swimming pool. The hall was owned by a wealthy retired antique dealer, a hospitable but lecherous old man, who liked to see young women in scanty swim suits disporting themselves in and around his pool — and pounced if given half a chance.

'You must meet Percy Muir,' I had been told. 'Interesting chap — clever, knows a lot about books ... speaks German and goes off to Austria on walking tours.

When we did meet, at a local party, Percy struck me at once as far more mature and knowledgeable than anyone else in the Bardfield circle. He was then thirty-eight, well built and broad-shouldered, with an erect bearing that made him appear taller than his height of less than six foot. His eyes were grey and wide-set, his mouth sensitive but resolute; a high broad forehead dominated a face thoughtful in repose, expressive in conversation.

As a clever, studious boy from a home where money had usually been short, his aim had been to acquire knowledge rather than worldly goods. Gifted with an excellent memory, learning had come easily to

11

him and he had never quite forgiven his mother for taking him away from grammar school to work as an office boy for a paint manufacturer, instead of letting him try for a university scholarship. His father had had little say in the matter.

After service in the London Scottish during the first world war (he had volunteered in 1914) he set himself to catch up on the studies he had missed, by intensive reading and attending classes at the Working Men's College at Toynbee Hall, where several of the tutors became his friends, including C. E. Joad. The discipline of study he imposed upon himself at this time was to serve him in good stead as a bibliographer.

A year on the music hall circuit, teamed up with a 'pro' from his army days, was enough to convince him that despite modest success life on the boards was not for him. But the year brought bonuses; it developed his natural talent as a raconteur and while his fellow troupers played whist, drank or slept it off, he was buying books in the street markets and second-hand shops which were eventually to start him off in his career as an antiquarian bookseller.

Although born in London Percy was more of a Scot than a Cockney, living by the high standards and principles of his Scottish forebears. Any form of cheating was an anathema to him; so was disloyalty. Those who cheated him once were not given a second chance. Beneath this self-imposed discipline was a man both sensitive and passionate, with emotions easily stirred, especially by music.

He talked fluently in a resonant baritone with no noticeable accent, often with humour; and people would listen. In congenial company he laughed easily, but if the conversation was only gossip and chit-chat he would say little, politely concealing his boredom.

The party was convivial that evening when we first met. We had little chance to talk together, but we were very much aware of each other. The evening ended in a sing-song as such evenings often did. As we stood round the piano I listened to his warm, strong baritone, easily heard above the rest, and watched his face light up with enjoyment. That was the beginning.

From that beginning, in the summer of 1932, here we were, driving out of London in our Lancia tourer to start a new life together in the country.

In those days few Londoners in our income bracket owned a car. Public transport was cheap, buses came by every few minutes; taxis were everywhere and relatively inexpensive. But as a commuter Percy was going to need a car, and a couple of weeks before the move he set off with the intention of buying a second-hand runabout, a Morris or a Ford.

The Italian dealer he consulted knew at once just the sort of car he really wanted, and abracadabra there she was — a raffish aristocrat of a car, with a long, greyhound-grey body that had seen better days.

'I would lika keep her for myself,' the dealer said, 'but — ' with an expressive shrug, 'business ees not good so, for a gentleman lika yourself I maka a special price.'

At the special price of £24 the bargain was irresistable. There was just 'a leetle work' to be done to the car and Percy, having paid a deposit, was asked to call the following week. When he did so the car was nowhere to be seen. Annoyed, he was walking away when the dealer drove up, in the Lancia.

'Hey!' Percy cried indignantly. 'What are you doing driving around in my car?'

Not a whit disconcerted the Italian got out of the Lancia, smiling broadly: 'Plees, I explain. To-day I must go to see my bank manager, you understand? So, I take da best car in my garage. Your car, yes?'

The Lancia proved a pleasure to drive and, though often a devil to start when cold, we never regretted buying her.

The first time we had seen the two dilapidated cottages which were to become our home for more than thirty years, the asking price was £450. Having exposed the old timbers and fireplaces, the enterprising agent who had bought the cottages as condemned property, was ready either to make a quick profit or, failing a buyer, to carry on with the conversion; in which case, he told us, the price would be £960.

'If you would like us to do the work we would be quite willing to fall in with your wishes as regards fittings and decoration,' he offered temptingly. 'And you would be able to come as often as you liked to see how the work was going.'

We thought it a reasonable proposition and fell for it. We found a building society willing, in principle, to grant us a mortgage of 75% and our savings would just about fill the gap. We had, as we later realised, trustingly given the agent the green light to complete the conversion as cheaply as possible, using cut-price materials and cut-price labour.

During the winter of '37/38 I had to be content with Percy's reports on progress, for without a car it meant a tedious journey by train and bus, with babe in arms.

'It's coming on nicely,' he would say, 'They've laid the floor in the kitchen.' Or — 'They've started on the bathroom.'

Eventually, a month before we were due to take possession, I left the baby with my mother-in-law and went to see for myself. On our arrival at the house, reached through mud and rubble, I barely looked into the

Taylors, part modernised, 1937.

sitting room and dining room before making my way to the kitchen. I wasn't expecting to find a bride's dream kitchen, glittering with stainless steel and shiny with ceramic tiles, but I was hoping for something approaching it.

The builder, who had agreed to meet us on the premises, and was being extremely affable, followed me. He was a biggish man and the ceiling was only a few inches above his balding head. I remembered it being quite a small room, only ten foot by ten. The floor still had the old, rough quarry tiles, the glaze long since scrubbed away, and although newly plastered the walls still bulged. There was a square earthenware sink and wooden draining-board; beside it the smallest possible Ideal boiler. Apart from this modest equipment the kitchen was empty. There was no means of cooking, no working surfaces, no storage space. The only cupboard was under the sink.

I looked around bewildered and dismayed. My dream kitchen had vanished like a mirage. 'But how am I going to cook?'

'Well, we reckoned you'd be usin' oil. That's what most folks around here use, bein' they've not got one o' them old kitcheners. There's an oil man come by every week.'

There had been oil stoves in the kitchen when I was a child, smelly

Beatrice stoves, brought into use when the kitchen range was left unlit during the heat of the summer. I had always hated the smell of paraffin. As there were neither gas mains nor a main electricity supply at our end of the village I had expected a solid-fuel cooker and said as much.

The builder fished the plans from his pocket and spread them out on the draining board. With a stubby finger he showed me that they did not include any provision for cooking, nor for cupboards or working surfaces. It was the first time I had seen that set of plans.

Sink units, wall cupboards and formica-topped working surfaces were not regarded as essential for housewives at that time, but in the kitchens of my childhood there had always been a painted pine dresser, with racks for plates and commodious drawers, and walk-in cupboards for saucepans, dishes and groceries.

I said I must have a solid-fuel stove that would heat the water as well, and he could take his Ideal boiler away. He tried to talk me out of it; there was, as we were to find out, a very good reason for this.

Before I went home I did get my own way over one glaring omission from the plans. I asked to be shown the airing-cupboard. The builder fished out the much creased plans.

'There's nothing about an airing-cupboard,' he said.

I said there must be. I wasn't going to share my sitting room fire with damp nappies. 'It's an essential in any house,' I insisted. 'As you're putting a hot water tank in the second bedroom you can build a cupboard around it.'

I could see he thought I was bringing new fangled ideas from London, but a threat to take up the matter with the agent brought me a grudging promise that he'd see what he could do. I did get my airing-cupboard, but we had to pay for our solid-fuel cooker.

These problems were all in the past as we drove along the A.11, with a fast run to Epping after Woodford Green, where the beech trees were already in bud; on through Harlow, peacefully unaware of its pioneering future, then the turn off to Hatfield Heath with its picture postcard green where white goats browsed and village cricket matches were held. From the green we wound through narrow lanes along the edges of Hatfield Forest to reach the A.120 and Takeley Street, a stretch of the old Stane Street, the one-time Roman road to Colchester.

Then it was only a couple of minutes before we drew up outside the old five-barred farm gate that the builder had used (because it was lying around) for the entry to the house we were to call 'Taylors' up-grading it, we felt, from 'Taylor's Farm Cottages'.

There it was! We gazed at it happily, the sort of picturesque cottagey house that makes Americans reach for their cameras. Cream-washed, the windows lattice-paned, the steep-pitched roof with its mellow old peg-tiles that had lasted more than 200 years, and the solid oak front door; it looked as friendly and welcoming as anyone could wish. Old, but no longer decrepit; three hundred years, perhaps? No one could be sure.

With broken bricks, left by the builder, Percy had laboriously laid the driveway from the gate to the garage. The effect was agreeable, not unlike French pavé, and about as uneven. Weeds were soon to grow up through the crevices, but the surface was to last out our time.

Only the cottage garden was lacking and the honeysuckle around the door. There was, in fact, no garden at all, not even a patch of grass, only a mound of rubble the builder hadn't bothered to clear away — and never did — and the straggling remains of a privet hedge.

We had arrived well ahead of the furniture van, with time to picnic in the empty dining room before it became full of packing cases, furniture and strewn newspaper. It was a bright March day, shafts of sunshine came through the curtainless windows, making patches on the red-tiled floor. While waiting for the van I left the cat to keep Helen company and as Percy collected firewood I wandered through the empty, airy rooms, delighting in each one and in a dream come true.

The rooms looked north and south; the sitting room was at one end of the house, the kitchen at the other end. In the middle was the all-purpose dining-room cum play-room, the heart of the house, with doors opening into the kitchen, the bathroom, back garden and the small, narrow entrance hall. From this room a twisting oak staircase went up to a tiny landing, leading to a small single bedroom and a double-bedroom with a fine open fire-place — unusual for a small house of the period. Leading off this room was a smaller bedroom we had earmarked as the nursery. From the sitting room, on the other side of the house, another staircase led to a second double-bedroom.

A big central chimney determined the separation of this fourth bedroom from the other three. It was a minor inconvenience that we accepted with the many others that we were to discover. It could have been overcome, and eventually it was, but only by our successors.

In every room one was conscious of the structure of the house; the ceilings were ribbed with oak beams, the walls studded with them; in one bedroom they made an arch across the room. In another bedroom the floor rose into a slight hump so that anything dropped promptly rolled away, to hide maddeningly under some piece of furniture. The builder had left the doorways as they were, no problem for anyone under five foot nine. Anyone taller needed to duck; usually they thought of it too late.

Starry-eyed about our new home as we were, we admitted it had its inconveniences, but like an eccentric yet lovable character, its charms persuaded us to over-look its deficiencies. Although it played us plenty of maddening tricks, we never quite fell out of love with it.

Eventually, rather later than we had expected, the removal van arrived. The cat, by then, had been let out of its basket and, deeply suspicious, it had retreated to a corner to sulk.

The appearance of two men bearing pieces of furniture must have seemed to it the last straw. Taking one look at them it shot up the big, open chimney.

Percy had been about to light a fire and wasn't pleased at having to wait for the cat to descend. When I peered up the chimney two yellow orbs glared down at me from a tiny ledge half way up to a patch of sky. Soft calls of 'puss, puss' had no effect, nor did offers of food. Thoroughly fed-up with the incomprehensible business of moving home, it was not to be tempted from its sooty refuge.

Meantime the removal men needed directing.

'Where d'yer want this 'ere to go, Lidy?'

We had it all worked out; everything was fitting in nicely until they brought in the painted Bavarian wardrobe, a curious piece of furniture that looked as if it had come out of a scene from *Hansel and Gretel*. It had a central panel of rather grubby lilies on a wide door which was fitted with a heavy lock and an enormous key. It had belonged to Percy's first wife who had sensibly left it behind. I had no more liking for it than Percy had for my cat, so that when the men pointed out the impossibility of getting it up either of the narrow twisting staircases, I said we could settle the problem by letting them take it back to London to be sold.

Percy demurred. 'Why can't it go in the kitchen?'

I wasn't keen, but I couldn't deny that there was room for it, and since Percy was determined not to part with it, the kitchen was a better home for it than the sitting room. So that was where it went, on a strictly temporary basis, and there it remained for years, fitted with shelves and doing service as a store cupboard, albeit a very inconvenient one.

'You're not going to get this 'ere box-spring mattress up them stairs, either,' said the greengrocer. Unlike modern box mattresses it was in one piece with no middle hinge.

'Well we've got to have a bed in our bedroom,' I said, 'even if the wardrobe stays downstairs.'

The greengrocer's mate thought it might just go through the window. A ladder was fetched, the central pillar of the casement was removed, a rope was slung and there was much struggling and heaving. All to no avail. There was only one thing left to do. The farmer's wife next door lent us a saw and we sawed the frame in half.

Folded into two it could just be squeezed through the window; there was then a fresh problem; set up on its four feet, its unsupported midriff promptly sank to the floor.

The greengrocer suggested bricks as suitable props, but Percy had a simpler solution to hand. A few books piled up on either side served the purpose very well, and continued to do so for weeks to come.

Up the ladder and through a window was the way most of the furniture reached the bedrooms, which didn't do the windows much good. In the sitting room tea-chests full of books were ranged against the walls, for bookshelves had yet to be made. As the last of the chests was being carried in a little girl came through the gate, carrying a tin tray bearing a teapot, milk, sugar and four cups and saucers.

'Mum said she thought you and the men might like a cup of tea,' she said shyly, as I went to meet her.

Her mother was the kindly, comely woman, who had cleaned up the house for us, after the builders left. This was the family who had lived in the larger of the two cottages that was now our house, and had moved for greater comfort into one of the two identical lodges a couple of hundred yards along the road.

The lodges stood opposite each other at the entrance to what had once been the drive to an imposing mansion. Now they were all that remained to testify to past grandeur. The drive had become a rutted farm lane, the trees that had lined it had been cut down for timber, the pair of fine wrought iron gates which had remained for a few years after the mansion had been demolished, had finally been sold. But the lodges were solidly built and were going to last for many more years.

The pot of tea was a kindly welcome and in the tradition of good-neighbourliness that we were to find in the village. The two removal men drank theirs gratefully and departed. With a little more coaxing the cat decided it was safe to descend and Percy soon had a fire blazing on the brick hearth.

To fetch drinking water from the pump up the road was a novelty, rather than a bore. For household water we had our own well, pumped up by hand. At least we had electric light; at the touch of a wall switch our generator started up. It was an A.C. model, petrol driven, and had cost twice as much as the D.C. paraffin fuelled model Percy had intended to buy. But I was anxious to have a generator that would allow me to use my vacuum cleaner and electric iron and thought the extra money well spent. Time was to prove me wrong.

We were blissfully happy that first evening, sitting tired but content beside a blazing log fire, the flames throwing shadows on the white, oak-studded walls, before we climbed the twisting little staircase to a bedroom that looked over fields without a house in sight. In the little room next door our daughter, tired out, was fast asleep in her cot and the cat, having finally accepted the situation, had curled up on a chair.

We had cooked a meal of sorts and unpacked the essentials. Time enough, we said, to get things straight on the morrow. There was still Sunday before Percy caught the commuters' train to London.

Since freeing ourselves from our former matrimonial partners after much difficulty, heart-searching and expense, we had had five years of living in different parts of London. We had surmounted various hurdles, including the libel action which had made Percy bankrupt and a crisis in the affairs of Percy's firm, Elkin Mathews, when it looked as if the business could not survive. Now we were looking forward to a peaceful and more stable life in the country.

It was the twelfth of March, 1938 and German troops and tanks were already converging on Vienna.

CHAPTER THREE

In the morning 'the boy Jones' reported for duty. He had been re-commended to us for the tedious job of pumping the water from our well to the storage tank in the roof. His father, we were told, was doing twelve months, there were six mouths to feed at home and his mum would be pleased for him to earn a few pence a day.

We'd been advised that sixpence an hour was a fair wage for a boy of twelve. It was boring work, but not arduous. All he had to do was stand in the stone-floored passage between the kitchen and the back door and move a pump handle back and forth until water spouted out of the overflow, indicating that the tank was full. This operation took about an hour.

He was a glum-looking lad with nothing to say for himself, and I soon gave up trying to talk to him. For a while he did turn up fairly regularly; if he failed to arrive I would, perforce, do the job myself, for by then Percy would be on his way to London and if no one pumped up the water the taps would run dry half way through the morning.

I found it quite easy to do the pumping whilst reading a book. The snag was that I'd become so absorbed that I'd forget to watch for the overflow, and the backyard would be awash before I'd become aware that it was time to stop pumping. After a while Percy discovered that Gamages (then in Holborn) was selling a small electrically powered pump designed to operate fountains in garden pools.

The salesman was dubious as to whether it was powerful enough for our purpose, but as it only cost £5 and Percy was easily tempted by mechanical gadgets (although far from being mechanically minded), he took a chance and bought one. To everyone's surprise it worked splendidly and the boy Jones became redundant.

The news of the *Anschluss* shocked and depressed us, Percy espec-ially, for he had fallen in love with Austria on his first visit there in 1929 in company with Ian Fleming. Ian, who was then a Reuter corres-pondent, had introduced Percy into his circle of friends in Kitzbühel and Percy had immediately been captivated by the women, the music and the wine — and the shoulder-shrugging attitude to life's problems amongst the young people he met, so much in contrast to his own fundamentally serious nature.

Thereafter he had gone almost every year — to Vienna to buy books and later first editions of music, to Innsbruck and Kitzbühel for holidays. And we had happily gone there together. To think of the Nazis in control sickened us both. But a move concentrates the mind on the present. World events, however shocking, take a back place when it comes to the need to put up a bathroom mirror or a book-shelf. Apart from getting things straight in the house and several hundred books on to shelves, we were both longing to tackle the garden.

As far as Percy was concerned this could only be done at the week-end, for he was now a commuter with an hour's journey at each end of his working day. Never one for early rising he had no intention of joining the usual scramble for a seat on the eight-ten, the so-called fast train from Bishop's Stortford to Liverpool Street; instead he settled for the stockbroker's 8.55 which enabled him to be in Duke Street, to where Elkin Mathews had recently moved, by 10 a.m. by which time the staff of three would have opened up. As for Percy's partner, Greville Worthington, the time was past when his presence could be expected at any regular time.

Greville was a lovable character and a loyal friend, but as Percy wrote in *Minding my own Business*, he never quite grew up. He had first joined the firm in 1927 and put into it a considerable amount of money. A few years later, after failing in an attempt to take over the company, he had resigned in disgust with, as Percy had thought, no intention of ever setting foot on the premises again. But Percy never lost touch with him and in 1936, when the firm was threatened with liquidation, Greville reappeared upon the scene with an offer for the business which Lord Cranbrook, then the major shareholder, was glad enough to accept. There was one condition; that Percy should agree to be managing director.

Not without some misgivings Percy did agree. Of the partners who had been present when Greville had been out-manoeuvred by A. W. Evans, then managing director, Percy was the only one left. A third partner was required by the firm's Articles of Association, so Ian Fleming, a friend of both Greville's and Percy's was invited to become a non-executive director.

This was Greville's third venture as an antiquarian bookseller and it was to last an even shorter time than his two previous spells of bookselling. He had energy and ability and a native shrewdness with money, but no staying power. Despite the side-whiskers he sported and his considerable height (once marked on the wall of the Spread Eagle Inn at Thame as 6ft. 5ins. plus) there was something of the over-grown school-boy about his appearance. His light brown hair was unruly, his

Greville Worthington, about 1936.

moustache bushy and unclipped, his eyes screwed up easily in amusement. Whether or not one shared his enthusiasms for taking part in the London to Brighton veteran car run, or for playing old seventy-eights on ancient phonographs, one couldn't help but find this trait engaging.

One enthusiasm he shared with Percy was for visiting music halls in the less salubrious parts of London and there was the occasion when, to Greville's delight, Percy introduced him to Kitty O'Shea, with whom Percy had once played in pantomime.

On another occasion when I went along with them to some long since closed-down hall, Greville warned us that if the orchestra played Gershwin's *Rhapsody in Blue* he would walk out, to show his disapproval of what he considered to be 'bogus' jazz.

I didn't believe him but when, after the interval, the first wails of the trumpets heralded this piece Greville immediately rose to his feet and, with a grin at Percy, stalked out.

When Percy and I were married at St. Marylebone Registrar's Office the Worthingtons gave us a wedding luncheon at their London house.

After lunch Greville announced that he was going to the Jermyn Street Turkish Baths.

'Why not come along, old boy?'

When Percy admitted to never having taken a Turkish Bath, Greville insisted on whisking him off to try this new and, to Greville, delightful experience. They were gone for two hours, leaving me with Diana uneasily wondering when he would return and in what sort of state. Eventually they reappeared with Percy looking as if he had been put through a mangle, while Greville was his usual buoyant self.

At the time of our move to Essex Percy was facing the prospect of another move, for Elkin Mathews' premises in Grosvenor Street were scheduled for demolition. With the firm still struggling to survive finding alternative premises at a rent we could afford wasn't easy. Meanwhile there was a Spring Catalogue to be prepared which would include a number of first editions of music by famous composers. This was a side of the business which was proving increasingly successful and, as far as the U.K. trade was concerned, there was little serious competition.

In 1934 Percy had returned from a buying trip in Germany with first editions of Beethoven (including the 'Emperor' Concerto in its 18 separate parts), Brahms, Berlioz, Chopin, Liszt, Mozart and other important composers. They had been surprisingly cheap to buy and he had catalogued them correspondingly modestly to try out the market. The 'Emperor' priced at £15 didn't sell but some of the sonatas and many of the Brahms and Chopin items did, at anything from 25/- to £2.

After this encouraging start music was to feature frequently in Elkin Mathews' catalogues, until the war brought to an end Percy's buying trips in Germany.

Another section of the Spring 1938 Catalogue offered a collection of Communist books and pamphlets, many of them concerning the progress of the Movement in Germany. Even to possess such material was a criminal offence in Hitler's Germany, so their Jewish owner was happy to sell them, especially as the money was to be paid into a London bank account to await his arrival in the U.K. Amongst them was a pamphlet by Rosa Luxembourg calling for a general strike — the strike which began the Spartacist revolution in 1918. Priced at 12s. 6d. it looked a bargain. A run of the suppressed *Kommunistiche International* with contributions by Lenin was another item in the catalogue — price £2. 10s. But at that time 20th century social history was a subject practically ignored by the book trade.

We had smuggled most of it out while in the guise of holiday tourists, with rucksacks on our backs. To be caught with such subversive 'literature' on us could have proved unpleasant. On one occasion when we crossed the frontier into France my waistline was thickened by a wad of pamphlets wedged under my girdle.

It had been the firm's policy, since the early 1920s, to be ahead of its time. Prices in the catalogue were aimed at enterprising collectors hoping to get in on the ground floor. One who did so was Ian Fleming, who put himself in Percy's hands. He wanted, he said, to collect 'books that made things happen', and he left it to Percy to suggest suitable titles.

Gerald Coke,* like Ian an old Etonian, was bent on collecting music, in particular Handel. He too, looked to Percy to find him what he wanted. It was fortunate for the firm that both could afford to indulge their tastes at a time when the trade was still struggling out of the Depression.

The move out of London meant adjustment for us both — a longish train journey for Percy, instead of a walk through Regent's Park and a bus up Bond Street — and for me a long day on my own without the possibility of dropping in at 78, Grosvenor Street, where I had enjoyed meeting the colleagues and collectors who would sometimes forgather at closing time. Like other commuter's wives, if I wanted the car to go shopping I had to bestir myself in order to accompany Percy to the station. This spelt *angst* for both of us. Percy was punctual by nature; I tried to be, not always successfully. His aim was to be on the platform at least ten minutes before the train was due to depart. I liked to arrive with a couple of minutes to spare.

I was willing, in theory at least, to accept his deadline for leaving the house. In practice I found this almost impossible. While he sat in the car, shouting at intervals that he would go without me, I would be tearing around the house searching for shopping bag, shopping list, or money. Somehow he always caught the train. Having the car for shopping meant meeting the train in the evening (shared transport didn't happen until war-time) which entailed more *angst*, for the Lancia proved to be a temperamental starter.

I would rush out, jump into the car and impatiently press my foot on the self-starter pedal. There would be a soprano whine, which would steadily descend the scale to a grudging baritone, and still the engine refused to fire. Cursing, I would jump out, grab the starting handle and jerk it upwards with all the strength I could muster. After a good deal of

---

* The Coke Handel Collection is now world famous. In the preface to a catalogue of the 1985 exhibition, held at Jenkyn Place, Bentley, Hampshire, Gerald Coke pays a generous tribute to Percy Muir's help in the formation of the collection.

expenditure of energy on my part there would come the welcome sound of the engine running, and putting my foot hard down I would manage to arrive in the station yard as the passengers came streaming off the train.

One evening, after we had been living at Taylors for about a month, Percy scribbled some figures on the back of an envelope.

'Do you realise it's costing us more than £1 a week to run the generator' he said. 'We simply can't afford it.'

Conscious-stricken because it had been my idea that we should have an A.C. petrol driven model, I said I'd buy a couple of flat-irons.

'You had better buy some oil lamps too,' Percy said.

I did, and in the evenings we would sit close together, reading or listening to the radio in a soft circle of radiance. Electric light became a luxury only to be used if we had guests, or if I forgot to hail the oilman when he came past the house each week, his travelling hardware shop hung with saucepans, tin kettles, enamel mugs, brooms and brushes. He sold candles too and when we went to bed we would climb the twisting, narrow oak staircase to our bedroom, each carrying a lighted candle, shielding the narrow flame as it wavered in the draughts from the many cracks and crannies.

Before we moved we had enquired of the local electricity company if there was any chance of getting connected to the supply, which was already available at the other end of the village. In reply they offered to send a representative to meet Percy at the house. No figure for making the connection was mentioned.

Percy duly arrived at the appointed time, travelling from London specially for that purpose. The electric company representative kept the appointment and announced that they would be happy to connect us.

'How much will that cost' Percy asked.

'Seven hundred pounds,' said the electricity man.

As the house itself had cost us less than £1,000 Percy told him, somewhat sharply, that it was a pity they had both had a wasted journey. The time was to come when the company would be made to have second thoughts about bringing electricity to our end of the village.

CHAPTER FOUR

My mother's probably erroneous belief that I was a delicate child had meant that I had no regular schooling until I was nearly ten. Thanks to an elder sister's disapproval of my illiterate state I learned to read rather earlier, picking up the knack quickly enough not to over-tax her patience. Soon I was reading anything that came to hand — if it was in print I read it. As we were living in furnished houses while my father was serving in the R.N.V.R. (in World War 1) the books I found on the shelves were mostly novels by the popular novelists of the day — Horace Annesley Vachel, H. de Vere Stackpool, Conan Doyle, Elinor Glyn, A. E. W. Mason and other best sellers. I enjoyed them all and determined that one day I too would write novels, as my father had done before he joined the Navy — and would do again after his demob.

As his father, Richard Gowing, one-time editor of *The Gentleman's Magazine*, had pulled strings to get him a job with Alfred Harmsworth at The Fleetway House, so he put in a word for his youngest daughter with his friend Willie Blackwood, a wily Scot and a director of the Amalgamated Press which had just been bought by the Berry Brothers.

A hopeful junior on *Answers*, the weekly journal on which Alfred Harmsworth had founded his newspaper empire and for which my father had been writing serial thrillers turn and turn about with Edgar Wallace and Augustus Muir, my wages were £2.10s. a week. Soon I was supplementing this by writing romantic fiction for house publications, articles and occasional light verse for Reggie Arkell (author of *Green Fingers*) who was just along the corridor as editor, for a shortish time, of *London Calling*. Reggie, a friendly kindly man, never looked quite at home in an editorial office and the magazine had a short life.

Not long after I joined *Answers* Hessell Tiltman, the editor, took on a young reporter whose job was to engage in exploits as Mr. Answers, one of these being to stand up to a round against Carnera, the Italian heavy-weight Boxing champion. His name was T. E. B. Clarke, known to his friends as 'Tibby', an engaging character, much given to ribbald and prankish jokes. At that time girls and gambling (dogs and horses) ranked amongst his chief interests, but neither was taken too seriously. Although then only twenty-two he had had his share of adventures including arriving at Buenos Aires in the middle of a revolution.

26

Excellent material for his first book, *Go South, Go West*, which was published in 1932 and went into three editions.

By the time I left *Answers* to get married (unwisely as it turned out) I had already written, re-written and torn up one novel and a number of short stories which I had submitted in vain to various literary periodicals not published by the Amalgamated Press. The A.P. had, in fact recently revived *T.P.'s Weekly*, and while I was there I would sometimes find myself in the lift with the Welsh short story writer, Carodoc Evans, a thin, melancholy looking man who worked on *T.P.'s* for a while. His books had brought him literary esteem, if little else and I would gaze at him with awe, longing for him to notice me so I could tell him of my own aspirations. But he never did.

After marriage I settled down to writing another novel which also failed to find a publisher. Divorce and the need to get a job put a temporary end to novel writing, but I did keep my typewriter from rusting with sporadic free-lance journalism, which brought in a few pounds now and then.

This was all very small beer compared to Percy's literary earnings. When we moved to Essex he already had two highly esteemed books in the *Constable Bibliographia Series* and a couple of bibliographies of modern authors to his credit, and he was regularly writing scholarly articles and book reviews for various periodicals, American as well as English. His pen was seldom idle and he wrote with a fluency and speed which I greatly envied.

Shortly before we moved to Essex the urge to write fiction once more welled up in me; my slumbering ambition to be a novelist awoke and on the advice of a writer friend I went to see his literary agent, who persuaded me that what I *ought* to do was to write serials for the woman's magazine market. If I succeeded, he pointed out, I should make far more money than I could hope for by writing an unserialised book. Reluctantly I agreed to try; it wasn't an idea that really appealed to me, but we badly needed money. The novel that would make my name would have to wait.

There was one problem to be overcome before I could even begin to write. I had to have some help in the house, if only to keep an eye on my delightful but demanding small daughter.

One day not long after our move a soberly dressed woman, with the quiet, respectful manner of a superior domestic servant, came to the house accompanied by her daughter. She was Mrs. Pacey, the wife of a groom-gardener, who had heard I was looking for a mother's help and had brought her fourteen-year-old Mavis for my inspection. The Pacey's lived two minutes walk away in one of a row of ugly, red-

bricked bungalows, built between the wars along the railway line. Left
a widower with six children, Mr. Pacey had speedily married his
deceased wife's sister and fathered a further half dozen. Mavis, a skinny
young girl with a narrow, solemn face, was the eldest of this second
brood.

Mrs. Pacey said that Mavis had done some cooking and was good
with children. With four young sisters and a brother to keep an eye on
she had had to be. She could start work straight away because she had
just left school.

I looked at Mavis; she kept her eyes down and said nothing while her
mother talked. I wondered if her wishes had been consulted, or if she
had taken it for granted that she would be 'placed' in service when she
left school. She was a shy girl and I never found out how she felt about
this, her first job.

Mrs. Pacey took it for granted that I would want Mavis to 'sleep in'
and she stated the wage she expected me to pay. So Mavis joined our
household for a wage of ten shillings a week. She turned out to be a
conscientious little worker and a devoted nursemaid. Helen took to her
happily and I, equally happy, would watch them set off together for a
walk and then hurry to my typewriter to achieve my stint for the day.
As I discovered later the walk was of short duration, ending a few
hundred yards down the road at the Pacey's bungalow where Helen
would be plied with sweets and thoroughly spoilt by the rest of the
Pacey family.

Mavis' board and wages stretched my housekeeping money to its
limits and sometimes beyond. This made it easier for me to impose a
tough discipline on myself in order to prove the investment worth-
while. To do this I fixed a deadline of eleven o'clock for starting to
write. If, for some reason, I failed to sit down at the typewriter by that
time I would be haunted by guilt for the rest of the day. Often the result
of two hours' work would be less than a thousand words, but as long as
I got something down on paper I would feel free to turn my attention to
the garden. There were, at that time, no other distractions, for we knew
no one in the neighbourhood and it seemed that no one was interested in
knowing us.

The weather was fine and dry that spring and my afternoons were
spent collecting the broken bricks, bits of plaster and other debris
spread over what had once been the garden and dumping them in the
pond at the back.

It was rather a dismal little pond, overhung by wild plum trees. In
summer it would partly dry out, exposing all manner of rusting
rubbish, but in winter it was deep enough to drown a small child, so my

aim was to fill it in, or at least make it safe. To the disgust of the resident moorhens I tipped in some thirty wheel-barrow loads of builders' rubble. At the end of this exercise the pool looked much the same, apart from some reduction in the scum of duck weed. The moorhens had stuck it out and were soon busy again, building their nest of floating sticks for a new brood.

Any hardware left behind by former occupants of the cottages was claimed by Percy, who made the building of a rockery his first priority in the creation of our garden. Into a grave alongside the bricked drive went an iron bedstead, several rusted cycle wheels, bottomless pails and holed saucepans. Topped with peat and loam, it looked like a miniature long barrow and I used to wonder what some archaeologist of the distant future might make of it. Studded with the rockery stones we had brought from London, it was soon a-bloom with pink saxifrage, purple aubretia and pink and yellow rock roses.

We had just begun the job of making a front lawn when Simon Nowell-Smith, our first week-end guest, arrived. Simon, then not so long down from university was one of the 'bookish' young men who used to forgather at Elkin Mathews after business hours for book talk and sherry. Percy had just begun writing a series of articles on important private libraries for the *T.L.S.*'s back page which was to run until 1943; and Simon was on the *Supplement*'s editorial staff. Of slight build, fair-haired and pink cheeked, he looked about eighteen. This boyish appearance was deceptive; his opinions were already firmly formed on most subjects. Whether or not he had been warned that there was to be little lounging in a deck chair, I'm not sure. In any case he accepted the role of gardener's mate cheerfully enough, trundling wheelbarrow loads of turves as Percy cut and lifted them from our piece of land across the road, and then stamped them down on to the ground that I had so laboriously cleared.

Simon was then a bachelor. As we sat over a well-earned dinner that evening I, as a recently married young woman, couldn't resist asking him if he had any thoughts of matrimony.

'I might, if I can find a girl with two thousand a year,' he said promptly.

This reply made me wonder if my duties as hostess included producing a suitable heiress or two for his inspection. Two thousand a year seemed wealth indeed to me; Percy and I were living on less than half that amount, out of which there was alimony to be paid and some financial help to his parents in London.

Simon's remark was in keeping with the conversation, for we had been talking of Jane Austen. It wasn't so long after his visit that he

found himself a very charming
wife, with no help from me. Early
in the war they came to see us
and Simon, leading Marion on to
our green, freshly mown front
lawn, told her: 'This was laid by
me!'

With the lawn finished and the
garden cleaned up I decided to
start keeping poultry. A few shillings bought me a small field ark,
a few more a secondhand roll of
wire netting to make a run on the
piece of land across the road. For
stock, I intended to buy day-old
chicks from the hatchery in
Bishop's Stortford where Japan-

*Taylors, shortly after
we had moved in, 1938.*

ese 'sexers' were employed to separate pullet chicks from cockerels,
presumably because no one else could. To rear my chicks I needed a
brooder, which I couldn't afford, or a broody hen, which I sought for
locally.

'Do yew goo an' arst Mr. Leyns, over at Great Hollin'bury,' said the
kindly tenant farmer next door. 'I reckon yew can borrow an ol' 'en off
of 'im, bein' yew asks 'im nicely.'

I acted on this advice after some hesitation, but I needn't have
worried. Mr. Leyns, a small, genial man in a buff overall, showed no
surprise at my tentative request and leading me into a long shed, full of
fat brown hens scratching about in a dusty litter, he pulled a fluffed-up,
squawking bird from a nest box and handed her to me.

'She'll be off laying for the next six weeks,' he said cheerfully, 'so
you'll be saving me her feed. Bring her back when you've finished with
her.'

My borrowed hen proved to be a conscientious foster-mother. That
evening, after dark, I brought a box of cheeping brown chicks to her
coop and cupping their soft, pulsing little bodies in my hand slipped
them under her one by one. As I did so her breast feathers lifted and
spread, gently covering each chick until they were all enveloped in
downy warmth.

Six weeks later, when my family of twelve were well feathered and
ready for independence, I duly returned the farmer's hen, with many
thanks. The time would come when he would be farming next door and
owning three other farms in the neighbourhood, for he was an astute

businessman and foresaw that the war would bring handsome profits to arable farmers.

Takeley Street was on a well-trodden route for the tramps, or 'roadies', who regularly made their way from the casual ward in Bishop's Stortford to the one in Braintree. In return for their night's lodging and a meal, they were supposed to do a day's work on the infirmary allotment, an obligation they resented and dodged whenever possible. I used to see them go by, dun-coloured figures, stooping over an ancient pram loaded with oddments of clothes and rags and whatever food they had been able to scrounge, a billycan hanging in front. Their leathery faces were seldom bearded, but bristly with a few days' growth, their age hard to guess. A few would look young and strong and would be pushing a bicycle, rather than a pram.

When they knocked on a door the initial request would be a modest one: 'A drop o' hot water' to pour into a tin mug, stained dark brown with tannin, a layer of tea leaves at the bottom. If the hot water was forthcoming it would be: 'maybe you'll spare a spoonful o' sugar . . . a bit o' bread an' jam . . . would there be an ol' jacket nobody would be wantin' . . .?'

It was said that once a housewife had given to one 'roadie' some sort of sign would be made by her gate, so that the rest of the fraternity knew where to call. Whether or not this was true the news soon got around that I was worth a visit.

Most of my callers were Irish, but there was little blarney in their approach. They came for hot water for their tea and food if they could get it, not for talk. My attempts to draw out these vagrants, in the hope of hearing romantic tales of life on the road, invariably failed. Dulled by meths drinking they were unresponsive and glum. They would take what they could get, mumble a word or two of thanks and go on their way, heads bowed over their prams, heavy, cracked boots stumping along the road, to cadge again at the next port of call.

In the pea-picking time there would be work for those who wanted it and the casual labourer would sometimes doss down for the night in the old barn next to us. It was rare to see a woman 'roadie' on her own, nearly always they would be with their man, but there was one old crone who came each year when our farmer neighbour's peas were ready. She would peer into the barn to see if it was unoccupied and make herself a bed of straw in a corner if no one else had got there first.

'I couldn't stop if any of them *men* be sleeping there,' she told me once, fearing I suppose, for her virtue.

Throughout May the rain held off, the pond dwindled to a scummy pool surrounded by baked mud, and although our electric pump still worked I didn't much care for the colour of the water. We had been promised main water by the end of the month, but when I pressed the local authority for a definite date they were cagey. I found it an increasing bore to have to go twice daily to the pump for our drinking water; there wasn't even the diversion of a gossip, for most of the cottagers at our end of the village had wells and drank the water from them as unconcernedly as their forefathers had done.

We hadn't fancied ours from the first and when one evening the bath taps spouted tadpoles I was glad we hadn't. For Helen, sharing her bath with pond life was great fun. All the same, I thought it as well to consult the local health inspector, known to the villagers as the 'Sanity Man'.

'Tadpoles? Don't worry, they're not unhealthy,' he said cheerfully. 'I expect what's happening is that the water from your pond is filtering into your well. You could have a filter put on the inlet, but you'll be getting the main supply soon, so there's not much point in spending money on your present system.'

Summer 1938

CHAPTER FIVE

'Hugh Walpole has invited us to stay in his house at Keswick while I work on his library,' Percy said one evening on his return from London. 'He can't be there himself because he has to go to the States, but the Elliotts will look after us. He says we can stay a month, if we like, but I think two weeks will be long enough.'

Walpole's library was to be featured in the series Percy was writing for the *Times Literary Supplement*. Two articles had already appeared, one on Michael Sadleir's library, the second on Lord Esher's. Hugh and Percy had known each other for several years and he was delighted that his library should be in the series.

I was even more delighted at the prospect of a holiday in the Lake District. Without Hugh's invitation any holiday would have been beyond our straitened means. But Hugh made one proviso. If we were bringing our small daughter, he wrote, it would be best for her to lodge in the gardener's cottage near-by.

I was hesitant about handing my daughter over to someone I didn't know, however kind the gardener's wife was said to be.

'Why not take Mavis to look after Helen?' Percy suggested.

I doubted if shy Mavis, who rushed home to her family every afternoon, would be willing to travel so far afield. To my surprise she seemed to like the idea, so one fine summer day the four of us set off in the Lancia for Keswick.

Percy's spirits always rose whenever we headed North. He had spent many walking holidays in the Lake District, several with Bertram Rota (always Cyril to Percy) when they were young men, and he was looking forward to stretching his legs on the fells once again. For me, a break from household chores and a change of scene was enough to raise my spirits to euphoric levels.

Mavis and Helen in the back of the car kept each other company contentedly. When we stopped to do some shopping in Skipton Mavis was fascinated by the Yorkshire accents of the shopkeepers, remarking

33

Percy at his desk, 1938.

shyly that the people 'sounded ever so funny', unconscious that her
Essex accent must have sounded equally funny to them.

We left her, with Helen, at the slate-built gardener's cottage at
Grange before driving up the winding, mountainous road to Walpole's
house perched high above Derwentwater. Built of local grey-green
flintstone it stood slightly above road level against the slope of the fell
which rose to the rocky summit of Cat Bells, with a glimpse of the lake
to be seen from the front windows through the steep, wooded descent
to the valley.

From the exterior it looked a comfortable, typical Lakeland house.
Inside it was far from typical. Thick pastel-coloured Axminster carpet-
ing covered the downstairs floors from wall to wall (by no means usual
in those days) with silky oriental rugs spread on top. Original paintings
by Monet and Cezanne hung on the walls, T'ang horses pranced on top
of a bureau which, with the rest of the furnishing, would have graced a
Mayfair antique shop. Looking round I could see why Hugh had
barred our small daughter from his house.

Walpole's taste could not be faulted; and yet, and yet — I thought as
we were shown around by the faithful and devoted Elliotts, wasn't it all
just a little too perfect? But there were the books to make us feel at

Brackenburn, Hugh Walpole's house.

home. The house almost over-flowed with them. One bedroom was lined with them from floor to ceiling.

Walpole, at that time, was one of the selectors for the Book Society which meant that every month he received a stream of novels from publishers. These, bright and clean in their dust-wrappers, gleamed from bookshelves and window ledges in every room.

His prized collection, which was largely of fiction and included manuscripts of Scott and Trollope as well as those of lesser novelists, was housed in a library in a new wing built to provide extra bedrooms, but largely used to accommodate more books.

As Percy wrote:

In this modern room (the library) then, are all the novelists from whose names not only Bloomsbury, but also some parts of Suburbia compiles its library list. Nothing could bring home more forcibly the increasing number of women novelists. Elizabeth Bowen, Virginia Woolf, Stella Gibbons, Clemence Dane, Sheila Kaye-Smith, Pamela Frankau, Marguerite Steen, Stella Benson, Katherine Mansfield — here they all are and dozens more.

Yet Walpole avoided the company of women — apart from one or two. Perhaps he felt safer reading them than meeting them.

The Elliotts looked after us quietly and efficiently. While Percy worked in the library every morning, sitting at Walpole's big desk in the bay window, making notes, or moving along the packed shelves, taking down issues of Dickens in parts, a Thackery or a Surtees, finding books he had sold to Hugh, I could laze in the garden, reading to my heart's content, with the widest possible choice. In the two weeks we stayed at Brackenburn I finished thirteen books; but not one was by our absent host. I felt absurdly guilty for slighting his novels in this way, but the truth was that, apart from one or two, I had never been able to finish them.

It was a blissful holiday, the last we were to have for some years. In the morning Mavis would walk up from Grange with Helen (who was allowed in the garden) and after lunch Percy would take a break from work and we would walk on the fells, or drive to Buttermere, our old Lancia taking the hills in style. At seven-thirty we would dine formally, with Elliott waiting at table, filling our glasses with excellent claret or burgundy from Walpole's cellar.

We were surprised by the number of people who came to stare at the house, presumably hoping to catch a glimpse of the creator of Rogue Herries. When, as they sometimes did, they saw a young woman sunning herself in a deckchair there must have been some speculation as to her identity, especially if Helen was there too, crawling about on the grass. Sometimes coach tours would pull up outside the gate so that the occupants could satisfy their curiosity. Once Percy happened to be in the garden on his own when a car stopped and a couple came to the front door. The Elliotts were out so Percy asked if he could help.

'We've come to see Sir 'ugh's 'ouse,' the man said. They were both short and stout and determined looking.

'I'm sorry, but I'm afraid Sir Hugh is away,' Percy told him.

'Well, can't we come in, then? I've brought t'wife all t'way from Leeds.'

Told it was not possible, they went away thoroughly indignant.

Just occasionally, during those two weeks, I felt guilty because I had not brought my typewriter and chided myself for reading other people's novels instead of getting on with my own. But I know that had I brought it I would have done little work. Halcyon days, free of chores, domestic or social, never sent me eagerly to my desk. Instead they produced inertia.

Back home the first thing I did was to turn on the kitchen taps. Clear water gushed out! We had been connected to the main. At least we now had one main service, but why only the one? The cost of our generator and its greedy consumption of petrol was rankling with Percy. If we did not use it then we had wasted money buying it; if we did use it we were spending money we couldn't afford.

It was a sore point and made more so when the *Daily Telegraph* published a special supplement extolling the benefits of electricity in the home.

This stung Percy into writing a letter to the editor pointing out that these delights could, apparently, never be ours because our dog-in-the-manger electricity undertaking refused to extend the supply to our small community, yet also refused to allow the neighbouring and willing North Met. to cross the boundary line and light us up.

Percy's letter was published and sent on to Rab Butler, our M.P. Within a week Butler had our electricity company apologetically agreeing to reconsider the matter. Very soon a representative was knocking on doors in Takeley Street and counting up potential customers. It was bad luck for them that the neighbouring North Met. was a public utility company for gas as well as electricity and not restricted as to where they laid their gas main. If they had once been hesitant as to the profitability of bringing gas to Takeley, now they hurriedly did their own survey, promising the housewives cheap and efficient gas cookers on the 'never never'. The result was predictable; women who had told the electricity rep. they would be happy to buy an electric cooker, promptly forgot their promise and signed up for gas.

The gas main came first; the electricity supply reached us in the summer of 1939 — just in time. But in the summer of 1938 I was struggling with a solid-fuel cooker that would neither roast joints nor heat the water. You had, it seemed to me, only to turn your back on it for the fire to sigh and die.

The young man from the manufacturers diagnosed the reasons before he walked into the house.

'That flue pipe you've got is useless,' he said. 'You'll never get your cooker to draw. What you want is a chimney.' He had come all the way from the North of England to tell us this.

I remembered how the builder had urged me to use oil, knowing very well that his flue pipe would be no good for a solid fuel cooker; but he'd installed a cooker all the same. He had, by this time, gone bankrupt, so we asked Mr. P. to build us a chimney.

He came and had a look and gave his verdict

'I can build you one, but that won't be as tall as it ought to be, not unless I move all the drains, and that's going to make it a big job.'

The drains, he explained, hadn't been put in to the statutory depth, which meant he couldn't get enough foundations for a tall chimney. He thought a smaller one might do the trick, so we settled for that. It cost £12 which we thought quite enough.

Shortly after our return from Keswick I had a letter from John Farquharson suggesting that I come to see him. I had sent him the first 20,000 words of my novel and he wrote that he would like to discuss it with me.

'Well if you're coming up to London we can go together and see Kot,' Percy said. Neither of us had seen Kot since we had left Acacia Road, for I hadn't been to London and Percy had been too busy.

The day came, I donned my one smart suit and with my mind absorbed with thoughts of my coming interview, rushed around the house making last minute arrangements for leaving Mavis to cope on her own. It was inevitable that Percy should be sitting in the car when the time came to leave, impatiently waiting for me to join him. Spurred on by threats that I was in danger of being left behind I scrambled in breathless beside him, no more than five minutes later than his usual time for departure.

We were half a mile down the road when I chanced to glance down at my feet and stared in horror at my old garden shoes, caked in dried mud.

'Oh, God!' My wail of dismay made Percy brake sharply.

'What on earth's the matter?'

'My shoes! Look! I forgot to change them after I'd been to feed the chickens. I *must* go back.'

Percy groaned. Punctual to a degree he knew he was now going to have a frightful rush, or even miss his train. The alternative was to spoil my day. To his credit he turned the car around, we sped back to the house, I snatched up my smart shoes and we caught the train with a minute to spare.

I had looked forward to a day in London but as the train neared Liverpool Street Station, rattling past the sad little back yards of smoke-smudged houses, ignoring Stratford and Bethnal Green, my confidence evaporated. By the time I walked into John Farquharson's office I was braced for him to tell me my novel was no good.

He greeted me genially. My typescript lay on his desk. He did not tell me it was no good, nor did he say that it was a masterpiece. He was encouraging without committing himself, in the tradition of literary agents.

'Well, I've read it and I think you should finish it. I can't promise you'll sell the serial rights; it's a difficult market just now, but carry on and finish it and we'll see.'

I had hoped for more than that. I longed for him to tell me what he thought of my characters, of the way I was handling my plot. I was hungry for a few words of praise, yet steeled to take criticism. I wanted a long, cosy talk about my book, as far as I had written it, with perhaps a pointer or two for its completion.

'But —' I began, 'What do you think —' and was headed off, kindly. Some general advice about the difficult serial market and then my hand was shaken warmly and I was on my way, my typescript tucked under my arm, my spirits if not high, at least higher than they had been, for if the book was no good he would not, I argued, have told me to finish it.

With no money to spend I window-shopped in Oxford Street. It was fun to be back in London. For an hour or two I was a Londoner again, knowing the bus routes and the side streets and, for once, not in a hurry.

It was high summer and the fashion models in the windows displayed cotton dresses and beach wear. They had round, innocent faces, rosebud mouths and short, wavy hair. Some wore bright coloured slacks with bell-bottoms, like sailors, but these were strictly for beach wear and the young.

In the men's wear shops the suits were sober grey or navy, the lapels narrow, the trouser legs cut straight; the bland wax faces of the display models had pale, straw-like hair, cut like an army recruit's. Holiday wear was equally formal, club blazers were striped green and white, or blue and white for wearing with white or grey flannels. In London the correctly dressed man wore a hat and gave some indication of his character by the angle at which he wore it. Percy, an individualist in his choice of clothes, was fond of the squashy black silk hat he wore for the evening and was once told by Greville Worthington: 'Only you and Winston Churchill would wear a hat like that!'

When we called on Kot that afternoon he seemed only moderately pleased to see us. It was strange to sit at his scrubbed-top table drinking tea, not to run upstairs afterwards to our own sitting room. The rooms we had vacated were still empty and I felt the house was unhappy at being less than half used. The garden looked sad, too, with only the ghostly white phlox in bloom.

Kot's long face was gloomy. He asked about Helen but clearly did not want to hear about our new home. I could see he hadn't forgiven us for leaving Number Five.

'Couldn't you come and visit us, Kot?' I asked. 'We could put you up, you know.'

He shook his head. 'I never leave London now, Barbara.'

It was true. In the three years that we had lived in Acacia Road Kot had never gone away and latterly he had seldom gone out in the evenings.

He must, we knew, be finding it difficult to pay the rent. His translation of Tchekhov's *Plays and Stories* for Dent's Everyman Edition was published in 1937 and money must have come to him from time to time for dramatic rights, but it would not have been much. Apart from literary translations (seldom well-paid work) his only regular source of income was the small sum which the Cresset Press paid to him as a reader.

We said good-bye, promising to visit him again soon. If he had missed us at first I doubt if he did so any longer. Marjorie Wells, and other faithful women friends would still be coming to tea with him. He and Number Five would survive the blitz, though part of Acacia Road did not.

As the summer wore on the German propoganda campaign against Czechoslovakia grew more and more vicious. We were both passionately anti-Nazi; we had been in Germany during the 'June blood bath' in 1934 and we knew that Hitler's ambitions for Germany were insatiable. We had been sickened by the Nazi treatment of the Jews, and Percy, during his business trips to Cologne, Frankfurt, Berlin and Munich, had done all he could to help Jewish colleagues emigrating to England.

To be drawn into arguments with Germans on trains or buses, as we sometimes were, was unwise, not to say dangerous. They were all too ready to press their point of view on English visitors and with my hackles rising frequently I found it hard not to show my disgust.

Business was slack in August, as it usually was, with no auction sales and few if any American buyers in London. To Percy's disappointment Greville Worthington hardly appeared at the shop, despite his considerable investment in the business. As Percy has written elsewhere, Greville's principle aim in taking over the shares had been to get his own back on those who had out-manoevred him five years earlier.

However, Greville's absence had not prevented sales from picking up and much as he regretted his partner's declining interest, Percy was enjoying running things his own way.

The real worry that autumn was the increasing threat of war. New premises for the business had been found in Duke Street, just around the corner from Fortnum and Mason, in a handsome house that was in part-use as 'gentlemen's chambers,' the landlord acting as valet to his tenants. Elkin Mathews was offered rooms on the first floor, plus a basement room for packing, for a rent of £200 a year inclusive of rates. Percy jumped at the offer. But if war came Duke Street looked like being unhealthy. Prudently, he set about making preparations for a quick evacuation to Takeley — just in case.

Amongst the horrors we were warned to expect was a gas attack. Everyone was to be issued with a gas mask and it was the job of the volunteer air raid wardens — middle-aged men and women, mostly — to deliver these.

In Takeley Street, Mr. Camp, our Warden, lived a few doors away in a nice little bungalow with a well-tended garden. He was a self-employed carpenter, a good craftsman who had already done several jobs for us. Stout and rubicund he always made the same little jokes, accompanying them with a high pitched giggle: 'Don't hit the wrong nail, will you?' he would say when he saw me wielding a hammer.

When he came one evening with our gas masks he told me, with a giggle, that there was 'a funny one for the little girl.' I opened the box and found a space-age Mickey Mouse mask. Presumably some well-intentioned Civil Servant had designed it to be less frightening to children. It was repulsive enough, but not quite as much so as the adult variety which made the wearer look like a mechanical pig. The masks came in square cardboard boxes; in the event of war we were instructed never to go out without one. One therefore needed a cover with a strap and it was remarkable how quickly enterprising manufacturers leapt on to this particular band-waggon. Covers were soon on the market in a variety of materials from the cheapest cotton to expensive pigskin.

We would read the news, shiver at the thought of what might be coming and switch our thoughts to the day's work — Percy to his next catalogue, or to his next article in the *Private Library Series* (Walpole's was followed by Lord Rothchild's) and I would get on with my novel. At the week-ends the garden would absorb most of our day.

On the eve of Chamberlain's departure to Munich, Percy put Elkin Mathews' evacuation plan into operation. The best of the stock was packed into tea-chests, together with the files and archives, and sent to Liverpool Street for despatch to the Takeley railway station.

We were far from being war-mongers, but we had had a bellyful of appeasement. For us Czechoslovakia was not a 'small, far-away country that few people had heard of,' but a courageous democracy that we were in honour bound to defend. We were convinced that we had to show Hitler we meant business this time.

On the afternoon that Chamberlain returned to London I came in from the garden and switched on the radio to hear the B.B.C. commentary on the Prime Minister's arrival. The commentator was building up the drama, describing the excited, waiting crowds of onlookers, the aircraft touching down, the Prime Minister emerging, pausing to smile, then as the reporters rushed forward, waving his worthless little piece of paper.

As the microphones picked up the cheers of the crowd I couldn't bear to listen any more and switched off. Did they really believe that Hitler could be bought off with our agreement to this shoddy deal?

A few days later Percy told me that Greville and Diana Worthington had attended a party in London that evening and that Robert Byron had stood at the foot of the stairs and asked every arriving guest: 'Are you ashamed to be an Englishman tonight?' This summed up the Worthingtons' feelings, and ours.

'Austria, the Sudetenland, what next?' I wondered dismally.

'Poland, probably,' Percy answered.

At least we were able to prevent the packing cases from being despatched to Takeley. Soon they were being unpacked in Duke Street and Percy concentrated on issuing his catalogue of *Fifty Famous First Editions*.

The first of these was two paper-covered booklets bound into one little book. It was written in Danish, published in 'Kobenhaven' in 1845 and on each of the two wrappers was a presentation inscription from the author.

One read:

'To my little friend Paul who never comes to see his old friend H.C.A.' and the other: 'To my dear little Paul Bloch. You know me well enough. H. C. Andersen.' In these little booklets Hans Christian Andersen's best loved fairy tales, with illustrations from V. Pedersen, had made their bow. Their price in the catalogue was £21 for the two.

Another famous first edition was Mark Twain's *Tom Sawyer*, £1 dearer than the Hans Andersen. A rather more sophisticated item was the *Memoirs of Casanova* (12 vols. published in Leipzig) at £18.

Elkin Mathews' catalogues had long been known for their literary quality and their exploration of little-trodden paths. They were intended to tempt, to be read with the relish of a gourmet studying an interesting menu. Percy was at pains both to keep up this tradition, and keep his prices low.

While the catalogues did sell books, Elkin Mathews' quarterly publication, *Bibliographical Notes and Queries* brought the firm esteem but little cash. Percy edited it in conjunction with Dave Randall, then in charge of Scribner's rare book department in New York. It was modest in appearance, an eight-page leaflet giving answers to earlier queries, each one being numbered, some being supplied by correspondents and some by the editors, with the rest of the leaflet setting out further queries, all numbered and in alphabetical order of authors. Amongst the 1938 queries was one from Bernard Shaw.

Bibliographical Notes and Queries was dear to Percy's heart. He mourned it sorrowfully when it became an early war casualty.

While my pen was adding nothing to the family income, Percy was taking on journalistic work when and where he could. Bobby St. John Cooper, an old friend whose Home Page Cat cartoon was a regular feature in the *Daily Express*, suggested that Percy wrote an article for that paper with the hopeful title, *Search Your Shelves*. The Features Editor agreed. There was always the chance that some reader, opening up a long-closed glass-fronted bookcase, might fish out a notable edition, which could make a real story.

The payment was in any case more generous than that of the back page of the *T.L.S.*, so Percy wrote the article and it duly appeared. Soon afterwards batches of readers' letters began to arrive with lists of books inherited from grandmas and grandads, aunts and uncles; books bought at jumble sales and uncovered in attics. One reader offered a first edition of *David Copperfield*. When, at Percy's request, this treasure arrived it turned out to be a Woolworth copy. On the fly-leaf the owner had written in ink the words 'First Edition'. Of all the books offered or sent not one had the slightest antiquarian value.

Winter 1938-1939

CHAPTER SIX

Our first winter in Takeley taught us a lesson in survival. We had already found that Taylors was a draughty house, but it needed a really cold winter to show us just how draughty it could be. If the doors had fitted, a roaring coal and log fire might have kept the sitting room tolerably warm, but not only were there gaps at the tops and bottoms, there were wide cracks in the doors themselves. They were the original old doors, made without panels; ostensibly they had not been replaced because they were 'in character' with the house. In fact the builder had ducked replacing them because none of the frames was square.

To huddle in the ingle nook was one way of avoiding icy air currents sucked in from the hall or from the staircase leading up to the spare bedroom, but that meant being kippered by wood smoke if a change of wind brought a draught puffing down the chimney.

The bedrooms had their own draughts sneaking in through the interstices between the wide oak floorboards. Friends admired these floors' mellow polish, but I used to lie in bed and long for a deep-pile wall-to-wall carpet to welcome my feet when I struggled out of bed on a winter morning. Fortunately the nursery was relatively warm, thanks to the presence of the hot water cylinder boxed into the airing-cupboard, put there because it was the only convenient place.

It was tempting to switch on an electric fire, but our guzzling generator made this prohibitively expensive, so we made do with a second-hand, smelly paraffin heater with a little mica window in the front and holes in the top.

One morning when I turned on the cold tap at the sink no water flowed. We were frozen up.

Eventually a plumber came and asked the whereabouts of the cold tank. I led him to the small, north bedroom where a cupboard door, high up the wall over the bed, led in to the roof space. There the tank was lodged, wedged under one of the supporting timbers. This made it impossible for anyone save a dwarf to stand erect beside it.

I offered the plumber a ladder but he preferred to stand on the bed and heave himself up through the little door, kicking the wall as he went.

'Yer ball-cock's froze up,' he reported. 'You did oughter 'ave sackin' around them pipes. There's a gret 'ol draught a-blowin' in from under the eaves. That's no wonder it's froze.'

He thawed us out and we bandaged the pipes with sacking; but it wasn't enough, the ball-cock continued to freeze. To avoid the expense of more visits from the plumber I learnt to thaw out the pipes myself. I would dress for the job as for a polar expedition, get Percy to give me a leg-up and squeeze myself into the space between the tank and the beam — a space too small for anyone of Percy's size — and apply poultices of rags dipped in boiling water. Usually this did the trick.

As I crouched in the half dark, pressed against the tank's cold galvanised side, my gaze would travel along the shadowy, cobweb-hung roof space with its age-blackened timbers held in place by heavy cross-beams. The Tudor builder had used wattle and daub to keep out wind and weather, but time, birds and probably rats had disposed of much of it. Once there would have been a straw thatch to keep the warmth in. Later, tilers had hung the thick, red roof tiles, securing them with elm-wood pegs.

As the weather grew colder I tried to prevent the tank from freezing up by keeping a trickle of water running all night. This was likely to cause a frozen waste pipe and a flooded kitchen. Percy's solution was to drain the whole system the last thing at night, letting the boiler go out to avoid a burst.

'If we *have* to do without hot water the first thing in the morning *and* come down to a freezing kitchen we might just as well *be* frozen up,' I said.

'At least you wouldn't have to climb up into the roof,' Percy countered.

Either way life was cold and uncomfortable as the bitter weather continued, and when I came down on Christmas Eve to find not only the ball-cock frozen to the top of the tank, but all the pipes solid as well, it was too much.

My mother was then living some forty miles away, sharing a largish house with her elder sister, while my father was away in Kenya. Blowing on numbed fingers I went to the 'phone.

'We're frozen solid. How are things with you?'

'Oh dear, how dreadful for you darling. Everything is quite all right here.'

I pictured her warm, comfortable house; hot water running from the taps, the big kitchen with its non-smoking Aga, and I poured out my tale of woe.

'Of course, you can't possibly stay where you are;' my mother responded generously. 'Helen might catch her death of cold. You must come right away. There's plenty of room and we've got a very big turkey ...'

Percy and my mother had never been on the same wave-length, but the civilities had always been maintained on both sides, so he was as thankful as I was to accept her invitation. A neighbour agreed to feed the cat and the hens, we packed up our Christmas fare, wrapped Helen in a rug against the rigours of a drive in our unheated Lancia and set off through the frosted countryside to West Mersea Island.

Islands have always had an appeal to those who seek a life free of conventional constraints, or at least a free and easy holiday. West Mersea, although only cut off from the mainland now and then when a spring tide flooded the Strood connecting it to the mainland, was favoured by a small circle of writers — members of the Savage Club — who would foregather at the Sailing and Social, the fishermen's pub, turning their backs on the yacht club members, smartly dressed in white ducks and navy blazers, who would foregather at the Victory, up the road. During the 'thirties my father would take them up the Blackwater for a sailing party, claiming that he had to be skipper, mate and galley cook rolled into one, while Victor Bridges, Bertie Shaw and other fellow Savages lazed on deck drinking the boat dry. But that Christmas he was in Kenya, recuperating from a serious illness and trying to finish the last serial he was to write; struggling to concentrate at an altitude of 6000 feet, a height at which he claimed 'the brain refused to work efficiently'.

After three days of warmth and good fare a thaw set in and we returned home well-fed and rested. Luckily the pipes had thawed out without disaster and in the milder weather it was possible to keep relatively warm.

By then Mavis had left me, tempted away by a wealthy family at the other end of the village. Much as I longed to replace her, for in her absence my novel was making hardly any progress, I could no longer afford to pay wages. Financially we were stretched to the limit. Percy's parents looked to him for support, Elkin Mathews was still struggling out of the Depression and he was having to make payments to the Official Receiver following a bankruptcy brought about by a lost libel action which had been no fault of his. There was also the mill-stone of alimony which hung round his neck for most of our married life.

It was just possible to manage, so long as things did not get worse. I would snatch an hour or so for writing while my daughter slept in her pram and, with the spring, out of the blue, came an unexpected windfall. An uncle I hadn't seen for years left me a small legacy.

My mother, who had gone to her brother's funeral in Wales, telephoned me on her return.

'I've got some good news for you, darling. Uncle Hugh remembered you three girls in his Will.'

'Good Heavens!' I couldn't believe it. 'How much?'

'A hundred and fifty pounds each. Don't you think it was good of him?'

I did indeed, and I felt a pang of remorse for not having been a more attentive neice.

My first reaction to any unexpected windfall is to start thinking how to blow it. But caution soon takes over. By the time the cheque arrived I had accustomed myself to the idea of having a reasonable in-credit bank account at last and no longer wanted to splurge out and then find myself once more on the brink of insolvency, albeit with a new wardrobe. Instead I settled for a modest shopping expedition and more money put towards domestic help.

As if in answer to a prayer, a nice looking, sensible eighteen-year-old arrived at my door to ask if she could come and work for me.

Like the legacy from my uncle it seemed almost too good to be true. Elsie had been a house parlourmaid in a largish local house where a staff of three maids was kept. To come and work for me looked like a loss of status, even if I was willing to pay her the same wage — £45 per annum all found. Then I discovered the reason why I was favoured. She had seen my small daughter out for walks with local children and wanted nothing better than to be allowed to look after her.

Spring saw Percy's rockery repaying him for his careful constructional work with a flowery carpet of pink and purple aubretia, to be followed by golden rock roses and shell-pink saxifrage, the flowers springing up from tiny green rosettes. We now had a flower bed bordering one end of the lawn, with flowering shrubs strategically placed to conceal the presence of our septic tank drainage.

In the vegetable plot peas and broad beans, carrots and lettuces planted by Percy were pushing up through the sticky clay soil in regimented rows, or in wavering lines where the planting had been left to me. It was not that I objected to using a garden line, but that I always believed I could succeed in sowing a straight row without one.

Indoors we had some of the more exposed pipes lagged, and we modified the big open fireplace in the sitting room so that it seldom smoked and was less voracious in fuel consumption.

Although we had made some friends amongst Percy's fellow commuters (wives coming by car to meet husbands who would chat to pass
the time when trains ran late, and friendships would form), our social
life was mostly with friends from London who visited us at week-ends,
and with Percy's one-time neighbours in and around Great Bardfield,
where he had once rented a country cottage a few doors from the
Edward Bawdens. Francis Meynell was living at Toppesfield, and
A.J.A. Symons at Finchingfield; so too was Tom Moult, poet and
author and for many years secretary of the Poetry Society.

A.J.'s handsome Georgian house, where he spent most week-ends,
faced the village green in Finchingfield. 'A noble house,' he had called it
when he had first set eyes on it in 1929, and immediately determined
that it should be his. Percy had stayed at Brick House on many
occasions and he and I had spent a night there not long after we had
parted from our respective spouses.

In the morning we had been awakened by the strains of Mendel-
sohn's Wedding March, played on one of A.J.'s collection of musical
boxes, or rather a polyphon (a man-sized version) which stood in the
passage upstairs, looking rather like an elaborate grandfather clock.
This anticipation of nuptials yet to come was a typical A.J. joke.

To stay with A.J. at Brick House was a stimulating experience, but it
could be mentally exhausting for one was drawn, willy nilly, into
participating in some ingenious, highly competitive game of A.J.'s
devising, or one long-since forgotten, which he had revived with his
own new elaborations.

We were invited to dinner one evening in June. Cyril Joad was
visiting A.J. and he and Percy were old friends. Natalie Sieveking, slim
and elegant, was hostess (A.J. and his wife Gladys had parted) and the
St. Loe Stracheys, who lived near-by at Shalford, were the other guests.
A.J. was, as always, an excellent host; the wine, which no doubt was
courtesy of the Wine and Food Society of which A.J. was secretary,
was not stinted; the food, although I have forgotten what we ate, was
certainly delicious and the talk, as A.J. intended, clever and competitive. Joad, I think had the edge on the others, but he, after all, was a
professional.

One couldn't help but like Joad. He was such good company and
there was no subject on which he could not produce instant information — not always to be relied upon. As a lad he was probably often
told, 'Cyril, you're so sharp one of these days you'll cut yourself,' and
there were occasions when he did.

That dinner party was memorable for me not only for the food and
drink and scintillating conversation; it was there that I learned for the

first time of the existence of disposable nappies. The Stracheys had recently been travelling in the United States with a babe in arms. Remembering my own problems with my first born when we took her on journeys I asked Celia Strachey how she had managed.

'Oh, you can buy disposable diapers anywhere in the States,' she said. 'All the mothers use them.'

I thought it a wonderful idea and wondered why one couldn't buy them in England, or, if they were obtainable, why I hadn't heard of them. Very likely they had already been introduced, but the paper shortage soon to come would have made them quickly unobtainable.

The Library at Chatsworth was to be one of the highlights of the *T.L.S.* Private Library Series. Arrangements were made that summer for Percy to spend a couple of days working on the library and he duly presented himself at the Librarian's house one Saturday morning. The visit began inauspiciously. Francis Thompson, an elderly bachelor (he preferred to call himself The Keeper of the Duke's Treasures) was not too pleased at having to give up a week-end to showing around 'the man from *The Times*' and his greeting was somewhat tart. 'I don't know how you think you're going to see the whole library in a couple of days,' he said. 'I've been here half a life-time and I don't know all the books there even now.'

However, it wasn't long before the two men were on the best of terms and that first visit was the basis for a friendship which lasted the rest of Francis' life. Two days were not nearly long enough to complete the job and on the next visit I went along too, staying with Percy in the little village of Ensor, a part of the Chatsworth estate. From the village a right of way runs through the park. According to Francis Thompson the old Duke was fond of strolling alone in the park wearing his oldest clothes, shabby corduroy trousers and an ancient jacket.

On one occasion he was stumping along down the middle of the road when a car came up behind him. As he didn't immediately move out of the way the driver leant out and shouted: 'Hey, move can't you? Anyone would think you owned the place!'

'And do you know,' the Duke said later, recounting the incident to Thompson, 'I was so taken aback that I never thought to tell him I did.'

Francis Thompson's own sense of humour was puckish. He was excellent company and he and Percy would sit over tea in Francis' cosy sitting room capping each other's stories. For years afterwards Percy dined out on tales of ducal eccentricities. I would sometimes wonder if Francis dined out, in his turn, on Percy's anecdotes.

Francis Thompson, in wheelchair, with Percy and Barbara Muir and Mme. Tulkens from Brussels, at Chatsworth.

Francis and I shared a love of Jane Austen; it was a great source of pleasure to him that Jane should have had Chatsworth in mind when she described Darcy's home. After the war Francis became so crippled with arthritis that he could only get about in a wheelchair, but although his legs failed him, his sense of humour never did.

On our way home from Derbyshire we spent a couple of days with the Worthingtons at Weston Underwood, the beautiful house they had recently bought in Buckinghamshire. It was the house where the Throckmorton family, the patrons of the poet Cowper, had once lived. Adjoining the formal garden was a wild garden where Cowper had spent many hours writing poetry. It was little changed since his time, with the summer-house, where he had sat writing his poems, still standing.

Diana Worthington was tiny — no more than five foot and looked even smaller with Grev's six foot five towering over her. She had fine eyes and rather brittle good looks. I didn't know her well (Percy knew her far better) and was unaware that her marriage was already breaking down, but I was conscious of tension beneath her welcoming hostess's manner.

The Worthingtons were not short of money; they had all the staff the house required, including an excellent cook and a kind, old-fashioned nanny who made no difficulty in adding Helen to her three young

Worthington charges. We found a small house-party in progress, our fellow guests being as well-heeled as our host and hostess. Grev, having pressed us to visit them, had gone off somewhere before our arrival — not untypical behaviour.

At dinner that evening the conversation turned to the Spanish Civil War. Though not particularly politically minded, Percy and I had been supporters of the Republicans from the start, so I was shocked to find that almost everyone present was backing General Franco. Unable to hold my tongue I began quoting *The News Chronicle* in support of my Republican views.

'But those poor nuns,' cried one of the women. 'They're doing such dreadful things to them!'

That was just Franco's propaganda, I retorted, and what about the atrocities committed by 'the Rebels', which was the way *The News Chronicle* always referred to Franco's forces?

'Oh, that's just Communist propaganda,' I was told. 'You can't believe anything they say.'

I don't think my fellow guests labelled me a communist — just misguided. As for Percy he sensibly kept out of the discussion, knowing that no conversion to our point of view was likely. As far as conversation at social occasions such as these was concerned, Percy had an easier time than I did, for the men enjoyed hearing him talk about books and book-collecting, while when I was left alone with the wives the talk invariably gravitated to the tiresomeness of nannies or the misdeeds of domestic servants — subjects to which I could make no useful contribution.

Much to Percy's embarrassment Diana confided her troubles to him on that visit. She was still devoted to Greville and sought Percy's help as Greville's friend and partner. Sorry as he was for Diana, he knew there was little he could do, for Grev was losing interest in his marriage.

On the second day of our visit Diana was summoned to the death-bed of her grand-mother, Frances, Countess of Warwick at Easton Lodge, only five miles from our house in Takeley. We already knew Maynard Greville, a likeable eccentric, but we had never met the Countess who was greatly loved by the villagers on the estate. The older tenants would recall, with parochial pride, Edward VII's arrivals at Easton Lodge station, where he would be met by a smart phaeton, driven by the beautiful countess herself.

After Elkin Mathews' move to Duke Street Greville ceased to take any practical interest in the firm, although he showed up now and then. He had taken on a new and absorbing job, that of selling air raid shelters to factories in the midlands. This he did with his customary zest for a new outlet for his considerable energies. As a salesman he had every-thing. His height made his appearance unforgettable, his grin and his sense of fun were infectious and he had the happy knack of getting along with people in all walks of life.

Ian Fleming, who in any case had done no more than lend his name to Elkin Mathews, was by this time in the Navy, working at the Admir-alty. Fortunately for the firm he was still buying books, on Percy's advice, for his collection. Many were surprisingly cheap, for the trade in general was not yet alive to the importance of, and therefore almost certain future demand for, the first publication of papers by Marconi and Rutherford, or even of Einstein. Art, philosophy, photographs, social history, sports and games all came into Ian's collecting field, as well as science and medicine. Percy was able to buy Florence Night-ingale's *Notes on Nursing** for £1, the same price that he paid for a first edition of R. C. Sherriff's *Journey's End*. Many of the books bought for Ian at this time would feature in the prestigious *Printing and the Mind of Man* exhibition held at Earl's Court in 1963, as part of the International Printing Machinery & Allied Trades Exhibition.

When, two weeks after Hitler's subjugation of Czechoslovakia, Chamberlain announced a combined British and French Guarantee of the Sovereignty of Poland Percy shook his head and said he feared it was too late. Yet we were thankful that Britain should at last be showing some resolution. Like almost everyone else we were surprised that Chamberlain should be willing to give such a guarantee, but as Churchill wrote later; 'He did not like being cheated'.

---

* Her famous indictment of the War Office' hospital administration during the Crimean war.

Spring and Summer 1939

CHAPTER SEVEN

As the weather warmed up so did the international situation. By August the German propaganda campaign against Poland had risen to a crescendo. Convinced that war was not far off Percy and his staff at Duke Street packed up the best of the stock and the archives, as they had done before Munich, and waited for the tip-off to evacuate which Ian had promised.

I had nearly finished my novel and I continued to work on it, more for the satisfaction of completing the task I had set myself, than with any real expectation of ever seeing it published. War, I assumed would put an end to anything as frivolous as the printing of novels even if the publishing houses weren't bombed out of existence. When not writing I hoed the vegetables, (subsequently known, hopefully, as 'digging for victory') salted down runner beans, cobbled up black-out curtains and pondered over a Government leaflet on how to make some part of the house into 'A Safe Room'. My name was already down as a part-time ambulance driver, based on Dunmow, but no one had taken me up on this offer.

Percy and I both found it incredible that so many people still appeared to think that war could somehow be avoided. Even after the signing of the German-Soviet non-aggression pact on August 23rd, *Mass Observation** recorded that two out of three people interviewed on the following day had said they didn't believe that there would be a war.

North-West Essex, having no large towns and no heavy industry to speak of, had been zoned as a reception area for evacuees. This meant it could expect to receive a mixed collection of pregnant women, mothers with babies or toddlers, as well as parties of school children. In Takeley, Les Frost had taken on the unenviable job of billeting officer. He was politically well to the left and had never hidden his views, so he was regarded with suspicion by the local Tories and labelled a 'Red'.

---

* Mass Observation. War begins at Home, Chatto & Windus, 1940

53

He was, in fact, an excellent head-master of our village school, firm but never harsh, a good mixer, respected by parents and endowed with a strong sense of humour — qualities very necessary for a billeting officer.

For those with large houses, to set aside a wing for an evacuee family was tiresome, but not unbearable; it was for the ordinary middleclass home that the prospect was daunting, especially for the house-proud, since it was supposed that the war would be a horrific one and there was no limit as to how long evacuees might be imposed on their host and hostess. For, with the best will in the world, few hostesses would be happy to accept a guest, however docile, for an indefinite visit and the docility of evacuees could hardly be guaranteed.

As we were having to put up Percy's parents when war was declared, we were not on Les's billeting list. This, from my point of view was not altogether a let-off: my mother-in-law was a strong-minded woman and, as Percy himself admitted, could be difficult. What was more she would bring her elderly, disagreeable little sealyham with her who would certainly not be welcomed by my dog-hating cat.

With no resident domestic help (Elsie, my new mother's help, lived just down the road) we could fit in one more adult so Percy suggested we should invite Elizabeth Marx who had been working for Elkin Mathews as a trainee for the past eighteen months.

Elizabeth was the eldest daughter of a Jewish lawyer who had moved his family from Germany to the south of France soon after Hitler came to power.

Percy had not been looking for more staff, but he was deeply sympathetic to the plight of Jews forced to leave Germany, and when asked by a German colleague if he would accept the daughter of an old friend as a trainee, he agreed to do so. Work permits were not then being given to foreign girls for anything except domestic work, so Elizabeth could only be taken on as a learner at a nominal salary, although she had had secretarial training and spoke excellent English.

She was only twenty in 1939, a friendly, willing girl with a round, pretty face, smiling brown eyes and dark, curly hair. Shy with strangers, she was sensitive about her German origins, hating everything to do with the country she had left, including its language.

'She's a nice girl and she has nowhere else to go,' Percy had said, one evening towards the end of August. By then the other members of his staff had already made their arrangements to leave London. 'I'll need someone here to help me and she says she would like to come. Do you think you could squeeze her in?'

I had never met Elizabeth, but squeezing one more person into one's home was the sort of thing one accepted without demur on the eve of war. As it turned out Elizabeth was remarkably accommodating and fitted easily into the family set-up, cheerfully accepting the rigours of our cold and inconvenient house and willingly taking on such extra-secretarial tasks as child-minding and deputising in the kitchen for the boss's wife.

Not long before the evacuation got under way the A.R.P. Centre in Dunmow told me to report at a local garage that evening to take an ambulance driver's proficiency test.

'We've just been supplied with an ambulance of sorts', said Mr. Smith, the garage owner, when I duly reported. 'You'd better see if you can drive it. I must warn you. It's a big 'un.'

He was right. Dunmow had been allocated a 10 ton Dennis truck, converted into an ambulance by having a rough super-structure resembling a sort of cage, covered with a tarpaulin, fixed on to the chassis.

I gazed at it doubtfully. I had never before driven anything larger than the Lancia.

'Well, come on then,' Mr. Smith said briskly. 'Jump into the cab, and we'll take it out.'

It was hardly a matter of 'jumping' into the cab, but I wasn't going to admit to my doubts. With a spurious show of confidence I managed to haul myself up unaided; Mr. Smith got in beside me and briefly explained the controls. When I tried them I found that to reach the self-starter, which was located on the floor beyond the clutch pedal, I had to shift myself along the bench seat. Mr. Smith thought this funny. His cheerful unconcern at the prospect of being my passenger was reassuring.

'Right!' he said. 'O.K? Then off we go!'

He had to help me release the hand-brake before we could move. Then, gingerly, I put the Dennis into gear and we lumbered off the forecourt on to the main road. My rear view was blocked by the built-on wooden contraption and the side mirror wasn't angled for my sort of height. Mercifully there was little traffic. The shops had closed and the town had settled down for the evening. I saw why I had been told to report at 6 p.m.

We lumbered through Dunmow at a cautious twenty miles an hour. To my relief the monster was obedient to my commands; it was rather like being put in charge of an elephant and finding it quite willing to go where one wanted.

'Come on, girl,' Mr. Smith said, giving me a nudge. 'I'll bet you don't always drive as slowly as this. Speed it up a bit.'

Obediently I let the speedometer needle creep up to thirty. When we were through the town I risked a bit more acceleration. Confidence returned and with it a pleasant feeling of power. There I was, at the wheel of a juggernaut, towering above every other vehicle on the road, yards of bonnet in front of me. The fat hedges and the grasses on the roadside genuflected as we passed. The occasional motorist we encountered gaped at me in astonishment. I was tempted to wave, but didn't. As we continued our majestic progress through the peaceful Essex countryside I glanced from time to time at my mentor. He looked comfortable and relaxed. Was he going to pass me? Suppose he wanted me to change a wheel?

We did a ten mile circuit returning to Dunmow through Easton Lodge Park, the home of the late Countess of Warwick, soon to be requisitioned by the War Office. After I had crept carefully through the narrow stone gate-way, Mr. Smith told me to pull up.

'Now reverse through it,' he ordered.

There was only about a three inch clearance. I took a deep breath and somehow managed it without loss of paint.

He grinned at me genially when I pulled up on his garage forecourt. 'Good! You'll do.'

For days I awaited the arrival of an official badge, or certificate. None came. Some weeks later I was told to collect a pair of navy blue serge trousers, a navy battle-dress jacket with metal ARP buttons, a tin hat and a splendidly warm navy blue great-coat. I was, officially, a part-time driver.

Three days before the German invasion of Poland Ian Fleming gave Percy the promised tip-off. Once again books, files and archives were despatched to Takeley station. This time they had left London for good.

Autumn and Winter 1939

CHAPTER EIGHT

Overnight our household doubled in size. As soon as the promised tip-off came from Ian, Percy and Elizabeth despatched the packed-up tea chests from Duke Street to Liverpool Street station and then they drove together to Takeley with some of the more precious books, the ledgers and a typewriter. The following day his parents and their dog arrived by train.

At first the atmosphere was almost jolly, so anxious was everyone to make the best of the situation. Only Susie, the sealyham, didn't bother to pretend. She was bloody-minded at having to leave her own hearth and didn't care who knew it.

Percy's father was an easy-going, likeable man, tall and spare, his bony face etched with tiny lines. He had once joined Percy and me for a sailing holiday on the Broads, cheerfully putting up with a cramped cabin in the bows and taking his turn as ship's cook. He and I had always got on well together; as Percy once said: 'My father likes personable young women'. As a father he had one drawback, he had never been able to save money for a rainy day. And these had come often enough in his life.

My mother-in-law was made of sterner stuff. She was small and determined. She had once gone to a fancy-dress dance as an Indian Squaw and looked the part to the life. The only interest she and I shared was the welfare of her eldest son. Her life had not been easy, but she was a woman of spirit and had never allowed adversity to defeat her.

There was only one possible room for my in-laws to occupy — the bedroom above the sitting room, reached by a narrow, twisting staircase which led directly into it. Should nature call during the night the occupants were faced with a tricky descent to the bathroom on the other side of the house. A chamber-pot was the alternative answer to the problem, which meant the surreptitious carrying of slops through the sitting room the next day — for frankness about such problems was not then usual. Earlier occupants of the room had no doubt found a simpler solution, but in Takeley Street in 1939 a cry of 'gardez-loo' might have sounded out of place.

Percy had his own problems. Elkin Mathews was to be carried on somehow, but with all the bedrooms occupied and the dining room of necessity a general purpose room through which everyone passed frequently, the sitting room was Hobson's Choice for bookroom and office combined.

It was not an arrangement I could view with enthusiasm. I had spent much time and thought on this room in particular. I was happy with its green and oatmeal colour scheme, the polished floor, the Kelim rugs, the bookshelves along one wall, filled but not overfilled, and a few nice pieces of furniture left in my care by my mother.

The installation of a filing cabinet, a couple of typewriters and cartons of books did not improve its comfort or appearance. Much of the stock had been left in Duke Street to await transfer to Hodgson's auction rooms, the rest was in packing cases stacked at the back of the garage; the more precious items were in boxes under our bed and in the bottom of chests of drawers. Inevitably, when a particular book was wanted it was somewhere inaccessible. During working hours entry into the sitting room by non-members of Elkin Mathews' staff was frowned upon; Helen found this hard to understand.

Elizabeth and Percy's parents had arrived a couple of days before the official evacuation began. I had volunteered to transport the Takeley evacuees to their billets on that day and duly reported to the village hall at the appointed time.

The scene when I walked in was one which was to become boringly familiar — a number of people, middle-aged to elderly, standing about waiting to be given a job to do, one or two business-like bodies sitting at tables, papers before them, apparently busy. Some harassed-looking organisers hurrying in and out.

We had been warned that a coach-load of London school-children would be arriving that morning. No one knew quite when.

I approached a middle-aged, trousered woman who was sitting at a card-table studying various lists, and explained that I had come with my car and was ready and willing to drive anyone anywhere. Could she tell me when my services would be required?

She had probably been asked the same question several times for she answered somewhat shortly.

'All we know is that the children are coming by coach and that they are on their way.'

I didn't know any of my fellow volunteers, but, comrades in the boredom of hanging about, we soon formed chatty little groups, indulged in some one-upmanship over just how over-crowded our homes had become (one would hardly have dared *not* to have had a home crammed to capacity) and swapped accounts of our domestic preparations for war-time. From the kitchen kindly women appeared with cups of tea.

The morning dragged on; no one said what was really in their minds. No coach load of children arrived.

After a hurried lunch at home I returned to the hall to find everyone still dutifully hanging around. Some news had filtered through, mostly of muddles and troubles. A large number of children had been dumped in a small near-by village which had expected only a dozen; other coaches had been misdirected or had lost their way. The afternoon wore on, the volunteer helpers began to drift away, drivers went home to look after their own families. It was already evening and growing dusk when someone called out:

'They're here!'

As thankful and relieved as a hostess when belated guests finally turn up, we who had stuck it out rushed out to the forecourt to greet our poor, tired little evacuees and make them feel at home. The fifty-seater coach had just pulled up and a young woman, infant in arms, was being handed down by the driver, behind her other women with babies or toddlers were waiting to follow her, all of them clutching bulging carrier bags. A few had large pink labels pinned on their coats to indicate a condition once known as 'interesting'.

'Well, they'll have to stop where they are now,' said the weary driver when Les Frost pointed out that this wasn't our consignment. 'I can't take 'em on anywhere else tonight, not with all them babies. It's been a rare old muddle.'

Weary and bemused, carrying their sleeping or wailing babies, the evacuees trailed into the hall, followed by smudge-eyed toddlers. Helpers bustled around boiling up kettles and fetching milk. Les Frost and his reception committee rose to the occasion. The unexpected guests should be bedded down for the night in the village hall and made as comfortable as possible. Someone was despatched to a near-by farm to commandeer a wagon-load of straw. Spread over the floor to a depth of a couple of feet it provided a tolerably comfortable form of bedding. Blankets were collected from neighbouring homes and issued to each family and I went off on a tour of the village to collect pillows or cushions. By the time I returned with a car-full the hall looked like an indoor camping site, with each little family settled on its own territory, having staked a claim by spreading a blanket and depositing thereon its few belongings.

Babies were being fed and changed, toddlers were bouncing excited-
ly on the springy straw, or straying away and having to be retrieved like
lost lambs. Soon everyone was settling down for the night with
exchanges of cockney humour and a remarkably stoical acceptance of
the situation.

All the same, it was pointed out that the straw bedding was a
considerable fire hazard; one dropped match and the whole place could
have been ablaze.

'Someone'll have to stop and keep an eye on things,' the committee
decided. By this time the helpers were ready to call it a day, but four
volunteers nobly came forward to take turns as night watchmen. I felt
I'd been absent from my family long enough and set off for home,
promising to return the next day.

When I cycled up in the morning the straw was being swept out and
the double doors of the hall left wide open to let in much-needed fresh
air. Of our guests of the night before there was no sign. A coach had
come and carried them all away. The night had passed relatively
quietly, I was told. Breakfast had been provided for everyone and the
straw was being taken away to be burnt.

The village had coped and it only remained to tidy up. But the
memory, hardly fragrant, lingered on, especially for the volunteer
wardens.

'Well, I shan't forget this morning in a hurry,' said one. 'When I went
in there first thing *the smell*, that fair hit you in the face. Should have had
me gas mask on.'

Later that day our correct allocation of evacuees finally arrived, a
coach-load of subdued-looking school children, boys and girls, labels
tied to their jackets, mouths sticky with sweets. A printed sticker on the
window of the coach read EVACUATION.

'Will you take these two?' I was asked. 'Their name's Donovan and
they're to go to Mrs. Taylor.'

The boy looked about twelve, the girl a little younger; both were
dark haired and sallow.

'Hello,' I said. They didn't return my smile. 'Hop in, then. It isn't
far.'

They obeyed apathetically.

'I'm sure you'll be happy at Mrs. Taylor's. She's very nice and kind.'
I wasn't at all sure for I hardly knew Mrs. Taylor, but I felt some
encouragement was needed, especially since the Taylor's house, when
we reached it a few minutes later, didn't encourage optimism. It was a
grey-brick double-fronted Victorian villa, standing a few feet back
from the main road behind a neglected, railed-in front garden.

I pulled up outside the gate and told the two evacuees to come with me. Mrs. Taylor appeared at the door as soon as I rang the bell. She was middle-aged and what used to be described as 'respectable looking.'

'Hello, Mrs. Taylor,' I said brightly. 'I've brought you your evacuees.' I saw her looking dubiously past me at the two Donovans who were trailing up the path with their suitcases.

'Is that them? But I *asked* Mr. Frost for a boy. I *told* him I wanted a boy to go in with my Michael.'

'Well they're brother and sister, you see, and of course they don't want to be separated.' I could see Mrs. Taylor was on the point of refusing to take them in. 'Perhaps you could manage them both just for the time being,' I urged, 'then we might be able to fix them up somewhere else and find a boy on his own, instead ...'

While I explained and persuaded, the Donovans stood waiting behind me, glumly silent.

'Well, I don't know ...' Mrs. Taylor considered her unwanted guests and sighed. She was not an unkind woman. 'It's not what I was led to expect ... well, I suppose they'd better come in.'

I watched the boy and girl follow her into the house. They didn't look back. The door shut behind them and I went back to the village hall. I was to discover later that there were several more Donovans distributed around the village, to be joined before long by Mrs. Donovan, mother of ten children, a matriarchal figure who was to prove a valuable addition to the community.

On September the third, shortly before eleven o'clock, I left the rest of the household gathered around the wireless set and cycled to the village hall on Elizabeth's bicycle, not having one of my own. Petrol, already pooled, was a commodity to be saved.

The nation had been warned to stand by for an important announcement at eleven fifteen. There could have been few households who were not tuned in to the B.B.C. Home Service that morning.

No one had asked me to report at the hall, but I knew that people would be gathering there and the previous few days had made me feel I was already knitted into the community and should be at hand in case my help was needed.

I found it already half full, with people sitting in rows facing the platform, as if for a public meeting. A portable wireless stood on a card table in the centre of the hall between the rows. People were talking quietly to their neighbours. As I found a seat I heard a woman telling someone that her sisters had arrived from London with their children and she had twenty people squeezed into her house.

'I just didn't know where to put them all. I kept on making pots of tea ... didn't get to bed until three this morning'.

The wireless had been droning away quietly with no one listening. Someone called out: 'It's nearly time!' The sound was turned up and the chatter died away.

'I'm speaking to you from Number Ten Downing Street ...' The voice that less than a year ago had told us that he brought us peace in our time now sounded thin and weary.

' ... a bitter blow ... my long struggle to win peace has failed ... cannot believe that there is anything more or anything different that I could have done that would have been more successful ...'

I couldn't accept that; yet, profoundly though I had disagreed with Chamberlain over Munich, it was moving to listen to his confession of failure, an admission that he had been tricked and out-manoevred by Hitler, and impossible not to feel sympathy for him. And now, at last, he was showing resolution.

'It is the evil things we shall be fighting against — brute force, bad faith, injustice, oppression, persecution — and against them I am certain the right will prevail.'

The fortissimo strains of the National Anthem brought us all to our feet. When it died away there were neither cheers nor protests. If some wept they did so surreptitiously. The long threatened war, discounted by so many, prepared for so belatedly and reluctantly, was now a fact. It was rather as if, having held our breath uncomfortably long in fear, we had released it with a resigned sigh of acceptance. All right, then, the oft-prophecied second world war had begun. Now we had to see it through.

For a start this meant sitting down again and listening obediently to a string of official announcements. Cinemas to be closed, people not to congregate in halls and other meeting places, air raid warnings ...

'No W.I. Meeting on Tuesday,' murmured the President, the wife of a retired general, who had already turned part of her house into a first-aid post. 'Pass the word along!'

The hall soon emptied. No more evacuees were expected so there was nothing more for me to do but cycle home and cook a meal for my houseful. There was no dramatic air raid warning in our part of Essex; we didn't hear about London's false alarm until later. According to reports it was the warblings of London sirens on that first morning of the war that panicked some families, who had opted out of the official evacuation scheme, to abandon their homes and Sunday dinners and light out for the countryside, only stopping long enough to snatch up a few belongings.

My black-out curtains had been severely criticised by Percy the previous evening after he inspected the outside of the house for tell-tale chinks of light. I was no needlewoman and I knew I had made an inefficient job of the black-out. My pretty chintz bedroom curtains did have a black lining, but it fitted badly.

'But does it really matter so much?' I asked despondently, 'if we *do* show a tiny chink of light? Will some German bomber, three or four thousand feet up, see it and drop a bomb? I can't believe it! And Charley Camp would never fine us.'

This wasn't the kind of argument to succeed with Percy. Our black-out should be total, he said. If I couldn't make it so we would go to bed in the dark.

I had slipped up over the larder window too, completely forgetting to make a curtain for it. Another problem was that if a window was left open the curtains might stir in the wind letting out slivers of light. So Percy made a rule: lights must be put out before a window was opened.

My preparations for war had been sketchy; as well as skimping on black-out material I had very little stocks of food against inevitable rationing. We had, indeed, been asked not to hoard food, but it was shortage of cash and not Governmental warnings that had deterred me. Far-sighted friends, I found, had not only stocked up with food, but had seen to it that their wine cellars were equally well stocked. This sensible precaution was soon to pay off as spirits began to disappear 'under the counter' and popular brands vanished altogether.

For weeks after the start of the war nearly everyone had their favourite evacuee story; nor were these all from the point of view of host and hostess. Shortly after our Takeley evacuees arrived a furious 'mum' stood outside the village grocer's telling anyone who cared to listen just what she thought of the accommodation provided for her and her children.

'A filthy place — that's what I call it — an' we're not stoppin' there another night. I'd rather chance 'itler's bombs. Just you look at this!'

A small boy, standing glumly beside her, was told to pull up his jersey to display the speckling of red spots on his thin white chest.

'Flea bites — that's what they are! Bitten to death nearly, poor little fellow. We all were.'

The family had been sent to a somewhat primitive little beer-house off the beaten track and were duly moved to more salubrious lodgings.

Then there was the other side of the coin. Disgruntled hostesses complained of wet patches on clean mattresses, of children who appeared not to know how to use knives and forks, of London mothers whose cooking was limited to warming up fish and chips, or opening tins of baked beans and pink salmon. Before long the initial good will began to evaporate and as the days went by without bombs, gas attacks or the arrival of German parachutists, and boredom replaced fear, the reluctant lodgers began trickling back to the familiar streets where they knew their neighbours, the shopkeepers and the local licencee. Mostly the school children stayed, accepted their situation as children will, settling down in village schools without too much trouble.

Meanwhile Percy was searching fruitlessly for premises for the business in Bishop's Stortford, having drawn a blank in the village. Fortunately the lease of the Duke Street premises was running out so we had little more rent to pay. The landlord's Crown lease would run out at about the same time; he had intended to renew it, but when war broke out he decided to join up and he therefore wanted to be rid of the contents of the house as soon as possible. Rather than store the furniture he was prepared to sell it at giveaway prices.

'There's a very nice glazed break-front book-case,' Percy said to me one day after going up to Duke Street to see what was on offer, 'and two Regency card tables, if you can fit them in.'

I was only too willing; the furniture we had brought from London was pretty ordinary stuff; elegant additions from Duke Street were to be welcomed, once the typewriter and the packing cases had gone. A deal was soon done, the landlord a thin, worried little man, asked the modest sum of £50 for the items Percy chose, and the bulk of the stock was allowed to stay on the shelves until it went into appropriate sales at Hodgson's auction rooms.

Percy's parents had by then returned to Highgate. We had all exercised restraint; tempers had been kept. In the evenings Percy had taken refuge in a book, while I perforce listened to accounts of the doings and mis-doings of his many relatives, most of whom I had never met. Nor did I expect to meet them, for despite his Scottish blood Percy had no enthusiasm for gatherings of the clan.

October saw the appearance of our first Elkin Mathews catalogue issued from Takeley. It was a modest little job of just a few pages, but at least it showed our private customers and the trade that we were still in business, albeit no longer operating from London. Few of our customers could have heard of Takeley then.

The catalogue that was soon to follow was more ambitious. On a green cover, with a device designed by Reynolds Stone, P. H. Muir announced that Elkin Mathews Ltd., were offering 'The Library of a Man of Letters'.* The cable code-word was 'Adventure' and an adventurous catalogue it was, listing books on Architecture and Art, Biography, History, Psychology, the Theatre, Travel and Typography, first editions and limited editions.

There were plenty of bargains; few of the items went into double figures, many were priced less than £1. A limited edition of Oscar Wilde's *The Sphinx*, one of only 25 copies, was offered for £25 — and failed to sell. A.J.A. Symons, in need of money as always, had given Percy several Corvo items, including a 'mint' copy of the first issue of *Hadrian the Seventh*. These did sell quickly. Gastronomic curiosities from A.J.'s library were also offered; one was *A Bin Book* for wine lovers to record their judgement of wines they had drunk, details of wine purchased and consumption. This was a handsome quarto volume in full morocco, issued by the Wine and Food Society in their palmy days — one of A.J.'s bright ideas — complete with index, tabs and labels, price £1.5s.

Percy had counted on these two catalogues doing well in the U.S. — it was very important for us that they should. Most of the work of preparing them had been done in London during the quiet days in August when business had been almost at a standstill. There was uncertainty as to whether the overseas batch would arrive safely, and for that matter, if mailed orders would. Predictably, few booksellers in the U.K. were keen to buy at that time. A number had evacuated with their stock, as we had, and were barely organised for business. And our private customers had other preoccupations. But orders did come from the U.S. — enough to have made the exercise worth while, for it also showed that we were still alive and kicking.

The packing and posting of orders was another problem, with new and complicated export forms to be filled in. For Elizabeth it meant cycling back and forth to Takeley post-office on her German bicycle, parcels of books strapped precariously on to the carrier. As time passed the challenge of 'making-do' was becoming a bore. It was obvious that Elkin Mathews could not live indefinitely in its suitcases — or rather packing cases — with part of the stock in London. Some other arrangements had to be made if the business was to survive.

---

* A.J.A. Symons

CHAPTER NINE

One day that autumn before we parted with the Lancia, Percy and A.J. drove off together to Norfolk. Percy was going to see another famous private library for the *Times Literary Supplement* and he invited A.J. to go with him for the ride.

The Private Library Series had already taken Percy into several splendid country mansions. Houghton, the family seat of the Marquess of Cholmondeley and once the home of Sir Robert Walpole, was the one that charmed him most.

A.J.A. Symons.

A visitor to the library at Houghton, he wrote, should be blinded at the entrance to the house and the bandage only removed when he is in the library, and the doors are closed: otherwise the edge of its perfection is dulled by the beauty of the rest of the house.

And, in describing the library, he went on: It is, in fact, as one facet of a gem of 18th century architecture and furnishing that the library is chiefly recalled ... every room is a picture. Its detail loses much of its meaning when detached from the whole and this is not less true of the library than of the rest of the house.

Nevertheless, when he was seated at the desk in Britain's first Prime Minister's ornate, red morocco-covered chair, he couldn't help noting that much of the contents of the library was rather dull, although the 18th century spirit of the room made that fact supremely unimportant. His tongue was, perhaps, briefly in his cheek when he wrote that it might not have mattered much if the recessed shelves had been filled with dummies, instead of real books. There were, of course, many treasures, including books containing designs by William Kent, together with his interior design for Houghton, and by Inigo Jones and, predictably for a Norfolk country house, Blomefield's *Norfolk*, to mention just a few.

It was on the outward journey, when they were nearing King's Lynn, that A.J. enquired of Percy: 'Do you hear what I hear?'

'Yes,' said Percy gloomily, 'I'm afraid it's the big end.'

The diagnosis was confirmed when they pulled into a small garage for first aid. Could the job be done that day?

'Cost you a tenner, Guv'nor,' said the man in charge, 'but you'll have the car by the afternoon.'

A taxi was hired, A.J. was left in Lynn to explore the town and retrieve the car, and Percy who had been invited to lunch went on to Houghton. Sure enough A.J. arrived with the car in time for tea and was graciously received by Lady Cholmondeley who was on leave from her duties as a senior officer in the A.T.S.

As always A.J. rose to an occasion; his conversation sparkled and his hostess, instantly captivated, reproached Percy for not having brought him that morning. 'But you must bring Mr. Symons another time, when there's no need for you to hurry away ...'

Alas, A.J. was not to have the opportunity of returning to Houghton, for a month later the mysterious illness from which he never completely recovered struck him down.

It was shortly after this trip that A.J. turned up one evening on his way to Finchingfield with 'a review copy' on which he said he wished to have Percy's opinion. This was a bottle of wine sent to the Wine and Food Society, of which he was secretary and co-founder with André Simon.

I watched him come up the drive carrying the bottle tenderly, a tall man with a suggestion of an Edwardian dandy in his dress. He and Percy had known each other for some years and always got on well together. In a copy of his book *The Quest for Corvo*, inscribed to Percy, he had written: 'For Percy Muir, this Quest, to which he contributed both mentally and materially, very cordially from his friend a (sic) colleague A.J.'

'I thought you might like to give me your opinion on this bottle,' he said, handing it gently to Percy. Percy said he would be happy to do so, which meant, I guessed (rightly) that A.J. would stay for what would have been supper but would be up-graded to dinner in his and the wine's honour.

Like Percy, I always enjoyed A.J.'s company although I didn't find him physically attractive. His lank, longish hair, his height and the

rather yellowish pallor of his face gave an impression of too fast growth
without sufficient light, a sort of dankness.

During the next eighteen months we were to see A.J. often. Despite
his illness he was always full of plans and projects; we were still invited
to play his own frustrating form of croquet around the garden, or
squails on a marble top table, but his health grew worse and the time
would come when Percy would have the sad task of valuing his library
and his collection of Victoriana for probate. Acquisitive but always
discriminating, A.J. had delighted in clever and amusing trifles;
mother-of-pearl counters and card cases, water-colours of scenery that,
when held to the light, showed not one picture but two, glass paper-
weights with their sealed-in patterns in beads or dried flowers, and all
over the house his musical boxes, some as tall as grand-father clocks,
some as small as snuff boxes, tinkling out their Victorian melodies at the
touch of a finger.

Some of 'these foolish things' Percy bought and time was to prove
that A.J. had chosen wisely.

That evening he was in excellent spirits, apparently not at all cast
down by the probability that the Wine and Food Society, his main
source of income, would be an early war-time casualty. His latest idea
would, he assured us, be a winner. He was going to publish an *Unration
Book*. This would be the same size as the little buff ration book which
was being issued to everyone — five inches by four and a half. But his
would be blue and the 'coupons' would be recipes for delicious dishes
making use of every kind of unrationed food. It would be issued by the
Wine and Food Society and would certainly be an instant success.

This, alas, was not to happen. It made no one's fortune and never
really caught on.

After dinner, the subject of the *Unration Book* having at last been
exhausted, he taught Percy, Elizabeth and me a word game which he
had either invented or adapted. It required pencil and paper, a quick
brain, and a bit of practice — and there he, of course, had the advantage
over us.

He was not a bad loser, it was not in his nature to be petulant, but he
did like to win and usually did so, for he knew all about 'gamesmanship'
long before Stephen Potter invented the word. The game he taught us
was a complicated one, as A.J.'s games usually were, and presently
Percy, who was not competitive, dropped out and Elizabeth went to
bed, leaving A.J. and me to fight it out. He won and eventually drove
off to Finchingfield in high humour. I felt I had kept my end up, but at
the cost of an over-stimulated brain. Percy slept, but I lay restlessly
awake.

As I tossed and turned, my mind kept worrying over our one predominant problem, the urgent need to find premises for the firm with plenty of room for the books; somewhere not too far away and for the duration of the war at least.

It must have been around two a.m. when inspiration came to me. One day in July I had gone to view a poultry farm sale in a neighbouring village; there, amongst the field arks and feeding equipment, I had noticed a thirty foot pantechnicon which had been used as an office and store. Rumour had it that the woman who had been running the farm was the ex-mistress of a rich business man who had set her up as a poultry farmer. The farm had been running less than a year when fowl pest struck, killing most of the stock and putting an end to the business.

'Wasted 'is money, the ol' fule,' one of the locals, who had come to observe the sale, commented sourly. 'Er didn't know nowt about 'ens. She weren't there five minutes afore she were in trouble.'

The sale was a failure; the news of the fowl pest epidemic had spread and no one wanted to bid for infected poultry houses. As there was a reserve on most of them, for they were almost new, few were sold. Warned off, I had bought nothing.

As I lay awake I could see the pantechnicon in my mind's eye. It was hardly ideal accommodation, but I thought it could be shelved for books and there was room for it to stand in the garden. I nudged Percy awake; it seemed rather a shame, but I couldn't keep the idea to myself until morning.

He listened sleepily and then with more interest.

'Mm, sounds possible,' he agreed. 'We'd better get on to the auctioneers first thing in the morning; see if it's still there and they're willing to sell.'

'Yes, the pantechnicon is still on the site,' the auctioneer said, when Percy rang up. 'So are several of the bigger hen houses. As a matter of fact we're anxious to clear everything as soon as possible because the field has just been sold. If you're interested we could meet you on the site today.'

We made an appointment for that afternoon and took our friendly builder, Mr. P. along with us. The big field was dotted with wooden poultry houses and there was the pantechnicon, even longer than I remembered it. The paintwork was peeling, but it still looked serviceable. An amiable young man from the auctioneers joined us and he and Percy inspected it together. Inside it was rather less promising. Lined with books it would have been like working in a tunnel and I couldn't see Percy and Elizabeth installed in its narrow confines, complete with files and typewriters, not to mention the stock. On the other hand I thought it might do as a store. But Percy already had a better idea. As we climbed out of the pantechnicon he nodded towards a large hen house with a pitched roof. 'Is that one for sale?'

The auctioneer said it was.

From the outside it looked as good as new. It was built of pinewood and there were windows along one side and a sturdy door. We peered inside; the mouldy droppings on the wooden floor discouraged entry, so did the rotting corpse of a hen which had, presumably, been lying there since before the auction.

'What do you think of this?' Percy asked Mr. P. who had joined us.

'Not much wrong with it, so far as I can see,' he said cautiously. 'It's been built in sections so it could be moved easily enough. The floor should be all right, with a clean-up.'

I thought that an understatement, but our builder knew his business. He pulled out a tape, measured up and reported that the hen house was twenty foot square, the wood was sound and it could be taken to pieces and transported to Takeley in a morning.

'All right, if the price is reasonable we'll take it,' Percy decided. Meanwhile I had spotted a field ark that was just what I wanted for my expanding poultry flock. Eager to dispose of it, the agent assured me that a coat of tar would kill off any remaining fowl pest bugs.

'If we can buy the hen house you can have the ark as a present,' Percy told me generously, and for good measure we added a handy little potting shed to our purchases. The agent asked if we'd like to make an offer and was told it was up to him to state a price. This he was not prepared to do without first consulting his client who lived at Southend. He would contact him right away, he said and let us know that same day. He was as good as his word. We had not been home long before he rang up.

'We've just spoken to our client. He says he will accept £26.10s. for those three lots you've selected.'

It sounded too good to be true. We had expected to pay nearer £100. Percy told the agent he would put a cheque in the post that afternoon, then he rang our builder and arranged for our three purchases to be collected the following morning.

'I'm not taking a chance on a change of mind,' he said.

Twenty-four hours later the dismantled hen house was lying in sections on our front lawn, the droppings still on the floor boards, the potting shed was being erected next to our coal shed (and very handy it proved to be for housing my electric brooder) and the field ark, big enough to hold fifty birds, was standing on our strip of land across the road, having been towed there behind the builder's lorry.

We were gloating over our bargain when the agent telephoned. He sounded embarrassed.

'Mr. Muir? We have just had our client on the 'phone. I'm afraid he has changed his mind about the price of those three lots. He feels they were too cheap.'

'I'm sorry, but I am afraid he is too late,' Percy said. 'We have already taken delivery and you have had our cheque. It was he who named the price and we accepted it.'

Our cheque was cashed and we heard no more either from the agent or his eccentric client.

The part of the garden which was to be allocated to Elkin Mathews was where we had originally planned to have rose beds. The sacrifice of this plan was made willingly but my hope of almost instant accommodation for books and an office was optimistic. There was planning permission to be obtained ('ask for a temporary building for storing books, and you shouldn't have any trouble,' advised Mr. P.), footings had to be dug, bricks ordered for the foundations and plaster-board for lining the wooden sides and for the ceiling. And in war-time we must not expect speedy deliveries, Mr. P. warned.

A month went by and the smelly wooden sections still lay spread about the lawn, catching my eye whenever I looked out of the kitchen window. My hens were occupying their new premises long before Elkin Mathews was able to move. The plans were passed but the builder couldn't start building without bricks and they, it seemed, were already 'in short supply'; a phrase which was to become all too familiar.

CWK-F

CHAPTER TEN

By the end of October expectancy of a German offensive on the Western Front had begun to fade as far as the general public was concerned. A writer in a Belgian newspaper was reported as saying that 'boredom constitutes one of the principal enemies on the British Home Front.' Disillusion might, I thought, have been a better word. The Germans had swept through Poland and all the R.A.F. had done was to drop millions of leaflets over Germany. We were losing ships — the submarine Courageous had been destroyed and then the Germans had sneaked into Scapa Flow and sunk the Royal Oak. There were rumours that some sort of deal was being worked out by Hitler, with a Swedish diplomat acting as a mediator.

The village had its share of Left-wingers and 'fellow travellers' who shrugged off the war as none of their business; other people one met were puzzled or apathetic. The wit who dubbed the 'phoney war' period the 'Great Bore War', summed it up for many. The black-out was a bore, rationing was a bore and even more so were snooping A.R.P. wardens and the endless exhortations from Government departments.

Through a recommendation from Ian Fleming, Percy was invited to an interview at M.I.6 where Ian thought Percy's fluent German and familiarity with parts of South Germany and Austria might be useful. He duly attended the interview, warning me not to mention where he was going; but nothing came of it. In November he went with less enthusiasm to be interviewed by someone at the Bishop's Stortford office of the Ministry of Labour.

'Well, Mr. Muir', said the official, 'although you are over-age for military service you are still required to register for civilian work. I see your present occupation is that of an antiquarian bookseller and that you drive a car. Have you any objection to being asked to drive a lorry?'

One of the least mechanically minded of men, Percy replied that he would drive a lorry if it was in the national interest for him to do so, but should the thing break down he wouldn't have the faintest idea of what to do. The point must have been taken for he heard no more from that quarter.

As the mother of a young child I was not required to register for national service, but having been accepted as a part-time ambulance driver I was expected to pass a first-aid test. This meant attending a course of lessons given in the back room of a Takeley pub by a jovial local doctor. There were about ten of us in the class, all women. We bandaged each other diligently, strapping splints on to each others legs and tourniquets on to arms and wrists. We searched for pressure points and took it in turns to lie on the floor and be resuscitated. I did my best, but the tight rolls of bandage had a way of leaping from my hand when I tried to wind them round someone's supposedly fast-bleeding head or limb, and when it came to the St. John sling — the mastering of which was the peak of achievement for the first-aided tyro — it only needed a tug by the doctor for mine to fall off.

The day came for the official test and I approached the ordeal with jittering nerves. It was held one evening in a bare, lino-floored room at the A.R.P. headquarters in Dunmow, the candidates going in singly to be examined by a doctor none of us knew. For some reason I was the last to be summoned.

The doctor, sitting at a deal table, gave me a weary glance. It was late and no doubt he had had a long day. He shot a few basic questions at me, accepted my answers with a brief nod and then turned to a lad who had been brought along to play the part of the victim. He was a tall, thin lad and must have been heartily sick of being pummelled and bandaged by strange women.

'Lie down on the floor will you, John' the doctor told him. 'Now,' he turned to me, 'that's a boy who has just been pulled out of a river, half drowned and unconscious. I want you to try to revive him.'

John had obediently lain face down on the lino. I knew about artificial respiration. I had practised it in the class. I knelt beside my victim with some confidence. The only trouble was that he hadn't attended our class where the routine had been to turn a patient over before attempting to revive him. With what I hoped was professional skill I heaved John over and began to apply the correct rhythmic pressure to his rib cage. His eyes goggled up at me in surprise, then he began to giggle.

I paused, disconcerted. Half-drowned lads shouldn't giggle. Somehow I'd got it wrong.

The doctor sighed. 'Do you really think that's right?' he said wearily.

'Oh!' Belatedly I saw what was wrong. 'He should be face down.' Instead of expanding his lungs I'd merely been tickling him.

'Well then, hadn't you better turn him over?'

Mortified I rolled John back on to his stomach and put my hands on to his skinny back.

'All right, that will do. Thank you.' The test was over and I fled, convinced that I had failed. My certificate arrived two weeks later. Everyone had passed. Volunteer drivers were needed and no one wanted to fail us.

Despite the absence of air raids we were expected to sleep at the Dunmow Foakes Memorial Hall on our duty nights. I had been teamed up with a neighbour a few years older than myself who ran a dairy farm and had a husband who was a naval reservist. He had already been called up and she was running the farm on her own. A member of the Red Cross, she was a far more efficient first-aider than I was and more used to driving heavy vehicles. In the interests of the casualties we might have to transport, we agreed that I should be the driver.

On our weekly duty evening we would drive into Dunmow with our sleeping bags, tin hats and gas masks, dispose our belongings in the projection room next to the ladies' cloakroom and then make for the kitchen, where kindly ladies would have sandwiches and coffee ready for us and the air raid wardens.

The sandwiches were invariably filled with sardines which would haunt us for the rest of the evening. All too often our duty nights would coincide with a dance. This was a great bore because then we couldn't go to bed until it was over, usually at mid-night. Neither of us fancied the role of uniformed wall-flower and, while in those days the dances were relatively sedate, sitting around on the fringe of the fun was a tedious business. To be sent out on an exercise was far more to our taste.

By this time the Dennis truck had been replaced by a smaller, more conventional ambulance. In this we were expected to find our way through dark, winding country roads, our headlights doused and no signposts to give us a bit of help.

In the feeble beam from our doused lights stretches of roads would look unfamiliar enough to raise doubts.

'I don't remember that barn ...we must have missed the turning.'

'Well, we can't turn here anyway. Better keep going.'

Peering into the darkness, crawling through anonymous villages with never a gleam from a lighted window to cheer us, we would search for landmarks, and the reassurance that we were heading back to Dunmow and not on the way to Chelmsford or Ongar. Back at the hall we would climb up the stairs to the empty, bare-boarded little room allotted to us for sleeping quarters, snuggle into our sleeping bags and talk ourselves to sleep.

Yda was a tall woman with a matter-of-fact manner behind which was a heart easily moved by the misfortunes of others. From my point of view she had only one disadvantage as a team mate; her devotion to her Jersey herd. This meant that she couldn't bring herself to leave the milking to her not very bright cowman.

I thought five-thirty an appalling hour to be up and away, but as our petrol allowance for our duty turn was for one car only there was nothing for it but to struggle out of my sleeping bag and leave with her.

I'd be only half awake as we drove along the empty road in what seemed like the middle of the night. Left at my gate I'd steal softly into the silent house; the curtains drawn, everyone still asleep, the ashes cold in the sitting room fireplace. By then I'd be feeling a pleasant sense of superiority at being up and about when everyone else was still in bed. I'd stir the kitchen stove to life, light the sitting room fire and tell myself that this was an excellent opportunity to sit down at my typewriter and get on with my book.

It had been nearly finished when war was declared. To go on with it at such a time had seemed pointless and I had put it away. At the end of September when, instead of the expected chaos and destruction, we were being subjected to nothing worse than inconvenience, I took it out, read it through and decided to finish it after all, adding a war-time ending.

If I did sit down to write, making use of the couple of hours of quiet, presented to me by the needs of Yda's Jersey cows, the time flew by until the family awoke and needed my attention, the poultry needed feeding and the sitting room became Elkin Mathews' office. But sometimes self discipline would fail and I'd potter in the kitchen, nibbling biscuits to assuage my wide-awake stomach, tidying up, watching the sky lighten, the night fade away.

By November I knew I was pregnant again. The knowledge made me determined to finish the task I had set myself — the completion and despatch of my book by the end of the year. I would send it to my agent and then forget it.

We had both wanted another child, but my timing wasn't very clever.

Neither of us expected the war to be over quickly, the firm's survival was uncertain and Percy's parents still needed financial support; despite all this we were both happy at the prospect of another child.

'Early June,' said the doctor and signed the form that allowed me free orange juice and half price milk. June then, seemed the best possible month to have a baby.

Winter 1939 — Spring 1940

CHAPTER ELEVEN

By the time winter came we had settled into a routine of a sort. Percy and Elizabeth made a weekly trip to London with the car, bringing back cartons of books to catalogue or for despatch to customers, mostly anglophile Americans who wrote warm and encouraging letters assuring us that they were backing Britain wholeheartedly.

While the Government was urging exporters to redouble their efforts to bring in much needed dollars, civil servants were producing complicated forms that made such business as difficult as possible. Percy, a law-abiding man, was none the less never one to suffer bureaucracy gladly, and he was soon campaigning on behalf of his trade association for more sensible regulations. As the war continued the file of letters to and from the Board of Trade (as it then was) grew fatter and fatter.

It was not long before some of the 'runners' began to find their way to Takeley. These were the small-timers with no shop of their own who made their living (and still do) by quoting a book they have seen in one bookshop to a bookseller in another and making a modest profit if the deal goes through.

Percy, having once done the same before setting up in his own shop, was sympathetic to the fraternity and made a point of treating them fairly. He was tolerant even with the rogues, as a few were, enjoying their cockney wit and guile. They were all sorts, from the Major with the stammer, always down on his luck, to the cockney carpenter who never asked more than a shilling or two for a book and volunteered to come and put up our bookshelves. Runners came by train and bus, arriving unheralded, with a suitcase full of books and the prospect of a couple of hours' wait before they could get a bus back to the station.

The war hadn't stopped the London book auctions and Percy would usually go by train to attend them, conserving our petrol allowance for the buying trip he was planning for the new year. The need to replenish stock is always in an antiquarian bookseller's mind; to buy at auctions is all very well, but to buy privately is far better. Because we were newcomers to Essex with no shop front, there was little opportunity locally for this. Nor were there any second-hand bookshops in our neighbourhood. While we were living in London we would set off on Saturdays to do the rounds of the outer London bookshops, usually profitably, returning to Acacia Road via the Charing Cross Road. At most calls there would be a pause for shop-chat, after the bill was paid, and sometimes a cup of tea and a privileged look at the dealer's own 'not for sale' books with a few treasures proudly shown. Those Saturday outings were my apprenticeship to the antiquarian book trade. I would study the books Percy selected and diligently search the shelves for titles he might want.

As well as the business petrol allowance there was a small 'basic' for non-business purposes. 'Without this allowance people in rural areas might not be able to get to church,' a Government spokesman had said piously when petrol rationing was introduced. Which didn't mean that the impious couldn't use their 'basic' for a Sunday morning visit to their local. But later even the 'basic' was withdrawn and a case for some special need had to be made.

Given the necessary coupons (and there were ways of getting hold of a few extra) motorists could fill up where they liked. It was all 'Pool' in any case. But when it came to food rations it was a different matter. There could be no shopping around for the best cuts of bacon, the freshest butter, the tenderest joints of meat. You chose your grocer and your butcher; the union was registered at the Food Office, and accepted by both parties for better or worse, for the duration of the ration book period.

It was not a choice to be made lightly on the strength of an attractive shop front; for though the goods in the window might appeal, it was those hidden away under the counter that made registration worth-while.

Mistakenly, as it turned out later, I took our ration books to Bishop Stortford's best grocery store, a private firm who catered for what was known as the 'high class' trade.

When we came to Essex, I had been tempted by their delicatessen foods and their continental cheeses, the sort of food I had bought in Soho. Besides, not only did they deliver my weekly order, they even sent a man round each week to ask me what I wanted. As for the butcher, he and I were already on good terms and I was happy to let him supply me, when I found he was willing to continue his deliveries at least twice a week and that he was not short of offal, which the Food Minister had decided not to ration. Game was also unrationed, but usually obtained by people with either guns or long purses.

Rationing killed off our little grocery-cum-sweet-shop at the bottom of the hill. It was run by a kindly widow and when only a few local families registered with her, she knew her turnover would be too small for her to carry on. Sadly she returned their ration books and closed down.

Elizabeth was rather dismayed by my sparsely stocked store-cupboard. She had a good appetite and must have feared that one day it would be Mother Hubbard over again. Not that she said anything; instead she began quietly stocking up a store of tinned foods in her bedroom.

The arrival of a German girl in our household had caused no noticeable interest in the village, so far as we knew, and certainly no antagonism against Elizabeth. Since Hitler had come to power, Germans, both Jewish and political refugees, had been arriving in England in a steady stream and been accepted sympathetically by most people, in the tolerant British tradition of welcoming persecuted foreigners. Unlike the early days of the first world war, there was no immediate spy scare as when unfortunate naturalised Germans, who had lived harmlessly in the U.K. for years, were ostracized and sometimes persecuted.

Although the outbreak of war didn't change attitudes as far as the general public was concerned, the Home Office took no chances. Germans and Austrians were technically 'enemy aliens', if not naturalised, and as such were required to prove before a tribunal that they were no threat to national security. Elizabeth was even required to have a licence for her push-bike. The Tribunal wasn't too alarming an ordeal, thanks to the good work of the British Jewish community, who made it their business to look after the immigrants, not only at their Tribunals but with finding them jobs and homes.

Not long after Elizabeth arrived we had a visit from Nancy Salaman, Sir Herbert Samuel's daughter, who was living at Newport a few miles away. She would, she said, see Elizabeth through her Tribunal when the time came. Some weeks later, armed with Percy's testimony that she was a member of our household and invaluable to Elkin Mathews, and supported by Nancy, Elizabeth was officially accepted as a non-enemy alien and, in theory, eligible to enroll in H.M. forces — which was what she was longing to do. In practice this wasn't so easy.

Meanwhile autumn leaves drifted down on to the smelly sections of the hen house that were beginning to turn the grass yellow. Winter had come and the builder had not. 'Why?' I kept demanding of him, 'are we still waiting? Why can't you start building?'

Planning permission had at last come through for 'a temporary building'. It was the plaster-board that was the trouble, Mr. P. said. 'It's a job to get any at all.'

But get it he did and one happy day the men arrived to dig the foundations. After that the operation moved fairly fast, though not as fast as I wanted. The trickiest part was when it came to balancing the two end sections on top of the three foot wall which was necessary to raise the shed to the requisite height. These had to be propped up with long planks while the side sections were raised and secured to the ends. The two halves of the pitched roof were then perilously manoevred into position, all this being done without the erection of any scaffolding, which meant waiting for a completely windless day.

Once the roof was on the men could work regardless of the weather, which was just as well because we were soon having snow.

With little news of special interest on the home front the saga of the Battle of the River Plate held us all enthralled. The successful outcome and a speech by Churchill was a great boost to our morale. Then came the news of the Russian invasion of Finland and to the delight of everyone (bar our 'fellow travelling' neighbours, who wouldn't admit it) we learnt that the heroic Finns were giving the invaders a bloody nose.

Although Percy's parents had returned to London, along with most of the evacuees, they did not want to stay there. Instead they planned to come and live near us in Takeley. As Percy's father had turned seventy and was not too well, this seemed the best thing for them to do and Percy, a dutiful son, found a bungalow for them to rent less than ten minutes walk from our house. It had only four rooms; two bedrooms, a 'front room', a small kitchen-cum-living room, and an after-thought bathroom. Adequate accommodation for the two of them, Percy thought. As for the rent, the landlord, who was a grandson of Haddon Spurgeon the non-conformist preacher, was asking 12 shillings a week, including rates, which seemed modest even for those days.

Percy's mother immediately took to Mr. Spurgeon who was known locally as the Bee Man for his skill in dealing with those, to me, dangerous insects. She was also delighted at the prospect of living so close to her son, a delight I couldn't altogether share. Meanwhile the work on the firm's new premises was proceeding steadily; the wooden sections were lined with plaster-board, the floorboards were scrubbed and stained and shelving erected.

The exterior, it is true, lacked architectural distinction, but as it was sited beyond the garage it didn't impinge much on the house and the purple swags of clematis which were soon to hang around the door (embellished with Elkin Mathew's brass plate) would give it a pretty, cottagey look.

Shortly before Christmas we were all given some morale boosting by the Ministry of Information which told us that victory depended on 'the will of the people to stand up to the strain of war'. We were 'The Home Front' and, the inference was, we could win the war by keeping our chins up and waiting for the Germans to lose it. 'We do not have to defeat the Nazis on land,' said the writer of the M.O.T. pamphlet hopefully, 'but only to prevent them from defeating us.'

Food was no problem that Christmas; I had fattened up a couple of my fowls, gift parcels arrived from friends in the United States and Elizabeth contributed some luxuries. Percy's parents joined us for Christmas dinner, after which we sat, replete, listening to George VI struggling bravely through his Christmas broadcast without a stutter. Later we heard on the nine o'clock news that the western front was still all quiet.

Early in the new year came the joyful day when the workmen moved out of Elkin Mathews' new premises and Percy and Elizabeth moved in. The desks and office furniture from Duke Street were installed, along with the stock, now much diminished. Handsome pieces of furniture selected by Percy from the gentlemen's chambers, were brought into the house. An unexpected bonus was three pairs of long curtains in heavy gold slub, which had graced the tall Duke Street windows. Made by Storeys, silk-lined and interlined, they were the sort of curtains I had never dreamed of owning — any more than I ever expected to own a mink coat. They were, of course, far too long and wide for our casement windows and I could hardly bear to cut them up.

At first the two regency card-tables, with their harp pedestals and brass inlay seemed rather grand for our sitting room, but we were soon taking them for granted, along with the equally handsome break-front bookcase that came with them. This, over the years, became the home of Percy's most prized books — presentation copies mostly, and those books that a wise bookseller puts away for himself to enjoy in his old age or for a rainy day. Apart from containing books, the polished top was to prove useful as a display stand for the automata Percy was beginning to collect.

Clockwork figures performing tricks under glass domes to the tinkling tunes from a musical box were not particularly saleable in war time; a few pounds or less would buy such toys and while Percy bought them for the best possible reason — because he liked them — he was pretty sure that they would also prove a good investment.

Some we bought locally, others came from Cameo Corner in

London. The time was to come when they would be sold at Christies for sums that took our breath away.

There was one snag to Elkin Mathews' new premises, and it never was entirely solved. This was the heating problem. A wooden building designed for hens could hardly be expected to provide cosy accommodation for human beings. Our chosen heating was by electricity, but even with two fires full on the temperature that winter seldom climbed into the sixties and Percy and Elizabeth, huddled at their desks in woollies and jackets, could see their breath condensing in the air as they worked.

Apart from this disadvantage the building made an acceptable office-cum-bookshop. The walls were shelved and sections of white glazed bookcases, brought from Duke Street, served as a room divider, with Percy's desk on one side and Elizabeth's on the other.

From the back window the view of a muddy pond was hardly inspiring and was soon partly hidden by accumulating clutter; but the south window compensated, with a view of the front garden and a bed of flowering shrubs. There was still no place for packing parcels bar the floor, which Elizabeth maintained was more convenient than anywhere else. This problem, too, was to be solved in due course.

At last it looked as if we really were in business again and when the occasional customer turned up they could, at last, see the stock on the shelves.

Pregnancy and ambulance driving don't go well together. By March my A.R.P. trousers had become too tight for my swelling figure so I resigned the job, offering to return in the autumn if I was still wanted.

I had finished my novel and despatched it to John Farquarson who wrote to say that he was willing to handle it, but that with the woman's magazine market contracting fast, owing to the war, he could hold out no hope of selling it as a serial. As it was on his advice that I had tailored my plot for this market it was discouraging news.

Too late I wished I had written quite a different book instead of trying to jump onto a band waggon that was no longer rolling. Yet, by and large, I had written to please myself, within the limits of my plot. I had believed in my characters, enjoyed telling the story and polished my prose to the best of my ability. It was finished, out of my hands, and I made up my mind to forget it. Once again I would put my literary ambitions on ice and concentrate on my home and family and helping the war effort locally. No more disciplining myself to sit at the typewriter when the sun was shining and the garden called me. No more surreptitiously slipping away to write when Percy and Elizabeth were reading by the fireside. Spring had come, our puddingy clay soil was beginning to dry out, it was time to sow early vegetable seeds, to get out the brooder and order a batch of day-old chicks.

Chicks, for the first few weeks of their lives, like birds in their nests, agree. In their brooder with no hen to gather them under her wings, nature tells them when it's time for a nap and, with one accord, they go into a tight huddle like a football scrum, heads down, beaks tucked in. From their little throats comes a soft trilling sound, as if they were reassuring each other. Later, as they start to grow feathers, a pecking order develops. Why some were more equal than others I never could discover; nor why those discriminated against meekly accepted their lowly situation.

In March Percy set off on a buying trip with Harold Edwards, a colleague who, like us, had moved his business out of London. They were old friends; Londoners with a similar background but utterly different in character. Both had read widely, but whereas Percy's reading never influenced his behaviour or attitude to life, Harold had been in turn a Marxist, a pacifist, and a vegetarian — and was at that time a Buddhist. Never reluctant to give his reasons for whatever creed, cult or political theory he was currently supporting, he thoroughly enjoyed opposition. But while giving the impression of pugnacity, his essential good humour always prevailed, however vigorous the argument on both sides.

This was not their first joint buying trip. At the height of the inflation in Germany they had gone there together to buy books; young, green and hopeful, with a few pounds in their pockets and hardly a word of German between them. They had made the rounds of the Berlin bookshops changing money each day into bundles of almost worthless marks, and somehow managing to buy enough to have made the trip worthwhile. Percy, looking back on that trip, would sometimes think of the bargains he had missed, through lack of knowledge as well as cash, but he had made contacts which were to stand him in good stead in the years to come. He also met the German girl who was to become his first wife.

The 1940 buying trip had become necessary because Elkin Mathews' stock badly needed building up. The North had proved a good hunting ground in the past and there were one or two ports of call en route.

'Have spent just about £200 all told,' he wrote to me in a letter from Grassmere, 'and am very pleased with what I have bought.' Many of the bargains came from Varty's shop in Ambleside, a happy hunting ground on other occasions.

Harold, too, was satisfied with the trip and presently, loaded up with books, they started back for Essex. By then the 'twilight war' as

Churchill called it, had ended. The Germans had marched into Denmark and were spreading through Norway. In the newspapers we read of the Norwegians' heroic resistance and speculation as to where the British Navy would mount a counter offensive. Few of us had heard of Narvik until then. Switching on the radio for every news bulletin we waited to hear that the Navy had triumphed. Instead the news was generally depressing. For a short time our spirits were raised by reports of British and French landings on the Norwegian coasts, and of allied troops pushing into central Norway, only to be dashed by the news that we were having to withdraw.

April was bad enough; May was infinitely worse. From the second week onwards, with the invasion of the low countries and the bombing of Rotterdam, it was a nightmarish sequence of defeats and disaster. Certain phrases began to crop up in the reports from the war zone, phrases which were to become depressingly familiar during the next two years. The situation was described as 'obscure', or more ambiguously, 'confused'. Another well-used phrase was 'regrouping seems to be taking place'. This always meant things were going badly wrong. In France we were told of a 'bulge' in the line, which was soon to be 'a gap'.

Percy was never given to useless speculation about events over which he had no control, and as we sat round the radio in the evenings, listening to harrowing accounts of peasants being shot up by low-flying Messerschmidts as they fled along the country roads, their belongings and young children piled on to handcarts, he would be silent. For Elizabeth it was worse, since her mother, grand-mother and younger sister were then living in the south of France with little chance of getting away to safety and she was powerless to help them.

My reaction to these horrors was furious rage. I longed to be actively involved in the war. Pregnant as I was, I felt useless and frustrated. Yet somehow my optimism as to the outcome never quite left me. To lose the war was unthinkable and I refused to believe it could happen.

Amongst our friends there was endless speculation as to what the French might or might not do; of what we could expect if we had to face the Germans alone. The war had knit our village community closer together. Early in 1940 we found ourselves drawn into a circle of friends who were mostly in the same circumstances as ourselves, relative newcomers to the neighbourhood. Like us they had bought old timbered cottages and had had the same problems over conversions and dilatory or incompetent builders. Most were still commuting to Liverpool Street.

Percy went to London by train often enough to be regarded as one of the fraternity and would be invited to join a bridge four to pass the time on the homeward journey. He was a good player, helped by an excellent memory. Often one of the four would be Rupert Cross a young, blind lawyer, and the game would be played with Braille cards.

Rupert and his wife, Heather had recently bought the oldest cottage in Takeley Street — a cottage that would one day be the home of Percy's partner, Laurie Deval and his wife and family. It was a sturdy example of Tudor village building, with a front door that opened directly on to the narrow footpath. The rooms were tiny and low-ceilinged and the Heath Robinson plumbing system had a way of flooding the next-door garden. When convoys went by, the cottage would gently vibrate. Rupert was tall and thin and, like most blind men, his head habitually inclined forward, which no doubt saved it from too frequent contact with beams and low doorways.

Both he and Heather were practising solicitors working for different London law practices. They travelled to London together, parted at Liverpool Street and usually came back on the same train. They coped with the problems of Rupert's blindness with a matter-of-fact good humour which made pity seem out of place. Blessed as he was with a first-class brain and an excellent sense of humour, Rupert gave the impression of enjoying life more than most. Later he was to become Vinerian Professor of Law at Oxford. A hospitable couple, the Crosses led an active social life and never let rationing prevent them from entertaining friends.

From bridge on the train Percy's friendship with Rupert soon ripened and we would play in each other's houses. For Percy and I the fascination of watching Rupert 'read' his hand and then, when it went down on the table 'read' the dummy, was never-failing. His memory was such that once having fingered the Braille cards he seldom needed to be told what was still on the table. On one occasion when a card unaccountably disappeared and we were all crawling about searching for it Rupert remarked cheerfully: 'You see this is where I enjoy an advantage. I can sit back and leave the rest of you to do the searching.'

Down Takeley Street, a little further on from the Crosses, were the Sharps in yet another modernised bit of Tudor England, although in a rather more up-market style. Geoffrey Sharp, a young man still in his twenties, was owner and editor of *The Music Review*, an intellectual music quarterly which he had founded and was subsidising from a comfortable private income. A professed conscientious objector since his Oxford undergraduate days, he was waiting to be called before a tribunal to show why he should not be conscripted into the Forces, while his nineteen-year-old wife, Mary, pretty and intelligent, was waiting to take over running the magazine when he went to prison. She did not share his views, but kept hers to herself and loyally supported him.

Heinie Fraenkel, author and journalist and a political refugee from the Nazis at the time of the Reichstag trial, arrived with his wife Gretel and two young sons a little later. Both spoke almost perfect English; Heinie, who had written film scenarios in Germany, was chess correspondent for the *New Statesman*. A small, slight man, warmly anglophile he was an eager talker; speech would bubble up from him. After the war he became well-known as the co-author of biographies of the Nazi war criminals; also, in curious contrast, as a translator into German of P. G. Wodehouse's novels. Gretel, practical and down to earth, had been a ballet dancer in Germany and was soon much in demand at village concerts. To call the old cottage that they had rented 'modernised' would have been a gross exaggeration; a temporary haven is the best word for it.

Another German Jew who had sought sanctuary in England and lived briefly in the neighbourhood at that time was Freddie Uhlman, the artist. Before coming to England shortly after the outbreak of war, he had been running a tropical fish shop in Paris — the sort of unlikely thing one might have expected him to do, for he was, as the French would say 'un type'. To the bewilderment of her family, he had married the daughter of a peer, a charming Mitfordish girl whose father caught the headlines when he advocated issuing pikes to the Home Guard if sufficient rifles weren't available.

Freddie was a natural entertainer, delighting in the absurd. He could take the floor and keep his audience happily chuckling as he described his encounters with the more conventional members of the British aristocracy. The Uhlmans settled in Hampstead later and Freddie became one of the Hampstead group of artists.

Ruthven Todd, a gifted young writer still in his twenties, had come to live in a cottage tucked away in a remote hamlet not far from Thaxted. One found it more by good luck than by following any directions, which was, perhaps, why he had taken it. He had already published *The Laughing Mulatto*, the story of Alexander Dumas, and some of his poems had appeared in anthologies.

A thin, rather pale young man, he looked to me as if he didn't have enough to eat, which was probably true. Percy, whose interest in young writers was unfailing, would find his way to Todd's cottage from time to time and probably made some helpful purchases. *The Lost Traveller*, Todd's first novel, appeared in 1943. We thought it an appropriate title. He was to write a number of detective stories as 'R. T. Campbell'.

The date of my confinement was the first of June. With my suitcase packed and all arrangements made for going to Braintree Cottage Hospital I waited impatiently for the baby's arrival. If Britain was to be invaded, and the prospect seemed increasingly likely, the last thing I wanted was to be in hospital away from my family. Although Braintree was only some fifteen miles distant it was in what was then known as a 'protected area' and might well be sealed off in the event of an invasion. It was too late to change the arrangement; I could only hope that the baby would not delay his appearance unduly, even though his future didn't look too bright. For babies born in 1940 it certainly was a case of 'into the dangerous world I leapt'.

Summer 1940

CHAPTER TWELVE

In the early morning of June 2nd I awoke from an uneasy sleep and looked at my watch. It was 2 a.m. For what seemed like another hour I lay in a state of indecision while Percy slept beside me. Then I nudged him awake.

'I think it's starting'.

'Mmm? What?'

My doctor had impressed on me that I mustn't delay once the pains began, and we had a longish drive with possible hold-ups.

I eased my cumbersome body out of the bed, wishing I was already in the hospital, feeling for my bedroom slippers.

'I think I'd better get dressed.'

The night was fading into the dawn as we drove to Braintree. Half way there we found the road partly blocked by an improvised check point. Percy stopped the car and a young soldier came up and peered through the window.

'Your destination, please?'

'Braintree Cottage Hospital — maternity ward.'

He stepped back with a grin. 'O.K. Carry on.'

He had only glanced at me. Our explanation could have been a good alibi for a couple of fifth columnists out on a demolition mission. A well-placed cushion was all that was needed.

There were no further check-posts and we reached the hospital without hindrance. While Percy parked the car I was led away to the private ward we had booked — at £6 a week. During the journey the niggling pains that had awoken me had gradually died away — much to my annoyance. I hadn't admitted this to Percy, but I confessed to the nurse.

'My pains seem to have stopped.'

By the look she gave me I knew she didn't believe that they had ever seriously begun, but she refrained from saying so. What she did say didn't help to raise my morale.

'I should think your husband had better go home. You're not going to have the baby tonight so there's no point in him waiting.'

It was a shocking anti-climax but Percy seemed glad enough to go home to bed.

When my doctor looked in some hours later he was jocular about my false alarm.

'Like's to take its time, this baby of yours.'

But I, as ever, was impatient with waiting.

'Couldn't you do *something* to speed things up?'

In normal pregnancies in those days babies were allowed to arrive in their own good time, rather than be induced to suit other people's convenience; but my doctor promised a little encouragement for the laggard infant. A hot bath and a dose of quinine should do the trick, he said.

Percy arrived after breakfast with A.J. They brought flowers and newspapers full of dramatic stories of the Dunkirk evacuation, then nearing completion. A.J. was apparently recovering from the serious illness that had struck him down before Christmas. He had come to Finchingfield to recuperate and get on with his book on Oscar Wilde, and he and Percy had been seeing a good deal of each other. The news from Dunkirk was so much better than everyone had expected that it was impossible not to feel cheerful. Soon the conversation turned from the war to A.J.'s latest writing projects — he was never without one or more in view, a book on the Glennconner family was the latest. Ideas still sparked from his ever-fertile brain, although his illness had sapped his will to carry them forward.

After the two men had left I avidly read the newspapers until the nurse came to begin the hurrying-on process and I had something else to occupy my mind.

There was no doubt about the pains that evening, and early the next morning my son made his belated appearance — a healthy eight pound baby.

Ten peaceful, blissful days followed. In perfect June weather I lazed in the hospital garden, breast-fed my son, welcomed visitors and gossiped with the dressing-gowned patients who were allowed to walk around. The wards were segregated, male and female, but in the garden it was unisex.

In the aftermath of Dunkirk, luxuriating in that concentrated happiness that follows on the advent of a wanted child, I could manage to persuade myself that the future wasn't as bleak as we had feared.

The days slipped by. Percy came to take us home. Elizabeth, he said,

A FOURTH
SELECTION FROM
OUR STOCK
M—Ω

SOME 18TH CENTURY MUSIC
AND A SECTION AT 10/- AND UNDER

Issued by

P. H. MUIR

for

ELKIN MATHEWS LTD.

from

TAYLORS, TAKELEY, BISHOPS STORTFORD

PHONE: TAKELEY 312   WIRE: MUIR, TAKELEY 312

1940

had managed splendidly. Helen had been good, the hens were laying, the vegetables were coming on nicely.

A day or two earlier he and Elizabeth had posted a batch of catalogues to the United States. This was the fourth catalogue to be issued from Takeley and, as usual, it included a number of scarce items, temptingly priced. Percy had been working his way through the alphabet and was now listing books from M to Q, which brought in Katherine Mansfield (four first editions of her books) Somerset Maugham's *Liza of Lambeth*, exceedingly scarce and a fine copy (£5.10s.) and, more impressive, 'a very nice and tall copy in panelled calf' of Milton's *Paradise Lost*, price £14.

Once again there were collector's items of musical works, mostly engraved first editions. It was four years since music had begun to feature in Elkin Mathew's catalogues and the response was still relatively small. It was, Percy believed, a case of being ahead of the market. Already a few percipient collectors were buying systemati-cally — Gerald Coke was one — and Percy's own love of music and enjoyment of the necessary research was enough to make him persist in offering it. When time and printing costs allowed he would sometimes add an extra tidbit to his notes. *Berenice, an Opera as it is perform'd at the Theatre Royal in Covent Garden*, this, he noted 'was the last opera of Handel's ruinous season … which cost him £20,000'. Although only priced at £4.10s. the engraved, calf-bound first edition failed to sell, at least in that catalogue.

All the same, at least three quarters of the items offered *did* sell, to our great relief, for sending out catalogues at that time was something of an act of faith. Certainly it contained some remarkable bargains. In an under 10s. section was the first edition of D.H. Lawrence's *Women in Love* and a book illustrated by Beardsley, *Evil Motherhood*, with the suppressed plate was priced 7s.6d.

The catalogues went off in two batches, those to the United States ten days before the U.K. ones. Few of our private customers in this country were interested in buying books — Hugh Walpole was a happy exception — and we were selling almost nothing to the British trade. The response from the States was therefore eagerly awaited and the first cable, telephoned through from Takeley post-office by Isobel, the post-mistress, was greeted with a sigh of relief, since it showed that the overseas batch had arrived safely.

The post-office was a snug little timbered cottage in the centre of the village. What must have once been a front parlour served as the office and Isobel would hurry in from the back room to attend to customers, her little dog at her heels. A thin, conscientious spinster, round shouldered and a little short-sighted, she preferred not to take a holiday in case her relief got things in a muddle. This had happened once and she wasn't going to risk it a second time.

Much extra work had been piled on to her shoulders since the outbreak of war. The post-office had been appointed the village depot for cod-liver oil and 'national milk', the dried-milk baby food supplied by the Ministry of Food and heavily subsidised.

It was rare for cottagers and council house tenants to have a telephone, so when the postman was off duty it would be Isobel who got on her bicycle and delivered telegrams.

On top of all this Elkin Mathews was bringing her piles of catalogues to frank, parcels to weigh and cables and telegrams to take down and telephone to us. To her credit, she never grumbled.

Busy as we all were, we would be drawn like magnets to the radio in the sitting room for the latest reports from France. Every hour or so I'd scurry in from the kitchen or the garden to switch on the radio — the only one we possessed — with the absurd hope of hearing that by some miracle the situation in France might be saved from collapse.

Percy would come over from the office to join me. Far more realistic than I was, he knew that it could only be bad news. When I rushed to tell him that Churchill had flown to Paris and offered the French nation a union with Great Britain he only shook his head, saying 'I'm afraid it's too late now.'

Prepared though we were for the fall of Paris, when it happened I felt utterly cast down and couldn't bear to read the account in the newspapers. At the same time my imagination insisted on tormenting me with pictures of German soldiers marching through the streets of Paris, of arrogant German officers enjoying the pavement cafés and the restaurants. I longed to believe that the ladies of the town would refuse to smile on their conquerors, but this seemed very unlikely; as indeed it was.

Churchill's broadcasts came like a shot-in-the-arm to all of us. After hearing him state with implacable determination that we would 'defend our island home,' ... and with the British Empire 'we shall fight on unconquerable until the curse of Hitler is lifted from the brows of mankind,' I felt heartened and resolute. With a babe in arms I could see no way of putting this resolution into practical use for the war effort, but I planned to get back to ambulance driving as soon as possible.

By this time the village had formed its own Local Defence Volunteers Unit under the command of a retired poultry farmer, a coarse-grained, heavily built man, assertive and pugnacious. He was by no means popular in the village, although chairman of the hall committee, (it was said he had never been known to give anyone a lift in his large, comfortable car) but no one was surprised when he was given the job. A true-blue Tory and a veteran of the first world war, his hatred of 'the Hun' was well known.

Most of those who volunteered for the Home Guard were local farmers or farm labourers (we were an agricultural community) armed with their shot guns and ready to use a pitch fork for want of a better weapon. The rest of us, while applauding their patriotism, couldn't take the LDV's very seriously. Before long Churchill had them renamed the Home Guard and they were soon an accepted part of village life, drilling in the hall, or out on exercises in the field with the C.O. barking out commands.

There were volunteers too for the Observer Corps, some of them farm labourers. One of these, during his training, went to his officer instructor to report a sighting: 'I seen a plane with two tails, Sir, an' I don't like the look 'ont.'

'That's no use,' replied the officer testily. 'You are supposed to identify aircraft.'

'Oh, ar, yessir,' said the man and dashed off. A couple of minutes later he was back. 'I bin an' asked me mate Sir, an' he don't like the look 'ont neither.'

The aircraft in question was, in fact, 'one of ours,' a Lightning, unfamiliar to most people at that time. Observers were sometimes posted on the top of church towers in the villages; Hatfield Broad Oak Church was one of these.

When the Germans began their attacks on our airfields Debden, only a few miles from Takeley, became a target. The siren on the roof of the fire station in Dunmow would suddenly assault our ears with its warbling wail and we would hear the throb of aircraft engines, not knowing whether they were 'ours' or 'theirs'. Looking up into the blue summer sky there would be the vapour trails and a momentary glint of silver as a fighter plane dived in the sunshine. One afternoon a farm labourer working in a field near Debden was said to have been killed by a bomb aimed at the runway, and soon afterwards a bomb narrowly missed the shed where the Canfield Hermit (later to be immortalised by Raleigh Trevelyan) was living his solitary, frugal and, I suspect, pretty boring life. Although the poor fellow escaped injury he was almost scared out of his remaining wits. But most people were less worried by air raids that summer, than by the prospect of German parachutists descending upon the countryside and catching the inhabitants unawares. It was expected that some, at least, would be in civilian clothes, having been sent to make contact with the fifth columnists supposedly in our midst. Strangers, therefore, were looked upon with suspicion, including such newcomers as ourselves.

Fortunately we were so busy that we had no time to worry about what might be in store — at least not during the day time. Percy and Elizabeth would hurry over to the office as soon as they had finished breakfast ('do you put on your bowler hat and take your umbrella when you walk across to your bookshop?' Simon Nowell Smith once asked Percy) and I would have David to feed and bath, nappies to wash, the cooking and housework, which I would attack at high speed in order to get out into the garden for the weather was giving the lie to a dark future.

The vegetable garden had become my province, along with the poultry. By then we were growing all our vegetables and soft fruit, as well as producing our own eggs and table birds. So long as I was working out of doors I was content. I had accepted that my writing was no longer important, or relevant to my war-time life; in the garden I could work productively. Housework only produced discontent, yet because of my middle-class upbringing with its built-in belief that standards must be kept up, as if to appease some domestic God, I grudgingly gave it priority.

Barbara with Helen at 10, Adams Road, Cambridge,
home of the Hirsch family.

The departure to a munition factory of my 'treasure' Elsie had been predictable, but I missed her sadly. I was breast-feeding my son and between the last feed at ten o'clock and the first at six a.m., the night seemed all too short. There were times when I would have given almost anything for a morning spent snuggled, undisturbed in bed.

After a while the strain of breast-feeding, broken nights, the problems of stretching the rations and the usual outdoor work with the poultry and garden, began to tell. The day was never long enough for what I felt compelled to do; the night too short for the rest I needed. It was depressing to be told I was looking far too thin, usually by friends carrying a couple of stone more than I did.

I had combed the village for a replacement for Elsie, my departed 'treasure', but without success. Then one day we went to Cambridge to see Paul and Olga Hirsch.

The Hirsch family had left Germany in the early days of Hitler and had thus been able to bring out Paul's important music collection (now in the British Library) as well as most of their household goods, including, literally, their kitchen cooker. To visit 10 Adams Road in Cambridge was like entering the home of a well-to-do family in Germany. Everything was of German manufacture; even the taps in the sink were labelled 'warm' and 'kalt'.

Paul, scholarly without pomposity, good humoured and the kindest of 'papas' may have been the titular head of the household, but it was Olga who ran the home, made the rules and was inflexible in seeing that they were kept. She was a small woman, with a round, firm face framed in dark wiry hair, which she kept tightly constrained. A devoted wife and mother and an indefatigable hausfrau, ordinary mortals could be daunted when they found themselves in her highly charged field of energy.

I, as a young woman, was given the benefit of her advice.

'If you need help in your home, Bar-bar-ra, you must write to Woburn House. They have many German women who have no home any longer and who have to find some work. Here in England they may only do domestic work or caring for children. So at Woburn House such work is found for those who need it.'

The Hirsches had taken several German Jewish refugees into their home and to each Olga allotted some useful task. After lunch I was sitting in the garden with one of them, a scholarly looking Herr Professor who suddenly broke off our conversation, looked at his watch and stood up.

'Will you excuse me, please?' he said politely, if a little wearily. 'It is now time that I cut the lawn.' And off he went to perform his appointed task.

I took Olga's advice and wrote to Woburn House. Within a matter of days a lively and attractive young woman arrived, speaking excellent English. From the start she made her attitude to the job perfectly clear; it was just a stop-gap.

'Soon, I shall find an Englishman to marry,' she said confidently.

It didn't take her long to realise that Takeley wasn't a good hunting ground for the sort of Englishman she had in mind. She stayed four weeks and during that time we lived largely on salads, tastefully arranged and decorated with raw carrots from my vegetable garden.

Rather less hopefully I applied to Woburn House once again. By then I knew that I was not likely to be sent anyone who would be taking the job because they actually wanted to work for me — it would be a case of *faut de mieux*. Before coming to England they had been warned that if they wanted a job it would have to be something in the domestic line, so these unfortunate secretaries, bookkeepers, shop assistants and civil servants whose Jewish origin made life impossible for them in Germany and Austria, hurriedly enrolled in crash courses in domestic economy and the English language. Arriving thus equipped, knowing above all, how to cook a boiled pudding, they put their names down on the job register at Woburn House.

I was next offered a widow with a six year old son. Frau Grüber needed the job badly, I was told, and the little boy was very good and would be no trouble. Touched by the poor woman's plight I said I'd be glad to have them both.

The next day Mrs. Grüber arrived on the bus, with little Hans in tow, a silent, glum child. She was thin, fortyish, nervous and apologetic. While I showed her around the house Hans trailed glumly after us, ignoring Helen's eager advances. I suggested putting a bed for him in the nursery, but Mrs. Grüber said quickly that he would share her single bed.

'It is best, I think, that he stays with me.'

I had hoped she would relax and cheer up a bit once the ice was broken but she continued to look as anxious as ever, even when assuring me that she would be able to manage.

'Yes, yes, I shall find everything ... please do not trouble yourself any more ... I shall cook the meal as you wish it ... Hans will stay with me until it is his bed-time.'

I took her at her word and put in a couple of hours in the garden. Later, when my two children were tucked up in bed, I put my head round the kitchen door. Saucepans were bubbling on the cooker, there was an appetising smell. Mrs Grüber looked to be managing; the distracted glance she gave me made it plain she did not want to be disturbed. I couldn't see Hans so I supposed he was in bed.

'How is she getting on?' Percy asked when I joined him and Elizabeth in the sitting room. 'We're getting hungry.'

'She seems to be managing. I don't suppose she'll be long now.'

Half an hour later I looked hopefully into the dining room. The table was laid and standing on tip-toe in front of the dresser was Hans; his back was towards me and he was busily spooning into his mouth the contents of one of the dessert bowls put out for the sweet course. At that moment the kitchen door opened and Frau Grüber stood in the doorway.

'Hans!' It was a cry of horror. *'Teufelkind, was machst du?'**

The wretched Hans shrank back, wiping his mouth. He had emptied one bowl and had just started on another. Grabbed by his mother he was bundled upstairs and no doubt well spanked. Presently she came to apologise. Had he broken or stolen some valuable heirloom she couldn't have been more mortified.

I tried to console her. 'Please don't worry. They looked so tempting, no wonder he couldn't resist them.'

Frau Grüber shook her head sombrely.

'Ach, nein, nein! I made a mistake to come. Tomorrow we will go. I am sorry, but it is better that we do not stay longer.'

I tried to persuade her to think it over, even though I couldn't regard Hans as a welcome addition to the household. I said I was sure she would feel differently in the morning, but she still shook her head, disappearing into the kitchen to repair the damage. The meal when we eventually got it was well cooked, but the gloom prevailing in the kitchen was a damper on our enjoyment. And Percy's attempt to cheer the poor creature with some German conversation met with no success.

The next morning Frau Grüber's determination to leave was still unshakeable. After breakfast, which she insisted on preparing, I drove her and Hans to the station and saw them off on the train to London. She had told me she had wanted to get away from London because of her little boy. Now she was going back to her bed-sitting-room and her fears of the future. I felt to blame, and at the same time a lightening of spirits at her departure.

'Shall I try Woburn House once more?' I asked Percy that evening, for I was beginning to doubt the usefulness of Olga's advice.

His reply, predictably, was that it was up to me to decide.

---

* Devil child, what are you doing?

'All right,' I said. 'I'll leave our name on their register a little longer. Perhaps it will be third time lucky.'

A few days later I was offered an Austrian cook who was looking for a residential job out of London.

'She's a Viennese,' I told Percy. 'That should make you happy. She'll be able to cook you a Wiener Schnitzel — if I can somehow scrounge some veal.'

With rising hopes we looked forward to the arrival of a pretty, pert Despina, or a Susannah who would charm extra rations from Woodford the butcher, bake feather-weight pastries and make delicious coffee.

Once again I went to meet the London train. There was no difficulty in recognising Fraülein Meyer. Invisibly labelled 'Woburn House', she was short and dumpy, with a round, pasty face, brown button eyes and crimped, mouse coloured hair. On the way back from the station she told me that she had been a bookkeeper in a business firm in Vienna, where, I was soon to learn, she had been highly regarded by her boss. She also made it clear that she did not expect to be other than a cook in our household; she had never looked after children and had no wish to do so. Her English was good, but my heart had sunk. This was no Despina.

By the time she had been with us a week I thought she would probably stay. Although the Blitz on London was still to come, the Battle of Britain was by then in full swing and London didn't look a very healthy place. She seemed to have accepted the limitations of my cramped and far from modern kitchen and her even more cramped bedroom. We had all done our best to make her feel at home without actually bringing her into the family circle. I had a guilty feeling that by not inviting her to sit with us in the evenings I was underlining the social divisions between domestic staff and employer and thus making it plain to her that she had lost social status, but Percy had firmly vetoed such an invitation. It was one thing for Elizabeth to share the sitting room with us, she was now one of the family, but he couldn't do with another female to disturb the peace with chatter when he wanted to read or listen to music. So I told Fraülein Meyer that she could use the dining room as her sitting room in the evenings.

Not long after Fraülein Meyer's arrival Ian Fleming came for a night. Percy had already boasted to Ian that we now had a Viennese cook — which meant he would be looking forward to Austrian cooking. The meal I planned was meant to revive memories of holidays he and Percy had spent together in Kitzbühl.

When I tentatively proposed the menu to Berthe Meyer her small dark eyes, like currants in a doughy bun, looked at me dubiously.

'Paprika chicken, yes, this I can cook, but for apfel strüdel you will need much butter.'

I said we were willing to sacrifice our butter rations for this special occasion.

'But that is not so much. Also, I think you do not understand. Apfel strüdel takes a *very* long time to make.'

She had already told me of the cookery classes she had attended before leaving Vienna, classes specially designed for Jewish emigrants hoping to work in England. A diligent pupil, she had learnt to make suet roly-poly and rice pudding. Was it possible, I wondered, that apfel strüdel hadn't been included in the curriculum?

'But perhaps you could make it just this once?' I wheedled. 'I know you'll do it beautifully and Commander Fleming will be tremendously impressed ...'

Berthe was not the woman to refuse a challenge to national pride so the menu was agreed. Ian duly arrived in his naval commander's uniform, looking slim and debonair. Uniform suited his sardonic good looks. I had never thought him handsome; his face was too bony with

Ian Fleming.

its high cheek-bones, deep-set eyes and sharp lines running from bumpy nose to full-lipped mouth. There was a suggestion of arrogance which made it attractive to women — the unconscious arrogance of an old Etonian, a member of 'Pop'.

He was in good spirits despite the country's perilous plight, of which he knew far more than we did. He wasn't long back from France where his job had been to keep in touch with Admiral Darlan, head of the French fleet, who was still avoiding any commitment to put his ships at the disposal of the Royal Navy. This had led to another mission to Bordeaux and finally to organising the last-minute departure from French soil of many panic-stricken British nationals, most of them well-heeled expatriates who had fled from their villas in the south with their pets and valuables and were clamouring to be evacuated to England.

Ian, with the help of another naval officer, had not only succeeded in getting them all away by sea, but had somehow found shipping space for King Zog of Albania who had decided that France was a less healthy place for a holiday than he had supposed and was fleeing with his royal retinue.

As none of this was secret Ian could and did make an entertaining story of it. No doubt it had its tragic side, but it was not his style to pull out the stops nor to stress his own part in rescuing these unfortunates, some of whom wept at the sight of their Rolls Royces and Daimlers abandoned on the quay, stuffed with Saville Row suits and Paris fashion-house dresses.

After Helen's birth Percy had asked Ian to be her god-father. I don't think we expected him to take his duties in this respect seriously, nor, apart from giving her a parcel of shares, did he, although from time to time I would remind him of her existence.

My co-ambulance driver Yda and Alan her R.N. commander husband, a veteran of the 1918 Zeebrugge attack, came in for a drink that evening and while they were all talking I slipped out to see how Fraülein Meyer was managing.

I found her flushed of face, with perspiration on her brow, rolling out wafer-thin skeins of pastry. It was a warm early August evening and the temperature in the kitchen must have been in the eighties. In making pastry for a *strüdel* the paste must be rolled for at least twenty minutes, then stretched to almost transparent thinness, before being stuffed with apples and raisins.

Her brief: 'Of course!' when I enquired if all was going well, was cross rather than confident. I felt pretty sure that this was her first attempt at a strüdel, but national pride was at stake and Berthe was a determined woman.

The dinner, when we finally sat down to it, was better than I had dared to hope. Berthe had pulled it off, and when every scrap of apfel strüdel had disappeared Percy called her from the kitchen to be congratulated by Ian in his excellent German.

As he and Percy chatted to her of Austria, and Vienna in particular, I watched her face flush pink with pleasure; for once she looked really happy. She had, poor soul, little to be happy about. In Vienna she had had status as a valued office worker, and her own apartment. Here she had neither.

Ian and Percy sat up late talking that night, after Elizabeth and I had gone to bed. Their friendship was a warm one, despite almost fourteen years' difference in their age. With his men friends Ian was generous, uncritical and loyal; his friendships lasted and did not turn sour over the years. He respected Percy's judgement and discussed his personal affairs with him as he might have with an older brother and took his advice on book collecting, although not invariably. He was friendly enough to me, but as an adjunct of Percy rather than as a separate entity. In general he had little interest in women if they did not attract him sexually and he did not go out of his way to talk to them. When bored he could be dismissive to the point of rudeness.

Before he left the next day, Ian took Elizabeth aside and asked her if she would like to work for MI6; the job, he told her, would involve broadcasting to Germany. Elizabeth was modest about her attainments and she replied that as she had never been to university she didn't think she would qualify for such a job; another obstacle was that she was already in a reserved occupation. As dollar earners, antiquarian book-sellers had (very sensibly we thought) been given this special status.

No doubt Ian could have surmounted this obstacle, but perhaps he had second thoughts about snatching away Percy's girl Friday to work for Naval Intelligence, for Elizabeth heard no more from him.

After Ian had gone Percy told me that he had been extremely gloomy about the war situation. This was not surprising since we were then in the most crucial period of the Battle of Britain. The daily claims on the radio of the heavy losses which were being inflicted on the Luftwaffe boosted public morale, as they were intended to do, but most of us took the actual numbers of enemy aircraft destroyed with a pinch of salt, while at the same time suspecting that the figures for our own losses were being minimised.

During the first phase of the Battle of Britain, from July 10th to mid-August, our part of Essex saw little of the action and mostly we slept at night undisturbed. During the day we got on with our usual tasks like everyone else and in the evenings listened to the reports of enemy action elsewhere. Amongst our friends there were those who believed defeat was inevitable and, in private, said so. Percy was not optimistic, but he did not put his fears into words. For the most part we avoided the subject of invasion and possible defeat, even when we were alone. Our attitude was rather like someone who has a loved one threatened by a potentially fatal illness; life is easier if one doesn't look too far ahead.

It was, I suppose, my fault that Berthe Meyer only stayed with us for three months. I should have realised that she would soon become jealous of Elizabeth. There is little love lost between the Germans and the Austrians at the best of times and not only was Elizabeth a German, but she lived as part of the family and Berthe did not. That Elizabeth was also Jewish and an exile from her native country apparently counted for less.

Good-natured as she was, Elizabeth did her best to be friendly. It was no use; Fraülein Meyer referred to her icily as 'Miss Marx' and made a point of speaking to her in English, if at all. As time went on her jealousy grew greener. One day, feeling off-colour, I went into the kitchen to tell her that I was going to bed before the evening meal. To my surprise she tried to persuade me not to do so.

'But why not?' I said. 'I'm tired and I'm not hungry.'

She gave me a meaningful look. 'I tell you as a friend, Mrs. Muir, if it was me I would not leave my husband and *Miss Marx* alone together all the evening.'

Avoiding laughing outright I assured her that her suspicions were unfounded and then, as I took my supper tray up to bed, I began to wonder if jealousy for Elizabeth might be the result of a secret passion for Percy. Could his compliments on her cooking, especially her triumph with the apfel strüdel, have awoken passion in that plump little body? Rather reluctantly I kept these thoughts to myself, knowing that Percy would dismiss the idea as one of my 'romantic novelist's' stories. To my relief Berthe Meyer offered me no more good advice.

The Blitz was in fully fury when she told me that she had taken a job in a Lyons restaurant and would be returning to London. Life must have been dull for her in Takeley, with no friends to meet on her days off and the two small cinemas in Bishop's Stortford the only local entertainment. All the same I was somewhat shaken to think that she preferred to face bombing rather than stay on with us — and Elizabeth.

We parted on friendly terms, wishing each other well. In Saki's immortal words 'she was a good cook as cooks go ...'

I never heard what happened to her, nor did I risk applying to Woburn House again. I had come to the conclusion that however much good-will there was on both sides, my domestic-help problem was not going to be solved from that particular source.

CHAPTER THIRTEEN

In August the Parish Council called a special 'Invasion Meeting'. Percy, never enthusiastic about parochial events, saw no reason to attend, but I went along to see what it was all about. I found the hall crowded; the atmosphere was of expectancy rather than anxiety. The Captain of our local Home Guard sat on the platform, looking pompous and bulging out of his khaki battle dress. Beside him was the Chairman of the Parish Council who was at pains to tell us that the meeting had been called not because invasion was imminent, but because to be forewarned was to be forearmed.

This was not particularly reassuring, since we all knew that practically no arms were as yet available, even for the Home Guard. The Captain then stood up and with some relish told us what would be expected of us if the Germans landed.

This turned out to be largely negative advice. We were to keep off the roads, collect children for whom we were responsible and hurry them into our houses, then lock the doors and stay there, having first immobilised all transport belonging to us. Those who had official duties, such as Wardens, or volunteers for first aid posts, were to make their way to their posts avoiding the roads. We were solemnly warned to speak to no one apart from members of His Majesty's Forces unless we knew who they were.

'Now I will show you how to use a rifle,' he told us, picking up a gun that was on the floor beside him. 'If you don't know, you'd better learn now.'

The audience stared at him attentively as he loaded and unloaded the rifle. I glanced around at the women, mostly middle-aged or elderly housewives, all dutifully following the demonstration. Perhaps there were one or two potential heroines amongst them, but it was hard to picture any of them snatching up a gun from a dead or wounded Home Guard and holding the invaders at bay, let alone actually firing a rifle.

'Any questions?'

There was a moment's uneasy silence as we contemplated the prospect of the Germans attacking our village; then a retired district nurse, a respected local spinster, rose to ask what we should do if we came upon a wounded German soldier.

The answer came promptly: 'Madam, if I have anything to do with it there won't *be* any wounded Germans — only dead ones.'

'He doesn't like the Germans much,' murmured my neighbour. 'He had his insteps broken with a rifle butt when he was a P.O.W. in the last war. I suppose he's hoping to get his own back.'

We had been told that if there was an invasion the church bells would ring throughout the land. For this reason they had been silenced for the duration, although an exception was made to celebrate the victory of El Alamein.

There were plenty of rumours circulating about a build-up of invasion barges across the channel. Along the roads leading to the east coast, block houses seemed to spring up overnight, not that we strayed far from home that summer. One hot August afternoon when Elizabeth and I were in the vegetable plot across the road, moving up and down the tall rows of runner beans decked with their scarlet flowers, picking the juicy green beans, a sudden roar of aircraft overhead made us glance up. Usually the thrum of aircraft engines was such a familiar sound that we seldom even looked up at the little silver planes from Debden or North Weald patterning the sky with their fluffy vapour trails, but these planes were coming over low, almost skimming the tall trees on the outskirts of Hatfield Forest. Then, as we stared up, we saw that they were not ours.

For a second we goggled at them, then we simultaneously ducked down between the double rows of beans — pointlessly since by the time we had registered that they were German they had already passed overhead. For a couple of minutes we waited, crouching down, expecting the R.A.F. to be on their tails, but the German pilots had the sky to themselves and zoomed away into the distance unmolested.

When, on August 17th, it was reported on the radio that the R.A.F. had destroyed 496 enemy aircraft for the loss of only 134 of ours the numbers seemed hardly credible. Percy, for one, was not prepared to believe them. In fact the actual total was 261. All the same it was the turning point in the Battle of Britain and three days later we listened to Churchill putting on record for all time the country's debt to the R.A.F.

With the onset of autumn the feeling in the village was that Hitler would be bound to 'have a go' before the end of September. Every day and night, from the top of church towers members of the newly recruited Observer Corps, fresh from a course in plane spotting, would scan the clear sky (for the weather stayed remarkably fine) by day and the star-lit sky at night, while the Home Guard drilled in the village hall or tramped across the stubble on exercises.

Although women were being recruited for the armed services no one suggested that they should join the Home Guard or the Observer Corps; as always, they were the tea and sandwich makers and, if they belonged to the W.I., community jam makers, picking and pooling all the fruit they could lay their hands on and taking it in turns to stir great cauldrons, bubbling with the extra sugar ration graciously allowed for jam making by the Ministry of Food.

The night of September 7th was fine. When the siren began to warble we didn't pay much attention. Then, after a while a roseate flush showed on the horizon; it could have been the red after-glow of a sunset, except that it was to the south not the west. We didn't know it, but the Blitz on London had begun.

A week or so later I was crossing the road to give my hens their afternoon corn ration when I noticed a small group of women and children walking along the roadside towards the village. Since the Blitz had begun I had seen several such groups trailing along the road, carrying bundles and hand luggage, looking for some sort of shelter away from London—a derelict cottage, or even a disused barn. Already Takeley had its share of these pathetic fugitives from the bombing.

As I paused, wondering how far they had already walked and where they were hoping to go, a flight of four aircraft came over at a fairly low level. For a second heads looked upwards in unison, then the whole party dived into the ditch.

'It's all right—they're ours!' I shouted. In their panic they had dropped their bundles and their fibre suitcases. When they slowly climbed back onto the grass verge I went to help them pick up their scattered belongings.

'They all look alike to us,' one of the women said with a rueful smile. She was young, her face peaky, her eyes black-circled. 'You see we've come from London, West Ham, that's where we live. It's terrible there. We just couldn't stick it any longer.'

'Terrible,' echoed another woman. 'We packed up what we could carry and came away.'

I asked if they had anywhere to stay. They spoke of relatives in this and that village, aunts or friends who would surely find some room for them. They were out of London, that was the main thing; they were too bemused and weary to look far ahead.

For the rest of that day I couldn't put them out of my mind. It was one thing to listen to reports of people fleeing from London, quite another to see them trudging along the road, tired and frightened, with no certainty of finding a roof over their heads that night. In my own village nearly every house and cottage was full to over-flowing, so it was easy to imagine the problems an unannounced arrival would cause.

'We can't all get around the table now,' a woman in the village had told me resignedly, 'so I feed 'em in relays.'

Well might the evacuees bewail the absence of a fish and chip shop. Some villages were lucky enough to have a fish and chip van coming round on a Friday night, but petrol rationing had mostly put paid to such a welcome enterprise and, as village pubs had never thought of providing bar food, the only way to get a meal out was to go into the nearest town — supposing one had some means of transport and the money.

The following day I borrowed Elizabeth's bicycle and went to call on Les Frost. The village school was still on holiday and I found him at home in the modern villa opposite the school where he and his wife lived with their three young children. By then I had learnt that the Blitz had brought more evacuees to the village. Some had taken over condemned cottages, empty for months, with neither water nor sanitation; mostly they were squeezed in somehow with long suffering relatives.

An idea for doing something to alleviate the situation had come to me the evening before. Once germinated it had grown fast, possessing my mind and driving me into action. If towns could run war-time canteens then, I argued, why not villages? Since the beginning of rationing, local authorities had been encouraged to open 'British Restaurants' to provide subsidised cheap mid-day meals, chiefly for the benefit of people working in the towns but anyone else was welcome to use them. The food was the 'transport caff' kind, the building often a local church hall.

I was determined to start a canteen in Takeley and the first step was to enlist the help of Les Frost who, as well as being billeting officer was also the Hon. Secretary of the village hall; for the hall was essential to my scheme. I found him gloomy about the future, but willing to listen to my proposition.

'I'd like to hire the hall so that I can serve a mid-day meal from Monday to Friday,' I said. 'Can you get me permission to use it?'

To my delight he saw no objection.

'Sounds a good idea. When the school re-opens there could be some of the parents glad for their children to have a hot dinner, if you're going to keep the cost low. Who's going to help you?'

I admitted that up to then I hadn't given that much thought.

'Well, you'll obviously need some help,' he said. 'If I were you I'd go and see Mrs. Bridges, the Secretary of the Women's Institute.'

'Well, I don't know, dear,' said Mrs. Bridges doubtfully, when I called at her bungalow. She was a retired hospital nurse, kindly enough,

but not, I felt, a likely ally for my scheme. 'You see the members did do
all they *could* to make the evacuees feel at home last year, but none of
them were at all grateful. All they wanted was to get back to London.'

I said I didn't think they would be in such a hurry to go back this
time.

'Well, I expect not,' she agreed. 'There's a committee meeting next
week so I'll tell the members about your idea and you can come along to
the hall and ask them if they'd like to help you.'

When I returned home I found that Percy had already taken action on
my behalf. 'I've got you a catering licence,' he said. 'I rang up Jones and
he promised to send you one. I told him what you were planning and he
thoroughly approves.' Jones was Clerk to our Rural District Council, a
genial character with no use for red tape. He and Percy were already on
good terms.

A catering licence meant that I could buy food for a canteen without
ration books. With this and the promise that I could use the hall, I felt I
was already in business. But helpers I did need and I soon found, as the
W.I. secretary predicted, that the ladies on the committee were by no
means enthusiastic about helping evacuees from London. It was a case
of once bitten. Besides, as a newcomer to the village, wasn't I rushing in
presumptuously where older residents feared to tread?

Yet, despite such understandable reactions, four volunteers from the
W.I. did come forward; soon there were others from the village,
including Mrs. Donovan, mother of ten, herself an evacuee, who
looked every inch a cook and had in fact been one in a city restaurant.

'She says she'll do the cooking three mornings a week,' Yda said.
Mrs. Donovan was living in one of Yda's farm cottages with some of
her brood. It was not so much an offer as a statement of intent and we
didn't argue. Mrs. Donovan was not a woman one argued with — and
she knew her job.

The hall kitchen was tiny, equipped only to supply light refreshments. There was an urn but no cooker, no crockery other than
cups and saucers, and no cutlery. As we had no money to buy equipment the answer was to borrow. Someone produced an ancient oil
cooking-stove, someone else a couple of large saucepans. Plates,
dishes and cutlery were harder to come by until, on the grape vine, I
heard that there was an antique dealer nearby who might be able to
help.

Garnett Piper had recently closed down his shop in Bishop's Stortford; he was getting on in years and the war had made trading hardly
worth-while, with more people inclined to sell rather than to buy. He
had been living for some years in an old farmhouse on land that was to

become part of Stansted Airport. Various outbuildings served as a store for the accumulation of years of buying at auctions and clearing out local houses.

I made a tentative approach and was invited to come and see what I could find; an invitation I accepted eagerly. On my arrival I was taken into an ancient barn where we picked our way through narrow avenues of forgotten furniture — wardrobes, chests of drawers, tables, chairs, commodes — once-polished surfaces dim under a grey layer of dust, speckled here and there by nesting house-martins. From tea-chests full of floral patterned crockery I fished out scroll-ended vegetable dishes, heavy serving platters and the dinner plates I needed. In an old trunk I found some blackened baking trays and a basket of Woolworth cutlery. The plates were browned-vein from over-heating in kitchen ranges but it was not the time to be fussy.

'Take anything you need,' Mr. Piper said generously. 'It's more use to you than it'll ever be to me and I'll give you a sack o' potatoes and some windfall apples as well.'

We opened the following week with twenty-four customers, mostly young mothers, pale and tired-eyed, with their babies or toddlers. They came into the hall hesitantly, in little groups, looking about them as if they doubted their welcome. Some were camping in derelict cottages with no water or facilities, yet they had managed to smarten themselves up for the occasion. We had set out the small tables used for whist drives and when our customers had settled down we bustled around waiting on them. Self-service would come later; for a start we gave table service and we didn't look for tips. We had played for safety that first day; the menu was sausages and mash with fried onions and greens, followed by stewed apples (courtesy Mr. Piper) and custard. We fixed the price at 6d. for a two-course meal for adults, with children half price and we didn't vary it, even when, as a special treat, we served chicken, or, to be accurate, boiling fowl not in its first youth.

When all had been served we stood in the kitchen doorway watching our customers set-to, as if it was a party treat. As they tucked into their sausages and mash the muted atmosphere of their arrival was slowly dispelled and the hall filled with chatter and clatter, punctuated by the high treble of little voices.

When we went round clearing the tables we asked: 'Shall we see you tomorrow?'

'You bet,' they answered. 'Ta ever so ...'

As we sat down to our own meal in the cramped, steamy little kitchen the smell of fried onions and cabbage still hung in the air; stacked up

beside the sink a pile of washing-up reminded us that we still had work
to do.

'There'll be more of them coming tomorrow,' Mrs. Donovan pro-
phecied. And she was proved right.

Not all our menus proved so popular. Macaroni cheese, gooey
beneath a crisp crust came back on some plates barely touched. Fish was
unacceptable unless fried with chips — but we had no fish fryer. I was
loath to serve fried spam, then an almost universal dish, but there were
times when it saved the day when the butcher's meat went missing.

Because there was no butcher in the village our meat had to be sent
out on the bus from Bishop's Stortford. This meant posting a helper at
the bus stop to collect the parcel from the conductor and in wet or cold
weather she would, not surprisingly, be tempted to leave it to the last
minute. It would have been easier if the bus had run to time, but this was
not the way of war-time public transport, so there were occasions when
the helper, haring down the road after a retreating bus, yelling at the top
of her voice, just managed to save the day's dinner from being carried
on to Braintree — and other occasions when we resorted to tinned
spam.

After we had been running for a couple of weeks the primary school
re-opened and we began providing meals for the school children who
lived at a distance. There were no school dinners at that time, at least not
for rural schools. Either the children went home at mid-day or they
brought sandwiches, usually filled with fish or meat paste, or jam. With
rationing in force mothers were glad enough for Johnny and Mary to
fill their little bellies at school with 'a proper dinner' at 3d. a time and
soon our numbers had doubled.

We had been running for a month when a land-mine fell at the back of
a row of council houses. The tenants were evacuated in the early hours
of the morning and herded into the hall by the air-raid wardens.

'Do you think you could manage another twenty-four today?' asked
the warden that morning, after explaining what had happened. 'We're
keeping them in the hall until the bomb disposal people take it away.
It's a miracle it didn't go off. They'd all have been blown to bits if it
had.'

It was the sort of challenge that puts volunteers on their metal. Mine
were no exception. We stretched our resources and provided meals for
all who wanted them. No one would have admitted to enjoying the
drama, but there were plenty who relished the village having its own
bomb story, happily one without horror. The tenants in the council
houses had been asleep when the land-mine had been dropped. Its fall
had been checked by a parachute which allowed it to glide slowly to the

ground where, had the mechanism worked, the explosion and resulting blast would have destroyed the row of houses and probably devastated much of the centre of the village. It was some while after a bomb disposal squad had removed the fuse and driven away with the mine on a truck, that I learned just what had happened that night.

Les Frost had been on duty at the Warden's post and he and our local P.C., whose name was Haynes, had been keeping the cold out with something better than tea. It was a noisy night over London and there had been more than one alert when they heard the thrum of enemy aircraft coming over.

The descending land-mine with its opened parachute had been spotted by the A.R.P. and its location marked. While it lay dormant in a field within a couple of hundred yards of the council houses, refusing to obey the manufacturer's instructions and blow up, the frightened occupants were roused and hurried away to the hall.

It was when the initial excitement was over and P.C. Haynes had been given his instructions to see that no one went anywhere near the mine, that he decided to have a closer look at it.

'Come on,' he said to Les Frost, 'Lesh see what the bugger looks like.'

'Don't be daft, it's liable to go off any time.'

But P.C. Haynes was not to be deterred. Torch in hand, Dutch courage in his belly, he set off in the darkness stumbling through the damp grass until he spotted the long, sinister cylinder lying close to a hedge, its collapsed parachute spread around it. Unwillingly Les Frost followed.

'Thash it!' He walked up to the mine with Frost hanging behind, and gave it a shove. Frost promptly flung himself down behind the hedge.

'S'all right. Nothing to worry about!' Haynes was enjoying his show of bravado. Frost was not.

'For Christ's sake man, come away and leave it alone.'

From the utterly inadequate protection of the hedge Les Frost raised his head, hoping to see that sense was prevailing. Instead he saw, to his horror, Haynes swing a leg over the mine and with a triumphant cry of 'Ride him cowboy!' seat himself astride it.

Cowering behind the hedge, his face pressed to the ground, Les waited for death. Nothing happened.

Eventually, amazed to find they were both still alive, Frost got Haynes back to the village and his duty as guardian of the people's safety.

By daylight all access to the mine had been cordonned off and the curious and daring sternly warned to keep away. A few of the more intrepid tenants of the council houses did manage to sneak home and collect what they most needed, but the rest obediently waited in the hall until the mine was removed by a demolition squad. It had been a lucky escape. Next time the village would not be so lucky.

Autumn and Winter 1940

CHAPTER FOURTEEN

One morning towards the end of October after London had suffered a particularly unpleasant night, Richard Curle, author and book collector, rang up to ask if we could give him a bed for a few nights. He said he had been sleeping on the platform of one of the underground stations, along with hundreds of other Londoners, and he didn't think he could stand it much longer. Could he come to us for a brief respite?

He was not a close friend, although Percy had known him over a number of years.

When last he had run into Dick, Percy had issued a vague invitation. 'If ever you want a bed do let us know,' he had said, in an expansive moment. And now Dick, badly in need of a bed away from London, was taking him up on it. I had not then met him and busy as I was with a young family and the canteen I wasn't eager for another mouth to feed; but it was not a request one could refuse at such a time.

To my great relief I had just managed to find some local domestic help, a mouse-like little woman who lived further along the road and was willing to come and do some cleaning and keep an eye on my children while I was at the village hall organising the canteen. Before the advent of Mrs. Friar it had meant dumping my daughter on her grandmother and leaving my son in the pram close to the office door, so that if his yells became desperate either Percy or Elizabeth (in practice usually the latter) would leave their desks and do whatever the situation seemed to demand. So when little Mrs. Friar took over, the relief was general.

Dick Curle lost no time in arriving with his typewriter and the typescript of the book he was currently writing. In 1940 Dick was in his early sixties, tall, heavily built with a smooth, pink, sharp-nosed face. He wore a monocle and a ginger wig to hide a head left bald by a disease which had destroyed all his hair, including his eyebrows. A vain man, he pencilled these in with a brown make-up pencil. He was the proud descendant of an ancient Scottish family, a fact which didn't prevent him from spending most of his time outside Scotland's borders.

111

His manner was expansive with the easy assurance of the well-born, well-to-do man of the world, and his self-esteem allowed him to take for granted other people's interest in his writings and utterances. Although, to be fair, these were knowledgeable and often entertaining.

He was the author of several travel books, some works of criticism, more than one book about Conrad, whose close friend and executor he had been. He had also written three novels and a couple of collections of short stories, as well as some works of bibliography. In short, he was always engaged on some sort of literary work. While he was with us it was a book to be titled *Women; An Analytical Study*. In common with many of his sex he enjoyed generalising about women. We were devious, inconsistent and more ruthless than men. Not that he didn't like us — he did, very much, especially if we were young and personable, but he wished us to know that we couldn't fool him. To be fair, when later I read his book on 'Women' I have to admit that I found it perceptive and by no means ungenerous.

Percy had warned Dick that the little spare-room would be a tight fit for a man of his bulk and that our household was hardly a haven of peace and quiet; but for Dick it was a case of any port in a storm. He was suitably grateful for our hospitality and to prove it he handed over to me his ration book.

This was useful; on the other hand it suggested his stay might be longer than we had anticipated. However, another ration book was not to be sneezed at and I accepted it in the spirit in which it was given. This, I soon discovered, was a hopeful one for Dick relished his food and had an appetite to match his bulk. He would come to the table with an anticipatory gleam in his eye, sniffing to catch any tempting aroma emanating from the kitchen. Put on my mettle I felt I had to strive not to disappoint his eager taste buds.

He quickly made himself at home and spent much of his time browsing in the bookroom or pottering about in the garden feeding our ducks. We had bought them to keep the duckweed down in the pond and to provide ducklings for the table. They were a great source of interest to Dick who would watch their development speculatively, suggesting to anyone who might be around a better use than as layers and garden pets. They were rather a mixed lot but there was one well developed young Aylesbury he especially fancied.

'What about that one?' he would say to Percy. 'In her prime, isn't she? Must be five or six pounds by now.' And he'd smack his lips and talk of apple sauce and sage and onion.

A week passed and Dick made no mention of returning to his flat in London. Before the outbreak of war he had been living in the United

States; being a patriotic man he had hastened back to England, as soon as war was declared and offered his services to the Government in any capacity.

To his chagrin none of the departments to which he applied had a job for him, not even the Ministry of Information which, by then, had found niches for all manner of diverse talents, including several of Dick's literary contemporaries.

When he came to stay with us he had not quite given up hope of finding some sort of useful war-time employment and he went up to London for the day once or twice to see if he could pull a string or two, or to do a B.B.C. broadcast on the Third Programme.

As a young man he had sought the acquaintance of men of literary eminence, not always with success. One who had persistently eluded him had been Swinburne. Watts Dunton would invite Dick to tea, an invitation assiduously angled for in the expectation of Swinburne appearing. Hopeful and punctual Dick would arrive at the Swinburne residence, Watts Dunton would receive him, tea would be served and Dick would wait — and wait in vain for the poet's appearance. On each occasion it would be the same. This non-event Dick contrived to turn into an entertaining B.B.C. script — 'On not meeting Mr. Swinburne'.

We were fascinated when he talked about his friendship with Conrad, less so when the subject was the family trees of the Scottish aristocracy, a topic on which he liked to expound after a couple of glasses from the half-bottle of gin that would be beside his chair when we were settled down by the fire-side after the evening meal. His knowledge of who had married whom and begat which heir or heiress could have made him editor of Debrett. With an ear cocked for the almost nightly warble of the 'Alert' Percy and I would give Dick our half-hearted attention and I would wonder, sleepily, how long it would be before I would be able to bring the children downstairs for the night.

Since the land-mine incident we had taken to sleeping on the sitting-room floor with the two children. David in his Karri-kot would be put under the grand-piano (bought by Percy for £5 at a local auction), Helen would be carried downstairs, half awake and tucked up on her cot mattress and then Percy and I would spread blankets on top of the sofa cushions laid on the floor and settle down to sleep as well as we could, in the belief that unless we were unlucky enough to have a direct hit, a near-miss might not do much worse than cover us with lath and plaster.

We didn't invite Dick to share the sitting room floor with us, and perhaps it was an understandable reluctance to retire to his cold little bedroom at the far end of the house that kept him sitting in my favourite

armchair by the fireside, drinking gin and reeling off pedigrees.
In the end, fortified by the house of Gordon, he would take himself off.

A couple of weeks after Dick's arrival when, perforce, we were all adjusting to his presence, the Special Branch Police came to investigate our household.

I was cycling back from the canteen, the usual heavy bag of coppers from the dinner takings suspended from my bicycle's handlebars, when a black saloon car with two men inside pulled up beside me. Could I direct them to a house called 'Taylors', the driver asked?

The sharpish, albeit smiling, scrutiny they gave me, when I said that was where I lived, was somehow disconcerting. But after I had told them Taylors was just along the road they said no more, apart from thanking me, and drove on. I had to call on one of my canteen helpers before going home, and by the time I got back they had left.

I found Dick pink with annoyance and Percy looking amused.

'We've just been investigated by the Special Branch,' Percy said, with a chuckle.

The two visitors had been a Superintendent and a Sergeant from Saffron Walden. They had come to the point at once. A report had reached them that mysterious strangers were staying in our house and that one was certainly German and owned a German bicycle. It was the business of his department, the Superintendent said, to investigate all such reports, from whatever source.

Percy had immediately called in Dick from the garden, knowing what his reaction would be.

'Dick, you've been reported to the Police as a suspicious character, probably a fifth columnist,' he said. 'You'd better tell the Superintendent who you are.'

Dick had then confronted the policemen, drawing himself up to his full six foot two and screwing his monocle into his eye.

'My name is Curle,' he said, rolling the 'r'. 'Do you know what a pipe roll is, Superintendent?' And he proceeded to tell him that it was a document on which were recorded leases of Crown lands, and that the name Curle could be found on pipe-rolls going back five hundred years. 'I can also inform you,' he continued, 'that when Mary Queen of Scots was executed by the English there were only six people on the scaffold and one of those was a Curle.' More historical snippets from the annals of the Curles followed.

The two policemen had listened impassively until Dick at last drew breath, when the Superintendent courteously assured him that he was under no suspicion. This assurance left Dick unappeased. Percy thought it a great joke.

The other supposedly suspicious character was Elizabeth, the owner of the German bicycle and indisputably an alien. However, the Police showed no interest in her presence in our household. What they made of Dick with his ginger wig and monocle and his claim to have descended from King Bruce of Scotland, heaven knows. In the event we heard no more from them.

We were not the only people in the neighbourhood to be visited by the Special Branch. Some friends in an adjoining village, known for their left wing views, were called upon at about the same time and questioned rather more closely than we were. It so happened that one of their sons was a keen radio ham and this, together with the label 'communists' (which they were not), had aroused local suspicions.

Inevitably suspicion was in the air. To ask the way, if one was in a village where one wasn't known, was to invite a stony stare, instead of information. With the signposts removed, finding one's way in the country was tricky, even if a route was not unfamiliar. It was surprising how alike one country road could be to another. To stop and study a map was risky if villagers were around, and could lead to being reported to the local Bobby as a probable Nazi spy who had concealed his parachute in the ditch.

Not that we drove around much at the time, for petrol rationing didn't allow it, although Percy would, from time to time, be asked to look at books in a private house and would set off with elaborate directions for finding it. We were allowed a business allowance as well as the small basic amount, the latter being discontinued later. But, as with other forms of rationing, there were ways of getting a bit extra.

Peter Murray Hill, who combined a career as an actor with running an antiquarian book business and, throughout the Blitz served in the Police Force Reserves, going on duty when he left the theatre, once remarked to Percy that he didn't find petrol too much of a problem.

'You see, old boy, what you have to do is to drive up to a filling station and ask them: "Have you got any of that *expensive* petrol?" You'd be surprised how often it works.' But Percy never attempted such strategies.

Dick stayed with us six weeks. I was tempted sometimes to give him material for his book on women, a subject on which he clearly saw himself as an authority, although I never succeeded in persuading him to disclose his sources. He had, I knew, once been married, unsatisfactorily I felt, from his occasional remarks about that state.

One day, to see his reactions, I remarked: 'What a bit of luck, Dick!

The grocer's delivery man has made a mistake and left me two lots of bacon — twice our ration.'

'Then you should return it, of course,' Dick said promptly. 'Another customer may be going without.'

'That's their bad luck,' I said cheerfully. 'They'll have to complain to the grocer. We shall be having it for supper tonight.'

I could see Dick making a mental note — 'dishonest, unscrupulous ...' All the same, he didn't refuse the bacon when I served it with liver that evening.

Living at such close quarters inevitably produced tension from time to time but basically the two men got on well together, enjoying each other's company and each other's stories, for Dick, when on form, was an excellent raconteur. Nor was he an ungenerous man and he was certainly grateful to us for letting him stay at that time, when the Blitz was at its worst.

As he could not face returning to his London flat and equally could not contemplate living in one of the small private hotels in deserted holiday resorts which catered for elderly residents with nowhere else to go, I offered to find him a room in a private house in the village, which wasn't easy. The neighbour who did agree to take him, being in need of money, was a good cook (essential as far as Dick was concerned) but also a lady who believed men needed to be 'managed'. This had worked well with her husband for forty years, but four weeks was all Dick could take.

During that time we continued to see a good deal of him, especially as another guest, a young woman, had been foisted on us after his departure and was occupying the bedroom he had vacated.

Esther had, like Dick, fled the Blitz at the insistence of a bookseller friend of Percy's who had become besotted with her. She was pretty enough in a plaintive helpless way which seemed to appeal to Dick who, in her lover's absence, took her for walks in Hatfield Forest and to lunch in Bishop's Stortford. In the evenings the bookseller, a married man with a suspicious wife, would arrive for a clandestine meeting with his love (his alibi being a business deal with Percy) and we would try to keep out of the way until their impassioned parting was over. All this made life complicated in our not very big house in winter time. It was a relief when, after a couple of weeks, Esther was taken elsewhere and Dick, too, found other lodgings and moved away from Essex.

One of the boring things about rationing was the monotony of everyday diet; another was queuing. For most housewives queuing for the scarcer foods became a way of life and an endless topic of conversation, not to say one-upmanship. Greengrocers' shops attracted queues as jam attracts wasps. Someone would pass the word that there were oranges to be had at Mr. Smith's and within minutes a queue would be stretching along the pavement. Some shoppers would tag on to any queue without knowing beforehand what the reward might be. Lemons disappeared from the shops that winter, to turn up at charity sales as a special attraction on the raffle table. Onions were soon to become almost as scarce, once the home crop was finished. We were urged by the Ministry of Food to eat plenty of carrots, one of the few vegetables not in short supply. Carrots, it was claimed, were not only a nourishing food, but they helped one to see in the dark; so that the sensible citizen who took this advice would get along better in the black-out, never walking into lamp posts or tripping over kerbs.

Predictably, scarcity made the foods we had once taken for granted seem desirable and delectable. To secure a bunch of bananas was to return home from shopping in triumph, but I wasn't often willing to queue for scarce foods when we had plenty of vegetables in the garden, including luxuriant nettles which, stewed and mashed, were vaunted as a tasty substitute for spinach — which they were not.

It was a time for making do with substitutes — the German word, *ersatz* was in common use. Fortunate in having hens, we could usually manage without the tasteless yellow powder supposed to be dried egg (we had to use it at the canteen) nor could I bring myself to follow a neighbour's example and make mayonnaise with medicinal paraffin. But I did use the dried milk provided by the Government for infants. Its big advantage was that the price was half that of the proprietory baby foods and it was, presumably, just as nutritious. Yet mothers in what would now be called the C/D social grouping, mostly turned up their noses at National Dried Milk for their babies, preferring to pay the extra for the commercial product. No doubt a tin of Messrs. Burp and Coo's baby food on the kitchen table conferred status.

The meagre meat ration could be supplemented by liver, kidneys, heart, tripe, oxtail and other more dubious forms of offal; and there were always sausages, filled mostly with breadcrumbs and seasoning and with *ersatz* skins. Game, too, was unrationed but a somewhat speculative purchase, unless the supplier was a friend with rough shooting. Coots and moorhens, conveniently unrecognisable without their feathers, were offered under the general heading of 'game', or sometimes 'black game'. For the unfastidious there was horse meat on the black market and even donkey meat. Venison, poached from Hatfield Forest, was enjoyed by one or two local families, sworn to secrecy as to its origins, but it never came our way. We once tried grey squirrels caught in the Forest. The taste was agreeable and slightly nutty, but there wasn't much meat on the little carcases and when skinned they looked horribly like rats.

By the winter of 1940 some of our good friends in the States had begun to send us gifts of food parcels; these were to continue for most of the war years. Some came to us from fellow booksellers, some from private collectors with whom Percy had established *rapport* by correspondence, or through his catalogues. The parcels varied a good deal in their contents, but almost all contained a tin or two of Spam, the American version of which was, to our own pork luncheon meat, as rump steak is to a beef burger. Rich fruit cake, chocolates, maple syrup, Californian canned peaches ... we would lift out the luxuries from the well-packed gift parcel and gloat over them. 'Ladies Weep no More' was the message on a packet of dehydrated onions. These gift parcels were to familiarise us with many popular American canned foods that we had never known before, including wild rice from Minnesota. One private customer, who was to become a pen-friend for years, included two quilted bibs for my new-born son.

The time was to come when, after the war was over, she would make the trip to London and invite me to lunch at Claridges. She was then very old, and travelling with a companion. She had lived in London in the past and wanted to see it again before she died. The visit was for three days and on the second day I travelled to London with a bunch of rosebuds picked from the garden, wearing my best clothes and hoping that in the flesh I would not prove a disappointment to Mrs. Laura B. Doolittle, generous provider of so many goodies.

The companion was a pleasant, but unnoticeable lady with an apologetic manner. She met me in the foyer and took me in to lunch. Mrs. Doolittle, she explained, was a little tired and was remaining in her room, where she had been ever since her arrival in London. I supposed I should eventually be led to the presence, but I was not, nor did Mrs. Doolittle descend. She had, I gathered, decided that after all we should remain just pen-pals. I had an excellent lunch and sent my thanks via the companion. After that our correspondence was not renewed and some months later I heard that Mrs. Doolittle was dead. I often wondered what sort of report the companion gave of me.

CHAPTER FIFTEEN

In the early days of the Blitz the banshee warblings of the siren sited on the roof of the fire station in Dunmow had the same effect on my stomach as a swift descent in a fast lift. The sensation passed quickly, followed by a need to stand still, with ears strained to catch the first sound of approaching aircraft. Usually all I could hear was the thump, thump of my own heart beats.

If the 'warning' sounded when I was getting a meal I would carry on with what I was doing, staying near the children until I heard the steady wail of the 'all clear' dying away into a sort of giant's gurgle. Helen, seeing nothing to fear, was untroubled by sirens and David was too young to be affected.

It was different at night. Then, as Percy and I lay together on our make-shift bed on the sitting room floor, I would fear for what might be happening to London and other towns and cities, and I'd hold on to Percy for comfort as the drone of the bombers sounded overhead, both of us listening, listening until the droning died away.

One night a stick of bombs fell in Bishop's Stortford, scoring a direct hit on a teachers' training college, destroying the dormitory block and killing some of the young girls there on a training course. More often bombs would fall harmlessly in the countryside.

By this time Percy's younger brother Alan, a civil servant in the Ministry of Supply, had joined his parents in Takeley, bringing his wife and son with him. It was an uncomfortable squash for the two families in a two-bedroom bungalow, but after a few weeks of the Blitz the need to be able to sleep at night became paramount and after London Takeley seemed to them blissfully quiet and safe, yet near enough to the city for Alan to commute to his job at the Ministry.

Although they were living near us, we did not see a great deal of Alan for he and Percy had never been close. They were alike, yet not alike. In appearance they were unmistakably brothers, in character completely different. Alan had no interest in books. He was outgoing, enjoyed his club and his golf and had a share in an all-in wrestling club in Baker Street. Tall and broad-shouldered, he lacked Percy's good looks, as he lacked Percy's intellectual power. Despite this he kept his end up pretty well when they were together.

One November night, not long after Alan and his family had come to Takeley, Percy and I were awakened by three heavy crumps in quick succession and the house quivered as if slapped by a giant hand. Instinctively we knew that this time the bombs had not fallen harmlessly in the fields; it had been a different sort of crump and unpleasantly near.

We got up, put on dressing gowns and looked out of the front door. Footsteps sounded, hurrying along the road, there were voices and little pin-pricks of light from the guarded torches. Like us, nearly everyone along the street had come out of their houses. There had been a direct hit half way down Takeley Street on cottages where evacuees from London were housed, in supposed safety. A German bomber had dropped death on a row of four brick cottages, killing seven people outright, including one of my rota at the canteen. Other houses had suffered damage but the occupants had escaped, shocked but unharmed.

The two evacuee children I had left with their less than welcoming hostess had had one of the many narrow escapes, and a nearby timber-built cottage had been shifted from its foundations, to be left standing, lopsided but whole. All the occupants of a row of four cottages had been killed instantly.

The grisly details, which I would rather not have heard, were told to me later by one of my fellow ambulance drivers who had come out from Dunmow to collect the bodies. I was, by then, back on duty with my co-driver, Yda, on a six day rota, for David was weaned and on my duty nights slept in Elizabeth's bedroom, she insisting that she enjoyed his company; an arrangement Percy accepted with some relief. Although by no means enthusiastic about this part-time job of mine, Percy never tried to persuade me to give it up. Quite often there would be an Alert before I left and I was very conscious of his disquiet as he saw me off. On one occasion, as we neared Dunmow, the darkness was lit by what looked like a fire-works display in a field. Bright lights flared and fizzed into the sky for two or three minutes — then it was dark again. A Molotov cocktail of incendiaries had been dropped there, presumably intended for the town.

After three months of serving a mid-day meal five days a week to some thirty children and a dozen or so adults, the Takeley canteen had £10 in hand, plus a small stock of groceries. Apart from the occasional minor crisis it ran smoothly enough. I had started it at a time when few schools in the public sector provided anything more than a drink of cold water for pupils or staff. But ideas were beginning to change and shortly before the end of the autumn term the Education Authorities approached me. They said they would like to take over, if I would agree. They would equip the kitchen, appoint a full-time cook and one assistant cook and rent the hall as a school canteen for the duration.

The adult evacuees who had been using the canteen had dwindled, most had found decent accommodation or moved elsewhere, but there were still some who looked to our service for a hot mid-day meal. I put in a plea for these and extracted a promise that they would be allowed to continue to use the canteen, but the price of a meal would go up to 1s.6d. A three hundred percent increase seemed steep, but in future there would be paid staff instead of volunteers and Mrs. Donovan, whom we recommended for the job and who was duly appointed, certainly deserved a fair wage. The £10 reserve we had hoarded bought a radio for the village school.

It was taken for granted by Percy's mother that all the Muirs should spend Christmas together, which meant that the feast would have to take place at Taylors. Blood relationships had never meant much to Percy, although he was always a dutiful son. Chit-chat about aunts and uncles and cousins bored him to tears and as this was apt to be the chief topic of conversation when his family came together, he would avoid such gatherings as much as possible. Still, he accepted that the Muir clan must foregather on Christmas Day and the traditional feast was planned. A goose had been booked some time before, sugar and dried fruit saved. Drink was another matter. Since our move to Essex we had been too broke to buy wine or spirits from a local dealer and so we were on no one's list for a bottle or two. Beer, at least, was not in short supply. It had to be beer or nothing.

'Stout' said my mother-in-law, 'does very well in a Christmas pudding'. As a substitute for brandy it was certainly better than nothing, but I didn't fancy it in the brandy butter.

Although we could not know at the time, it was to be the last Christmas when Percy's mother and father and their two sons and respective families were all together. Uncompromising in her beliefs, her likes and dislikes, there was something indomitable about my mother-in-law. She was proud of her two tall sons; they were first and foremost *hers* and this was never to be denied. I could admire her but this claim did not make our relationship an easy one.

We all did our best to be jolly, despite the gloomy war situation.

There is nothing like a baby at a family gathering for bringing disparate elements together in amity. Fascinated by the yellow points of light from the tiny candles on our Christmas tree (fairy lights were unobtainable), David lay gazing up at them, as good as gold, admired, approved, petted, while his sister was indulged by her older cousins.

Like any other family Christmas the day climbed to its climax with the big feast, then dwindled away drowsily, with a brief revival for yet another meal, hardly wanted or needed, and less than enthusiastic participation in the latest parlour game.

Alan wondered why we'd managed so badly over Christmas drinks, but forbore to say so. And my mother-in-law, looking critically at her grand-daughter remarked, not for the first time: 'I don't know anything about little girls; I only had sons.' A statement made with pride rather than regret.

As Christmas days go it was a reasonably successful one.

At least there was no wailing from the Dunmow siren.

Winter and Spring 1941

CHAPTER SIXTEEN

January came with snowfalls and hard frost at night. Our house looked like a Dickensian Christmas card, with snow frozen on the roof tiles and white-capping the dormer windows. Hatfield Forest had a cold, still beauty. When I walked to the lake, the usually muddy rides were hard and rutted under my feet, the frosted dead leaves curled and crisp, the silver birch trees along the rides etched delicately against an icy blue sky. The scene when I came to the lake was like a painting by Breugel with the skaters cutting their elipses on the wide expanse of tree-fringed ice, the children in bright-coloured pixey hoods sliding and tumbling.

Indoors we stuffed newspaper into chinks around doors and windows. Despite our cat, a few of the resident mice we had taken over when we bought Taylors had managed to survive. It was a hard and precarious life in war-time, with few pickings. Desperate for food one little creature found its way into a chest of drawers in our bedroom and assuaged its hunger from a packet of Rendell's Wife's Friend, the pessaries with a coconut oil base which I used, perforce, against another pregnancy. What effect this diet had on the mouse's reproductive system I never discovered.

After my usual spell in the loft, thawing out our water supply, I would restore my circulation by taking Helen for a brisk trot to the lake. On the way we'd look for the footprints of small rodents and rabbits threading in and out of the trees. Sometimes there would be the heavier indentation of a fox, the fainter feathery trail of its brush behind the paw marks.

There were too many foxes in the forest for my liking. I had already lost more than one of my birds to a daylight marauder. The deer, too, could be a nuisance in hard weather, when they would sometimes leap the fence and cross the single-track railway line to raid the gardens for greens, or even spring bulbs. Their beauty, as well as the fact that they were a protected species, was usually enough to save them from retribution, but not invariably.

Since the onset of the Blitz I had avoided going to London, but business made it necessary for Percy to go up fairly frequently for he was still writing the *Notes on Sales* for the back page of the *Times Literary Supplement*; and as a committee member of the Antiquarian Booksellers Association he attended the monthly meetings held at Browns' Hotel. Apart from these commitments he viewed and attended sales at Sotheby's, Christie's and Hodgson's Rooms and contacted friends and customers too busy with their war-time jobs to make their way to Takeley.

The bitter cold in January and February, combined with the Blitz, made travelling by rail a miserable and often unpredictable business. The London termini were prime targets for the bombers and Liverpool Street got its share. If a commuters' train did manage to pull out at something like its evening scheduled time it was too soon to rejoice; the chances were it would jerk to a halt at Bethnal Green or some other dismal East End station and there it would stand, the lights dimmed, the heating system apparently non-functioning, a prisoner awaiting release.

Our blind neighbour, Rupert Cross, had the advantage over other commuters; when the lights were too dim for reading he had his Braille books. Sometimes there would be days when Heather would be unable to collect Rupert in the evening; then he would manage on his own. With much of the city in ruins where his office was, this could not have been easy. He was philosophical about the danger from bombs, and maintained an enviable imperturbability when travelling.

On the days when Percy had to go to London he would make a point of catching the same train as the Crosses. It was an understood thing that the first aboard the train would jealously guard seats for the others, for it was invariably full to overflowing. If Rupert was on his own one of the party would be looking out for him as he made his way along the platform, head slightly forward, listening for a welcome hail. Once settled in the compartment the pack of Braille cards would be produced and under the shaded light of the steamy, blacked-out compartment, the long, slow journey could be made tolerable.

Although Greville had completely lost interest in the running of Elkin Mathews he was still the main shareholder. After the outbreak of war he had been posted to Dover with the rank of Lieutenant. When he first heard that Ian Fleming, his junior by a few years, had been promoted to the rank of Commander he refused to believe it — it was all far too quick. Persuaded at last that there really were three gold bands on Ian's arm he remarked, with a wicked grin: 'Well, I always said he was a fixer.'

Percy made a point of meeting Greville when he came up to London on leave, but fixing a rendez-vous during the Blitz didn't always work out as planned. On one occasion they had arranged to lunch together at the In and Out Club in Piccadilly. On getting out of his taxi Percy found Greville standing disconsolately on the pavement, behind him the shattered ruins of the once handsome building.

'There you are old boy,' he said resignedly, 'that's my last club gone. Heaven knows where we can go for lunch now.'

Percy never stayed in London for the evening during the Blitz, much to my relief, nor did he take the car up, if he could help it. We had, by then, regretfully parted with the Lancia. It had served us well but its petrol consumption had condemned it. Instead we had accepted Peter Murray Hill's offer of his Ford Anglia, a sedate little car which served us obediently for the duration. After a vain attempt to sell the Lancia to our local garage Percy had driven it to a nearby car breaker. It was almost as bad as taking a family pet to the vet to be put down. To make matters worse the dealer, having looked over the car disparagingly, had offered a grudging 'thirty-bob'.

'I'd rather leave it rotting in a field than sell it to you for that,' Percy had retorted and driven away. The following day he had tried again, further afield. This time he thought he saw a gleam of interest, as the dealer ran his eye over the Lancia's thoroughbred chassis.

'Wot yer askin' for 'er, Guv?'

'Ten pounds,' Percy said at a venture.

'O.K. Guv, I'll take 'er.' And he paid out the cash straight away. Nor did he break her up; instead he was to be seen driving around in her for some months afterwards.

January and February's bitter weather did, at least, deter the Nazi bombers for some of the time and we were all wonderfully cheered by the continuing good news from North Africa. Names most of us had never heard of cropped up in the news bulletins; Bardia had fallen, our forces were pushing on to Tobruk.

Elizabeth had volunteered for the A.T.S., and as the winter reluctantly gave way to a late spring, Percy began looking for someone to take her place before her call-up papers came.

Anxious to help, Elizabeth suggested a cousin who was living in North London and not averse to taking a job thirty miles out.

Her credentials sounded excellent, but after our experience with Woburn House we were wary. She turned out to be a large, humourless young woman, a few years older than Elizabeth and not at all like her. Her secretarial qualifications were as good as we had been led to believe, which was embarrassing because the prospect of taking her into the family circle dismayed us. I could see her organising the household, as well as the office work.

Then we discovered that she couldn't ride a bicycle.

This is not one of the skills normally required of a secretary, but for Elkin Mathews it was useful, if not essential, to have someone who could jump on a bike and nip up to the post-office with a load of parcels, or to collect stamps and the forms that were now needed for the despatch of foreign mail. The time would come when the Post Office conceded that we were good enough customers for a van to call to collect our parcels, but that was some years in the future.

Elizabeth, kind hearted as ever, volunteered to teach her cousin to ride a bicycle.

'It's just a knack. You can try on my bike. Anyone can learn.'

Nervous and disbelieving the cousin agreed to being given lessons. These dragged on for several days with Elizabeth bearing the brunt of her cousin's temper, and weight. She would hold the bicycle fore and aft while a large bottom would be settled down on the saddle and nervous fingers gripped the handlebars, reluctant feet pressed down on the pedals. With Elizabeth still providing support they would proceed down the road at a wobbly 5 m.p.h., the pedals moving in slow motion. At intervals Elizabeth would cry: 'Now on your own!' The cousin would promptly panic and stop pedalling, wobbling to a standstill. Tempers frayed. Sly attempts by Elizabeth to withdraw support unnoticed invariably failed, and usually brought the lesson to an abrupt end.

I couldn't resist watching this performance and would follow the cousins unnoticed.

'Now *pedal*!' Elizabeth would urge. 'Why *should* you fall off? If you keep pedaling you won't. Go on, *faster, faster!*'

But it was all to no avail. Whatever talents Elizabeth's cousin may have possessed, riding on two wheels was not one of them.

'I think we must make being able to ride a bicycle essential for the job,' Percy said rather craftily. So to everyone's relief the cousin gave up and returned to London.

Not long after this episode a pleasant and competent young married woman from Bishop's Stortford applied for the job. At that time she had no children, which made her liable to be directed to a job. She was both willing and able to cycle daily to Takeley to work; we were glad to have her share the family mid-day meal and she would bring me bowls of bacon fat as a contribution to the rations. The time would come, but it was our good luck that it was not for several years, when she would start a family and leave us.

Fewer aid raids in the early months of 1941 persuaded Alan and his wife that life would be more tolerable in their own home in Putney When they invited Charles Muir to stay with them for a change of scene no-one admitted that he was dying; the word 'cancer' was taboo although by then it had reached his lungs. He enjoyed the visit as far as he was able, but soon after his return to Takeley he took to his bed. When Percy and I went to see him, he no longer wanted to talk and seemed only half aware of our presence. I had never before watched anyone being eaten away by disease and thought my mother-in-law's matter-of-fact acceptance of the situation unfeeling, not appreciating that it was the best way she could cope with the unremitting task of nursing her husband. Percy, who had always had a greater affection for his father than for his mother, never holding his fecklessness against him, sadly accepted the inevitable and said little.

CHAPTER SEVENTEEN

Rural Essex was a part of England that attracted many writers and artists. It had big advantages over counties south of the Thames; house property was much cheaper, there were plenty of attractive villages which had not been 'discovered', and London was within an hour's journey by rail.

Living in one of the more remote parts of the county, not far from the Suffolk borders were Margery Allingham, her husband Philip Youngman Carter and Alan Gregory who was then working as Margery's amanuensis. I had known the Carters and Alan before I was married, so one spring day Percy and I drove over to White Colne to see them. Staying with them at the time, evacuees from London, were Bobby St. John Cooper, his wife Philippa (who was later to marry Alan) and their baby son. Bobby, a clever cartoonist, was the creator of Mr. Cube, Tate and Lyle's little Lump Sugar Man, whose mission was to tell housewives how to make do on the half-a-pound sugar ration. Throughout the war this bossy little fellow, encased in a sugar cube, was as familiar a figure to the public as was the gas company's Mr. Therm.

Bobby and Philippa were old friends since the days when 'Tibby' (T.E.B.) Clarke and I were both working on *Answers* and Bobby was a staff artist at the Amalgamated Press. Tibby and Bobby had shared a flat for a time and lived a somewhat chaotic life until both got married.

Margery Allingham's Campion novels were then at the height of their popularity. She was a pretty but voluminous woman, billowing with fat, which didn't appear to bother her in the least. She was very much in command of her household and when we sat down to a plentiful evening meal it was Margery who did the carving.

When she was writing one of her 'who-dun-its' it was her habit to read out chapters to Philip and Alan and if they stopped her, declaring 'Oh no, Campion would not have said (or done) such and such', Margery would rewrite the passage.

Not long afterwards on a bright May morning, I went downstairs to collect the mail while Percy was still in bed. Never an early riser, he liked to have his mail brought to him in bed whenever possible. I sorted it as I came upstairs and I saw that there was a letter for me from John Farquharson. Tearing it open I steeled myself for disappointment;

almost certainly he was writing to say he had failed to sell my novel.

The letter began with his regrets that he had failed to sell the serial rights because 'that would have meant quite a considerable sum of money for you'. Then the letter continued:

> However, I have got an offer out of Hutchinsons of £40 outright for the book rights. I never like selling literary work outright but in view of the fact that new authors are finding it almost impossible to get their work published at all, you may feel that this is an offer you should accept.

I hardly needed any convincing. It was not much of an offer, but that was the way Hutchinsons signed up new authors desperate to be published. It was, at least, a start. Percy, characteristically, rejoiced with me that the book was sold.

A plot for my second novel was already developing in my mind when I went along the road that afternoon to see Mrs. D., the kindly woman who had sent us tea the day we moved in and whose daughters had sometimes taken our children out for walks while I was busy.

My proposal was that her daughter, Betty, who was still at the village school but a sensible, reliable girl, should come to me after school, give the children their tea and look after them until bedtime. With the prospect of some money to come I felt I could afford to pay the going rate of a shilling an hour.

I began my new regime the next day and found that it worked. The school bus would come lumbering along the road around four o'clock and a minute or two later there would be Betty coming through the gate. The children would run to meet her, I would hurry indoors to my typewriter and work steadily for the next two hours.

John Farquharson did his best for me in our dealings with Hutchinson. As I learned later, this firm was in a better position to take on new authors than were most publishers at that time. The bombing of Paternoster Row had destroyed large quantities of far from saleable stock for which they had been well compensated by their insurance. They also had their own printing works and a good supply of paper. Farquharson arranged that the copyright would be returned to me at the end of five years and I was to retain the film and dramatic rights. The book was to be published within six months and the price was to be 7s.6d.

With my contract came a request for a photograph, if possible taken when I was eighteen.

'Don't misunderstand me, I beg,' wrote John. 'You're very young still, but a youthful photograph has a great appeal to readers.'

Barbara Kaye.
A photograph used for a later novel.

I ignored this, no doubt good, advice. Percy took a snapshot of me out in the garden, holding our black cat for luck. I liked this photograph (Percy was a good photographer) but presumably the publishers did not, for they never used it.

That summer Percy sent out his most ambitious catalogue since the move from London. There were more than 1,200 items of autograph letters, manuscripts, literary portraits and music, many of them from the library of Paul Hirsch. It made fascinating reading with pages of facsimiles of letters and writings of such diverse writers as John Stuart Mill, Arnold Bennett, Francis Thompson the poet, and others. Amongst the autograph letters was one from Winston Churchill who wrote in reply to a suggestion that he should contribute to a periodical:

> I do not like the idea of articles of a personal nature such as you suggest and I am extremely doubtful of my ability to write fiction. My friends think that serious subjects are best suited to my pen ...

This letter was dated 1916, when Churchill was out of office. The price was £2.10.

The catalogue included a remarkable collection of letters from Russian royalty, including Frederick the Great, Prince Kropotkin, and a document favouring the release of the imprisoned Maxim Gorki amongst many other treasures.

Overseas customers were invited to send their orders from this catalogue by Air Mail and advised: 'We will credit you with the extra cost, if you wish.'

The response, especially from the U.S. was encouraging and brought in much needed cash.

A catalogue of such a size and scope entailed a tremendous amount of work and organisation in accumulating the material; at the same time Percy was keeping up his journalistic work — the weekly report on book auctions for the *Times Literary Supplement* back page, his Private Libraries Series which was to be completed in 1943, and an occasional book review. All this was possible because he had the gift of writing as effortlessly as he talked. Having marshalled his thoughts and the facts he needed, the words would flow on to the paper in the green ink he invariably used. He did not often use a typewriter, except for letters when there was no one to type them. Nor did he ever bother to learn to type with more than two fingers.

After Elizabeth had left us to join the A.T.S. (the army, in its wisdom, ignored her fluency in three languages and gave her a job as a cook) our spare-room became unoccupied, at least for a while, although Elizabeth would visit us when she was on leave. But there were

frequent week-end guests, glad of the chance to get away from London.
Ian Fleming would come for the odd night, usually on the way to visit
William Plomer. He said little about his war-time activities but we
knew he had been involved in the planning of the St. Nazaire raid, and
he had some entertaining stories to tell about his mission in Tangier
where he and a friend daubed a big V sign on the main runway of the
airport. A gesture which earned him some official disapproval.

Peter Murray Hill, best known at that time as a West End actor,
would visit us for a respite from his night work in London as a Police
Force Reservist. He and Percy were old friends and would usually
improve the occasion with a little useful business, sometimes in the form
of a 'swap'. Peter had considerable charm and was a welcome, undemanding guest. A tall, handsome man, he was a talented actor (he was a
splendid Captain Look, with his wife, Phyllis Calvert, playing Peter
Pan) but bookselling was more to his taste than the stage and the time
would come when, as a full-time bookseller, he would be elected
President of the A.B.A.

With the coming of spring air raids were less frequent in London, but
it was still an uncomfortable place to live in and those who had fled to
the country, and had no need to be in London to earn their living, were
hesitant to return. One of these was the poet E. H. W. Meyerstein who
had left his flat in Gray's Inn for the shelter of his old college in Oxford,
from where he made his contribution to the war effort by working a
few hours a week at a Red Cross depot. When not so engaged he spent
his time writing poetry and observing, with some malice, the ways of
the academics around him, most of whom he disliked.

He took his meals in College and found that his neighbours at High
Table each brought his own little pot of butter and sugar to the table
and guarded it jealously. The war, Meyerstein maintained, had brought
out the worst in such people and 'academic malevolence' prevailed.

He had been an occasional customer of Elkin Mathews, but I had
never met him until the summer of 1941. He was, I think, the strangest
man I have ever known. A novelist and a poet, Eddie, as his friends
called him, was the only son of a South African millionaire and
philanthropist. His parents were no longer young when he was born
and he was subjected to a regime of Victorian discipline. Any small
misdemeanour brought the threat of being sent away to a 'refor-
matory'. Clever, a loner and not the slightest interested in sport, he had
a miserable time at his public school, but found some freedom and
friendships at Oxford, graduating with a second in 'Greats'.

Early in the first world war he impetuously enlisted in an Irish
regiment, only to be ignominiously discharged after a few weeks as

unlikely ever to make a satisfactory soldier. After that he had worked for a time at the British Museum, eventually resigning to devote his time to writing poetry and the occasional novel, doing research on neglected writers of the past, keeping up a correspondence with literary friends and taking an interest in men who had been in prison for homicide. His father, whom he had detested, had provided him with a comfortable income for life, so he had no need to earn his living. This didn't prevent him from stinting himself in many absurd ways, wearing frayed shirts and resenting having to pay to have his suits cleaned.

A confessed masochist, he would recount how he had once manacled himself with a pair of handcuffs, to experience the sensation of being a prisoner, and then found he had lost the key. 'So there was nothing for it but to walk through the streets, handcuffed, to the locksmith,' he told us, with a wry chuckle.

'You would be doing a great kindness if you would have Eddie to stay now and then,' an Oxford friend had said to Percy. 'He longs to get away from Oxford, but he won't stay in an hotel and he hasn't many friends willing or able to put him up.' We suggested a long week-end and Eddie duly arrived in time for lunch and on his best behaviour.

He was then in his fifties. He had a round, rather crumpled face in keeping with his usually crumpled suit. A partial paralysis of a facial nerve had caused his mouth to be slightly distorted and affected the muscles around one eye, so that his smile seemed to be accompanied by a wink. Not that he was the sort of man to wink; women had no sexual appeal for him, although he had several women friends with whom he corresponded, including Dorothy Sayers, the crime novelist.

Eddie loved to talk and would pounce on any new subject introduced and toss it around wittily. If the talk was of successful writers his wit was apt to be barbed. That first day he won Helen's heart by talking to her as if she was an adult.

Although a confirmed Londoner he enjoyed walking in the country and would make his target the church of a not too distant village. I took him for a walk in Hatfield Forest after lunch and although I had said at the start that Hallingbury church was rather too far, we pressed on at Eddie's insistence until we found ourselves in sight of it. Delighted, he leapt up and down in front of me, waving his arms and grinning like a middle-aged hob-goblin. 'I was RIGHT,' he shouted. 'I told you we could get here, and you see, I WAS RIGHT.'

When he visited friends his latest poems would be in his pocket. After the evening meal, when his host and hostess were sitting by the fireside with their coffee, relaxed and attentive to their guest's conversation, out of Eddie's pocket would come a sheaf of paper. His audience's assent would be taken for granted.

'I would like to read you something I've been working on,' he would say.

Neither Percy nor I were familiar with Eddie's poetry then, nor did it ever greatly appeal to us. In any case Percy was not a great lover of poetry. I am, but unless it is read by a professional reader I prefer to read it to myself.

Eddie's verses were seldom easy to understand. Sleepy from fresh air and the evening meal we did our best to be attentive.

After a while, Eddie paused for comment; Percy murmured something suitable and escaped to bed. I stayed, by then part-hypnotised by the drone of the poet's voice. A line or a verse would light up in my mind and I would want to think about it, but his voice went on until I lost the thread, wondering what I should say when the reading was finally over.

My comments must have been acceptable for the visit went well. Eddie was delighted to find we had a piano, for he had missed his own. We introduced him to some carefully selected friends, including our neighbour Geoffrey Sharp and his wife Mary, with whom he was to form a friendship that lasted longer than his with us. Geoffrey, a clever but intellectually arrogant young man, was always on the look-out for contributors to the *Music Review* who were not only expert in their particular musical field, but prepared to write for the *Review* for little more than the satisfaction of seeing their words in print. Such contributors were not easy to find, but Geoffrey could be persuasive and the *Music Review* became, under his editorship, a publication of some standing in the world of serious music.

Because the Sharps were neighbours and because he admired Geoffrey's dedication and technical knowledge of the science of recording, Percy sometimes obliged with a contribution. Eddie was at once regarded as a possible recruit to the columns of reviewers and wooed in that light.

One poem, 'Pussy Willow' was written that first week-end with us, and the book, *The Visionary*, in which it appeared, came to me after another visit as a bread-and-butter present.

A visit to Finchingfield to meet A. J. A. Symons was less successful. A. J.'s collection of musical boxes, distributed around the house, depressed Eddie. Their dainty rendering of Victorian favourites did not amuse him, nor could he admire their handsome mahogany cases — many as much as three feet long.

'Like a lot of children's coffins,' he said gloomily as Percy drove him home. While approving of A.J.'s wish to write a book on Oscar Wilde, he couldn't approve of his interest in Corvo, remarking maliciously:

'Wilde was a genius. Corvo was merely ingenious.'

'You must come and stay again,' we said when he left us to catch the bus to Witham, where he was to stay with Dorothy Sayers.

He took us at our word. Soon he was inviting himself at regular intervals, and his best behaviour began to change to second best.

Later, one of his oldest friends told us, more in sorrow than in anger: 'Sooner or later Eddie never can resist biting the hand that feeds him.'

Was it a form of masochism which drove him to turn with sudden malice on those who took him into their homes and showed him kindness? Was he deliberately provoking his own rejection? Or was it jealousy of domestic happiness which he knew he could not achieve?

In a poem, 'Drankness' which appeared in *The Visionary* he wrote:

To the necessity of human tact
In me *will* stronger than desire I find ...

And the poem ends with the line:

How hard to teach our instinct not to speak!

It was a lesson Eddie never learned, perhaps never tried to learn.

We were all greatly depressed by the news of British reverses in North Africa. After Tobruk was encircled and eventually captured I learnt that amongst those taken prisoner was my first husband, who had been serving with the Fifth Essex. Much later, some well-intentioned friend sent him a copy of my first novel. In a letter to me, while still in a P.O.W. camp, he wrote bluntly: 'I didn't think much of it!'

The further bad news of our evacuation of Greece, then Crete, increased the general gloom. The Nazi forces had taken control in Bulgaria and after devastating Belgrade from the air without warning and killing some 17,000 of its citizens, it looked as if they would soon be subjugating the whole of Jugoslavia.

They were spreading, the Nazi hordes, across the body of Europe like some horrible invasive disease, a psoriasis erupting again and again in some new area. Although Britain had survived in 1940 and might now be strong enough to defeat an invasion by sea or air, the possibility of pushing the German armies out of the occupied countries seemed to us hopelessly remote, at least while we stood alone.

Then on June 22nd. came the news that the Germans had invaded the

Soviet Union. That night we sat round the radio listening to Churchill in a broadcast to the nation, declare:

> 'We shall give whatever help we can to the Russian people. We shall appeal to all our friends and allies in every part of the world to take the same course and pursue it, as we shall faithfully and steadfastly to the end ...'

And he went on to stress that this invasion of Russia was no more than a prelude to an attempt on the British Isles. In effect he was telling us that our feelings about Communism and the Soviet system of Government were irrelevant; we were now all in it together fighting against a common enemy.

This view was accepted by most sensible people. Undoubtedly there were many who wished for the Russians and Germans to fight each other to a standstill, destroying Communism in the process, but the initial successes of the German armies soon raised doubts as to the Russians' ability to fight back. In the village we were rather intrigued to see the reactions of our left-wing friends. Most of them were 'fellow travellers' as the term then was, readers of the *Daily Worker*, but not paid-up members of the Party. In any case they were all labelled 'reds' by the village.

Mostly they had accepted the party line on the war after the outbreak of hostilities. They scoffed at the idea that it was 'a fight to save democracy', declaring that the British worker was being conned and the only winners were going to be 'the international merchants of death', the current left-wing jargon for armament manufacturers.

Their rather smug, holier-than-thou attitude had sometimes strained our tolerance. For their part, they were prepared to tolerate our middle-of-the-road Liberalism, reserving their dislike and contempt for the local Tories who naturally returned the compliment.

With the invasion of Russia their *volte face* was immediate; Anglo-Soviet groups sprang up all over the place; apathy to the war effort changed to ardent support; overnight it had become a just cause, the Workers fight against Fascism.

I had friends in both camps (Percy generally found the 'Lefties', as they called themselves, rather a bore) and though it was true that both sides could be boring with their political clichés it was usually easy to switch the conversation to the unfailingly absorbing subject of food. Most of our Tory neighbours held no clearly defined political views. All they wanted was to live as they had been living in peace-time, and keep their capital and their children's schools from the 'Reds', whom they rightly thought had designs on both. As Percy and I posed no threat to either, we were considered socially acceptable, if somewhat misguided in our allegiance to the *News Chronicle* and the remnants of the Liberal party. But the 'Reds' (which included anyone who voted Labour), though their support of non-political village organisations was generous and their accents impeccable, were given a wide berth, even after June 1941 when Uncle Joe was our good friend and the U.S.S.R. our valued ally.

However depressing the war news the July sun shone hotly, the corn in the fields ripened and there were gooseberries and raspberries to be made into jam with the extra sugar ration graciously allowed by Lord Woolton for this purpose. I was never an enthusiastic jam maker, but to allow fruit to go to waste was practically a sin against the Holy Ghost and in those days, before the Deep Freeze became the busy housewife's friend, there could be no putting off the task. The members of our Women's Institutes dutifully got together for communal boilings — but that was something I couldn't face.

CHAPTER EIGHTEEN

Nineteen-forty-one was the year when at first things seemed to be going better; then they began going from bad to worse. Each time one picked up a newspaper or turned on the radio the news was of reverses, retreats, withdrawals. Although we did not hear much about the 'Battle of the Atlantic' at that time, rumour had it that our losses at sea were heavy. The epic story of the sinking of The Bismark lifted everyone's spirits, then came the news that we were withdrawing from Crete.

With the long-term future looking bleak — years and years of war ending, most probably, in a stale-mate — there was little point in making any long term plans; to do so seemed like tempting fate. This didn't prevent endless speculation about Hitler's likely plans and strategy — not that one of our circle had predicted his invasion of the U.S.S.R.

Percy was not one to waste his breath in this sort of guessing game; in any case the struggle to keep the business afloat absorbed most of his thoughts and energies. In London customers could call in to collect a book they had ordered and, browsing along the shelves, find something else they fancied. No one, except an occasional dealer making a diversionary visit, could be expected to find their way to a small Essex village thirty miles from London. Runners still came now and then, by train, catching a bus to the gate which usually meant that it was hours before there was another bus to take them away again. Whether I knew them by sight or not they were always identifiable — the not-so-smart London suit, the bulging brief case. Percy, remembering his own apprentice days, would see even the most importunate, and never quibbled over a price. He had always disliked bargaining. It was either 'yes' or 'no'. And when the deal was done there would be time for a chat.

It was a sad year for him; with A. J. A. Symon's death in August he lost a valued friend. Then came his father's death.

His mother, small and resolute at the funeral, contained her grief and soon began to make a life for herself in the village, joining the Congregational Church Women's Guild and the W.I. After seventy years in London she was content to spend her widowhood in the village where her eldest son lived.

With our eggs, a cockerel now and then, or a fat hen which had come to the end of her productive life, our vegetables, rabbits when in season, (long before myxamatosis decimated them) and the full rations allowed on David's book, we lived reasonably well, swapping the children's tea ration for extra sugar and using soya flour from a vegetarian shop to put a bit of protein into vegetable dishes.

Agricultural workers' pies were a great stand-by. These were delivered in the village once a week by the W.V.S. for fourpence each and were a meal in themselves. They saved rations, time and, what was more, they arrived hot. They were filled with potatoes, onions and a few bits of unidentifiable meat and were always tasty.

Our house became a depot for the pies for a time. Neighbours who had ordered them would come to collect them, or I would deliver them. After a few months the orders began to dwindle. Alarmed that the delivery for Takeley Street might cease I asked one housewife why she had cancelled her order.

'We're sick of them,' she said flatly.

Eventually the deliveries did cease, much to my disappointment; it had been a relief to have one morning a week when I didn't have to contrive a meal.

The news of the Japanese attack on Pearl Harbour came as an even greater surprise than the German invasion of Russia. We rejoiced to know that we should have the Americans fighting with us, with their vast resources. Inevitably it was the eventual defeat of Germany that was foremost in most people's minds; the danger to British possessions from the Japanese was a secondary consideration. Morale rose. Those like Percy old enough to have served in the first world war, remembered the impact of the American entry into the war in 1917 and the turning of the tide, just in time.

American friends were soon writing warmly 'Now we really are on your side,' and: 'so we're all in the same boat.' Christmas parcels full of seasonal goodies arrived from the U.S., from my parents in Kenya (my mother had joined my father there just before the war) and from my eldest sister who had a war-time civil service job in Singapore. It didn't occur to me to worry about her safety then, although already British wives and children of personnel were being sent home.

Our butcher sold us a rather smelly Irish goose and with some extra rations allowed by the Ministry of Food everyone was able to over-eat as usual. That time we had something better than beer for the loyal toast through a useful contact with a colleague who had inherited a pub with an off-licence. Sensibly, he had let the former but kept control of the latter — a recipe for popularity in war-time.

Spring came and with it the Americans. The news of their arrival had everyone abuzz with excitement. They had come to build an airfield with a runway long enough to take heavy bombers. A minor road was promptly closed, and eventually absorbed into the airfield. Grey, tunnel-like Nissen huts appeared like mushrooms on the flat farmland behind our house and in the coppices where the children picked oxslips and bluebells.

Prefabricated huts and squat administrative buildings went up, almost overnight it seemed, on the road to the adjoining village of Stansted. Patches of concrete lay on the fields like grey scabs and soon a long, wide ribbon of the stuff stretched from one parish to the next. A nice 17th-century farmhouse became expendable along with many acres of farmland. There were other less obvious losses; local chaps lost their girls and the girls lost their innocence. There were gains too; the Americans were friendly and free with their money. They gave parties for the village children and swelled the takings at the local Saturday night dances — and they were our allies in the fight against the Nazis.

Doors were opened to them as soon as they arrived. Everyone in a position to do so, wanted to show them hospitality. Mrs. D.'s daughters along the road who, as school children had taken Helen out in her pram, soon had a 'Yank' apiece, hefty young men who looked as if they had been reared on T. bone steaks. From my fifteen-year-old mother's help, Joyce, youngest of the five Pacey sisters, I heard stories of parties at the base; of the girls who passed our cold after their first introduction to 'the hard stuff' and were slung into the back of a truck and dumped on the doorsteps of their homes. Takeley Street had one acknowledged tart, a dim-witted, slatternly young woman who drifted about in the flotsam of village life and was only too happen to open her cottage door to American soldiery who had had no luck elsewhere, or were too drunk to get back to base before 'lights out'.

Apart from the four local pubs the Saturday night dances were the only popular form of entertainment the village could offer. The band was usually a group of enthusiastic amateurs and refreshments at that time non-alchoholic, but as the Four Ashes was only a minute's walk away from the hall that didn't matter too much. In any case the 'Yanks' usually carried their own supply.

Once the pubs closed the dance floor would be thronged, the couples tightly clasped together, dodging, weaving, bumping as the band beat out foxtrots, quick-steps, now and then a waltz danced under dimmed lights, and the occasional valeta to make a change. Now and then the M.C. would announce a 'Paul Jones', to give the wallflowers the chance of a male partner. Then as the girls in their circle faced the outer circle of men, eyes would eagerly scan the passing faces, 'Oh, if only the music would stop when *he's* opposite me — or *she* ...'

The dances were run on behalf of local organisations or charities, the football club, the Legion, the W.I., the hall itself and so on; but it was invariably the same people who actually ran them, willingly giving up their Saturday evenings week after week to act as M.C., look after the door, or do the catering.

It was taken for granted that old Frank should be M.C. A retired local farmer, a big, dependable man, he could be relied upon to keep order. The hall was dear to his heart, as everyone knew; he took as much pride in its maintenance as he did in his meticulously kept garden just down the road, and there wouldn't be any cigarette butts stamped into the polished floor if he was around.

The coal merchant who sat at the door good humouredly taking the money, never showed any signs of boredom. Someone had to be there and he was used to the job, sitting beside his table, chatting to the 'regulars', the half-crowns and florins in neat little piles in front of him.

The women helpers too were nearly always the same. They'd turn up with their aprons and tea cloths for the washing-up and settle down at the scrubbed-top in the little kitchen, steamy with water heating in the urn, to cut up the loaves of bread for the sandwiches, spread on the margarine and meat or fish paste for the filling. Somehow they always managed to find enough margarine, and sugar for the tea and coffee. Once the interval was over, the sandwiches all eaten, the washing-up done, they would fold away their aprons, pat their hair tidy and in their artificial silk dresses, floral patterns emphasising hips and bosoms, they would file into the hall to sit in a row near the kitchen door and watch the dancing. Sharp eyes would follow one couple, then another.

There was Mrs. Brown's Maureen dancing with the boy Clark. It looked as if it was all off between her and young Reg. Well, she never did stick to anyone for long. And there was Doreen with a Yank, a different one too, and her with a kiddie at home and a husband away in Africa ...

A daughter, clasped by her boy, would glance towards the kitchen door and murmur with a giggle: 'There's Mum sitting by the door, now, I bet she's watching us.'

While making a fuss of the Americans individually or in twos and threes, the village was critical of them as soldiers. 'They don't march like our boys' was the comment of older people. It was true. When they were on a march, which was not very often, they looked like a number of men ambling down the road, rather than soldiers marching. Had we said this to them they would probably have replied that they were there to build an airfield, not for military displays. They did indeed build an airfield, with a two mile runway, dispersal points, admin. buildings, gun emplacements and the rest of it, in remarkably quick time. Then they went away and the U.S.A.F. moved in to find the village children had acquired a taste for chewing gum and the girls were smoking Camels.

One unit from the South was coloured and when some of them turned up at the Saturday evening dances the girls who danced with them soon learned that this was not acceptable to their white partners.

'If yuh wanna dance with that black man we're thru.'

'But you're all *soldiers*, aren't you,' the girls protested. 'These coloured boys are fighting the war the same as you, aren't they?'

'Honey, yuh jest don' know what you're talking about,' was the usual reply.

There was some disapproval of this attitude amongst the girls, and our young, good looking and unmarried District Nurse showed what she thought of racist discrimination by making a point of dancing with the coloured boys, often in preference to the whites. On occasion trouble began brewing up and not always between blacks and whites; but the Military Police, in their white helmets, were usually in evidence before the dances came to an end, so that trouble seldom came to boiling point.

Village hops were not for Percy, nor for me, except when my involvement in a local organisation or charity made me feel in duty bound to lend a hand. When this happened Percy would be more than content to stay at home as baby-sitter. For our social life we turned to the small group of friends in and around the village within a few minutes cycling distance. There would be bridge, according to Culbertson, with beer and disintegrating 'bangers', or as a treat one of my less productive hens. No one asked for or expected any more.

With the news of the Japanese landings on the Malayan peninsular I had been naturally concerned for the safety of my eldest sister, who was working there. Was Singapore really so impregnable? We had all been lead to believe that it was; so it seemed, had the British community. Years later I was to be told by a friend of my sister's who had been sent there to organise the colony's civil defence a bare six months before the Japanese arrived, that he had been horrified by the lack of organisation and readiness for the attack.

Thanks to his initiative and foresight both he and my sister did escape before the Japanese took over, but only by the skin of their teeth. In the last few hours it had been everyone for himself and the devil take the hindmost. Only when they eventually arrived in

Bombay two months after the fall of impregnable Singapore, several stone lighter after a sea journey in a boat with rations for five hundred and a passenger role of fifteen hundred, did I learn that she was alive and free.

Spring and Summer 1942

CHAPTER NINETEEN

One evening I answered the telephone and it was Ian Fleming on the line. He had just heard that Greville Worthington had been killed.

As a security officer at the port of Dover Grev had gone out one dark, wet night with his driver to check that the various sentries guarding different parts of the port were all on the alert. His idea had been to see if he could catch the guards napping and drive through one of the posts without being challenged. He did, in fact, succeed in doing so and was just telling his driver that they had 'caught the bastards out' when a sentry, panicking, fired a warning shot, which ricochetted off the road, went through the rear of the car and struck Greville in the back. He died in hospital three days later.

He was buried at sea, with full naval honours, a moving and impressive ceremony. Percy, greatly saddened by the loss of a friend for whom he had had much affection, went to Dover to attend it. On the coffin was a bunch of violets and snowdrops from the garden at Olney, but Diana was not there. She had stayed away rather than face meeting the woman with whom Greville had lately become entangled. Not long after Greville's death Percy went to Olney to see her. He found her changed, looking thin and drawn and talking strangely. She was, she told him, being spied upon. Deserted as she had felt she was, by Greville, she had been hoping against hope that he would one day return to Olney and she could not reconcile herself to his death, despite her three young children. Some months later she was found drowned in the river that ran past the garden.

Greville's death at once put a question mark over the future of Elkin Mathews. The Worthington estate was a large one and Greville's holding in Elkin Mathews a fairly small part of it, nevertheless, it was a going concern and could be regarded by the Executors as a saleable asset. So long as Greville was alive Percy had felt reasonably secure. With Greville dead the Executors might well, in the interests of his heirs, propose to realise on his shares as quickly as possible.

Negotiations soon began. Percy, as always, wished to play fair. Apart from our house, which was on a mortgage, we had no realisable assets except his shares in Elkin Mathews, a business that was having a struggle to survive in war-time conditions. Our accountants made the very reasonable point that at such a time a buyer for Greville's holding would not easily be found. The stock was by no means spectacular and, as the good-will was bound up with Percy's expertise, without him the business was not a very saleable property.

Ian, as a sleeping partner with a nominal holding could do no more than give moral support. An offer for Greville's holding was made, negotiations dragged on. With our future still in doubt Percy issued a catalogue of two private libraries. One on behalf of Dr. R. W. Chapman, an authority on Jane Austen and a well known bibliophile, included only the less important books in his collection because he had 'not been able to brace himself to jettison the authors he had most studied ...'.

This catalogue has been compiled at odd moments and under some difficulties, Dr. Chapman wrote in a foreword to the catalogue, for any errors of description the owner, not his friendly bookseller, is to be held accountable.

To this Percy added truthfully: 'The scholar and bibliographer takes a mournful farewell of his books while the friendly bookseller welcomes them and cries his wares, not the less that they belong to the "unfashionable" eighteenth century ... similarly this bookseller welcomes the rank and file of a library — the bread and butter books ... there may not be a cake in the catalogue, but there is a not inadequate proportion of jam, the whole affording a repast suitable to digestion constricted by the tightened belt.'

Few of the books listed were priced at more than £10 and most were well below that figure, including a set of the first editions of Mary Woollstonecraft, the author of the now highly priced *A Vindication of the Rights of Women* (one of the five titles by women to be listed in *Printing and the Mind of Man*) which was offered for £8.

With Elkin Mathews' future still in the balance the catalogue was 'issued by P. H. Muir, for Elkin Mathews Ltd.'

After Diana's suicide her three children came under the care of their grand-mother, Lady Marjorie Beckett. The Executors, burdened with the complications of the two deaths, signified their willingness to sell Greville's shares to Percy over a period, at a figure settled amicably by the lawyers on both sides; and one day I was presented with a single share certificate and told that I was now one of the firm's three directors.

I was rather pleased to find myself a company director and somewhat disappointed that I was not expected to attend meetings of 'The Board'. My one new job, I learned, was to write my signature on the firm's cheques, which rather tiresomely required those of two directors. Ian, the third, somewhere in the Admiralty, or off on some secret naval mission, could hardly be expected to oblige. To save everyone's time I would usually sign a whole bookful, my signature becoming more and more illegible as I came to the end of the task.

It was with mixed feelings that I awaited the publication of my first novel which was announced in Hurst and Blackett's Spring List. When the galley proofs had arrived some months before, I had read them with increasing despondency; in the interval of eighteen months since its despatch to my agent I had half forgotten it. Distanced by the lapse of time from my involvement with the characters and situations (and my passionate wish to finish the book), I could see its weaknesses and faults too clearly to fool myself into thinking it was likely to achieve any real success. I knew it had no chance of being reviewed in the *Times Literary Supplement*, or in the serious Sunday papers, nor would readers of torrid romances pant through its pages. In fact I couldn't imagine who, if anyone, *would* read it.

There is nothing new in an author being depressed by his galley proofs; they are tiresome, unpleasing things to handle, in any case. To have second thoughts of any significance is dangerous.

Minor revisions will get by, but no publisher will foot a heavy correction bill and the author who insists on many corrections will find his royalty cheque woefully shrunken.

Once the proofs had been posted back I settled down again to finishing my second novel. Its publication would depend largely on the sales of the first one, but I was too deep in it to look far ahead. Naturally it was going to be a better book, for this time I had not the constraint of trying to write for the women's serial market.

'You'd better stick to novels now,' John Farquharson had advised; and my father in Kenya, who had put aside his typewriter and joined the Kenya R.N.V.R., had given me the same advice.

Soon after I returned the proofs I had been asked to write my own 'blurb'. I had thought, in my innocence, that this potted summary of the story, embellished with such words as 'absorbing', 'enthralling', or perhaps 'impressive' was produced by the publisher and I hardly knew how to respond to this request. Honesty forbade me to describe my novel as impressive, or even unforgettable; nor could I bring myself to add any fulsome adjectives to my brief outline of the plot. In the end I left it to the publisher's editor to supply the term he thought appropriate and was rewarded with a phrase out of the cliché drawer. The reader

E. H. W. Meyerstein reading poetry to friends.
Sketch by Sarah Atkinson.

(potential) was told that it was a book for those who could 'still enjoy a genuine love story'. The adverb 'still' seemed to suggest that they were a decreasing band, which time has certainly proved untrue.

My six free copies arrived one May morning. There was a girl on the dust wrapper wearing an evening dress and a simpering smile. I disliked her on sight. It was better when I turned the pages, reading snatches. There were my characters, all the people who had lived in my mind for months. For some reason they had not lived in the galley proofs, but between the covers of the book they did — for me, at least.

Percy, always helpful over my literary ambitions, sent off copies where they might prove useful.

It so happened that Eddie Meyerstein invited himself for a long week-end a few days after my novel was published. Much to my embarrassment he picked up a copy and said he was going to read it. When I protested that my guests were not expected to read my writings, he merely gave me one of his sly smiles and marched off with it into the garden.

It was a fine afternoon and as I worked amongst the flower beds I would catch sight of him every now and then strolling about, his nose in my book. Once I saw him set off down the road, book in hand.

I restrained myself from asking for a comment when next I saw him and he made none until the evening when he suddenly remarked: 'That was a good name for an office boy. Mm, yes — Julep.' Then, after a moment's reflection: 'And I *liked* the way you made the young woman get rid of that dishonest housekeeper.'

It was a small bouquet, but I was grateful. It allowed the book to be decently laid to rest and forgotten, as far as Eddie was concerned. It was characteristic that he had enjoyed the discomfiture of a female character, a devious woman who had cheated her boss.

During the following weeks a few brief reviews arrived from a press cutting agency, mostly from provincial papers. There were, also, one or two kindly ones from the local press. I resisted the temptation to ask at bookshops where I was not known, if they had the book in stock, remembering my embarrassment when my mother had done this in a well-meant attempt to push the sales of my father's novels. Another of her promotional ploys had been to leave printed postcards advertising his latest books in the ladies' 'loos' in shops and hotels, where she reckoned there wouldn't be competition from other reading matter.

Nevertheless, I could not resist walking around the book departments of the London stores in the hope of seeing my novel displayed with all the other shiny spring fiction titles. I failed to see a single copy in the stores, but when I went into Bumpus, in Oxford Street, then one of London's top bookshops, there it was, thanks to J. G. Wilson's kind heart and friendship with Percy. In fact there were several copies.

It was a time when people bought hard-backs to read on trains and in air raid shelters and other boring places where there was nothing to do but read something that would help one forget the war. Like everything else books were in short supply and were still relatively cheap at seven or eight and sixpence for some 80,000 words — the standard length for a novel. The big buyers were the commercial circulating libraries, Boots and Smiths in particular, with their branch libraries all over the provinces. Alas, their hideous stamping and labelling spoilt many a first edition of novels, later to be much sought-after by collectors.

When my first novel went out of print after a few months, Hutchinsons did not reprint; but by then they had accepted my new novel, offered to them by John Farquharson ('I think it is an improvement on your first') who negotiated a contract on a royalty basis with an advance of £150 and the option on two further books 'of a similar kind'.

I signed this contract with no qualms at committing myself to writing more 'light romance', nor with serious doubts as to whether I could continue to do so. The carrot of a regular income was too tempting to refuse.

I had written my second book, *Home Fires Burning* in time filched from domestic tasks during the day. Percy made a point of leaving his work in the bookroom, so I would put the cover over my typewriter, sometimes reluctantly, before our evening meal. Afterwards, if we were alone, there was the diversion of favourite radio programmes — undemanding entertainment interspersed with neat little catch phrases that were common currency during the war years, some wink-and-nod sex jokes and some wry wit in keeping with the times. I.T.M.A., Monday Night at Night, Gert and Daisy, Clapham and Dwyer ... we listened to them all, I with my knitting, Percy with pipe in mouth, filled with the tobacco for which I would queue each week. Just occasionally I would slip away, nagged by the thought of a chapter I hadn't finished, a scene that wouldn't 'come right', intending not to be out of the room for more than five minutes. Huddling by the stove in the dining room I would scribble away in a note-book, oblivious of passing time. Returning, guiltily to the sitting room I would find it in darkness, with only the cat to gaze up at me reproachfully from the hearthrug beside the dying embers of the fire.

One fine day in the early summer of 1942 I was called upon by a farmer's wife from a neighbouring village, a forceful committee lady, locally known as Mrs. Tom, whom I had met once or twice through the Women's Institutes.

'I need a billet for a couple of landgirls,' she said without any preliminaries. 'You've got a spare room, haven't you? You'll get paid, of course. Twenty-two and six a week for each girl. I know it's not a lot, but it'll cover the cost of their food. They're decent enough girls, won't be in your way much. Out of the house before eight o'clock and not back again until five. They'll be hungry then, mind you. So they'll need a decent evening meal ...'

We gave in without a fight and Lily and Lizzie duly arrived, two strapping factory girls from London, cheerful and uninhibited, taking life as it came.

Unmarried girls were required to register for national service at the age of eighteen. As well as the armed services other options were open to them; nursing was one, the Women's Land Army another. Although by no means a cushy option the latter meant a less regimented life, a room of one's own, or shared with one other girl, and a good deal more freedom. The uniform, green jersey, breeches and a splendidly warm great coat, was popular and not unbecoming.

Lily and Lizzie settled in without trouble, sharing our double spare room. In the evenings they took themselves off as soon as they had finished their evening meal. Where they went we never asked, there was little enough to do in the village, apart from the Saturday dances. As both were over twenty-one I didn't feel responsible for their morals. Besides they looked well able to take care of themselves.

They were working with a gang on a near-by farm and would come home ravenous. I would fill them up with a North country high-tea and we would see them no more until bed-time. Sometimes when I crossed the road at dusk to shut up my poultry I would catch a glimpse of shadowy figures standing close together in the pool of darkness cast by the big, black barn beside our gateway.

They had been with us for about a month when one day they arrived back midmorning in a high state of indignation.

'The girls 'ave gone on strike, so we came 'ome.'

'Good heavens! But why are they striking?'

'Well,' said Lizzie, 'we was all put to 'oeing the sugar beet and this Foreman that's in charge, 'e started tellin' orf some of the girls for not doin' it as 'e'd said, an' there was one or two said they weren't goin' to be talked to like that, an' next thing they'd all stopped work. So the foreman 'e said 'e'd report them. Well, Lil an' I didn't 'old with strikin' — we didn't want to get mixed up in it, so we both cleared off.'

'They was startin' to sabotage the sugar beet,' put in Lil in shocked tones. 'We didn't think that was right.'

The strike was soon settled by sending the ring leaders to another hostel and Lizzie and Lil, who were probably regarded as 'scabs', were sent to work at a market garden down the road, on their own. They stayed until the end of summer, leaving to go to resident jobs on farms in the north. We missed their cheerful presence and cockney wit, but I was rather relieved that I was not asked to take in any more landgirls. By this time the policy was to send girls either to resident jobs or keep them in groups in hostels. Before long there was a Land Army hostel in Takeley.

If there was a dance at the U.S.A.F. base a truck would be sent to collect the girls from the hostel.

'There was this girl, asked me to feel her bicep muscles. *And* she sure had some. What d'ya know about that?' said one surprised G.I. Another summed up the girls succinctly with the one word, 'rugged'.

From being a landgirls' landlady I graduated to area Welfare Officer, responsible for the well-being of any girls working on farms in and around the vilage. I didn't seek the job, but there was no gainsaying Mrs. Tom.

'They need someone to keep an eye on them, make sure they're being paid their wages and there's no funny business going on,' she said crisply. 'They'll be properly treated by most farmers, but there's always a rotten apple or two in the barrel and if there *is* any funny business we want to put a stop to it right away. Can't afford to lose workers through them getting in the family way ...'

I had no idea how I was to prevent such a calamity if the parties concerned, or one at least, was inclined towards 'funny business', but I promised to keep a watchful eye on the eight or so girls in my area, two of whom were going to work from their homes. I was issued with a badge to prove I had some authority but, mercifully, no form of uniform.

With the petrol coupons that went with the job I rather enjoyed driving around the various farms, arriving unheralded when the girls were at work, following them into the cowsheds at milking time (few farms had milking machines then) or into the fields to watch them perched on a tractor, ploughing chocolate brown furrows up and down the stubble fields. I usually found the girls cheerful and without problems, at least confidable ones. Living as one of the farmer's family they were seldom lonely and likely to be too tired at the end of a working day to be looking for bright lights.

To my considerable relief no girl complained of randy old farmers trying to seduce them, but one was soon 'going steady' with a farmer's son, a romance that ended in a happy marriage and the father handing over the farm to his son when the war was over.

I would invite my girls to foregather at Taylors once a month for a supper and get-together. This was a party Percy would usually dodge. They would arrive on their bikes, healthy and pink-cheeked, in their green jerseys, breeches and thick green socks and chatter cheerfully about their jobs. They had all opted for the Land Army because an out-door life was what they wanted, especially if there was stock to be looked after. Maternal instinct flowed out to the calves and the piglets. There was no drill or jumping to attention. They worked as individuals, doing a job on their own, and it suited them.

We heard nothing more from Lizzie or Lily until after the war when Lily came to call on me. She looked a fine young woman, comely, nicely dressed and wearing a wedding ring. After we had greeted each other she flashed it at me and gave me one of her sly grins.

'Remember that sailor that used to see me 'ome?' she asked.
I said I did.

'Well, I married 'im!' Her grin made it clear that the sailor was now safely in port, and would stay there.

CHAPTER TWENTY

One of the many tediums of war-time is the constant nagging to which the hapless citizen is subjected. We were nagged about travelling ('Is your journey really necessary?') about avoiding waste, carrying our gas masks, talking out of turn ('careless talk costs lives') and we were exhorted to 'dig for victory', eat carrots (to help us see better in the black-out) 'make-do and mend' in the home and to put our savings into war bonds. It was rather like being put on one's honour at school.

From time to time there would be a Government-sponsored campaign when we would be urged to make a special effort to render up our garden railings for scrap, our old rubber tyres for re-cycling or our books for pulping at the paper mills. Unfortunately some over-conscientious citizens reacted to these appeals with misplaced enthusiasm, donating fine examples of wrought iron work, or valuable books for pulping. Soon the Press was tut-tutting over such desecration, pointing out that irreplaceable treasures were being lost.

When it came to saving books Percy was predictably called upon by the Local Authority, whose job it was to organise the campaigns in their areas.

'There is to be a Books for Salvage Drive next week,' said a voice on the telephone one morning,' and we wonder if you could spare the time to help us, Mr. Muir? The Council has suggested that we have a small scrutinising committee to make sure that nothing of value goes to the pulp mills.'

It was a request that Percy felt he couldn't refuse even though he hadn't the time to spare. His fellow scrutineers, he was told, would be George Edinger, (a future Liberal Candidate in the 1945 election) author and journalist who had a cottage near Dunmow, and Lancelot Cranmer Byng, editor of *The Wisdom of the East* series and, as Vice Chairman of the Essex Education Committee, an obvious choice.

The Drive was well publicised. Householders with books to give away were made to feel that here was an opportunity to help the war effort and, at the same time rid themselves of useless dust-gathering clutter. All they had to do was to notify the council that the books were ready and a van would come and collect them.

On the first day of the Drive Percy arrived at the Council Offices

153

punctually at the appointed hour. A room had been made available and
books were already being stacked up on the floor. No one else was there
so he settled down to sift through damp-stained sets of the Waverley
novels, Dickens, Thackeray, dog-eared volumes of *The Family Doctor*,
innumerable reprints of romantic novels, grubby cookery books with
the covers gone, scribbled-on children's annuals and much unreadable
theology. He had been working for half an hour or so when Cranmer-
Byng turned up. By then the books were covering half the floor space.
Greetings were exchanged, Cranmer-Byng settled down in a chair,
picked a book from one of the growing piles and began to read. An hour
later he closed the book, replaced it on the pile, muttered that he really
must be off and wandered away. It was the only time Percy saw him
during the three days of the Drive. As for George Edinger, he never
turned up at all.

Predictably, it was a boring job. Amongst the hundreds of books
brought in there was not one to bring a gleam to a dealer's eye. On the
second day, as he arrived at the Council Offices, Percy spotted a
volunteer about to unload a handsome set of the Encyclopedia Britannica. Noting that it was the 11th, the most sought-after edition, he
assumed it had been given away by mistake and told the volunteer
driver he had better leave it where it was. According to the regulations
for the Drive, books once unloaded couldn't be taken back by their
owners. The traffic was one way only — either to the pulp mills or, in
the rare case of anything turning out to be of value, to the auction rooms
to be sold on behalf of the Red Cross.

'Where did you get these?' Percy asked. 'From an old lady,' said the
driver and supplied her address. At the end of the day Percy set off to
visit the donor and found her to be an elderly gentlewoman living alone
in a comfortably furnished house in a nearby village.

When she learned the reason for his visit she invited him in and
assured him that she had intended the 29 volumes to go to be pulped.

'It was such a lot of paper I felt I ought to give it away, but if you
really think it would be better to let it be sold for the Red Cross then of
course I will agree.'

Percy had glanced around her pretty drawing room as he went in
and, as all booksellers would do, his eyes had rested on the books in a
bookcase. There he saw another set of Britannica, the 9th edition. As he
was leaving he couldn't resist remarking:

'I see you have another set with even more weight of paper. I rather
wonder why you didn't give that one and keep the 11th, which is
smaller as well as being a better edition.'

The owner gave a rather embarrassed laugh.

'Well yes, perhaps I should have; but you see the one I've kept is rather a nicer *colour* than the other and I do think it *goes* better in this room, don't you agree?'

To disagree would have been churlish. The lady had been patriotic, according to her lights.

Meanwhile I, too, had been active in the paper saving campaign. It was, after all, one of the campaigns in which I had a vested interest. Books were already being published in eye-straining type to conform with economy requirements, editions were limited to three or four thousand copies, periodicals had been drastically slimmed, wall-paper was practically unobtainable, greengrocers wrapped up vegetables in old newspapers, paper bags (polythene ones didn't exist) were so thin they were likely to split and spill their contents and the only toilet paper to be had was a dingy grey and as coarse as brown paper.

Percy, who was apt to be sceptical about my schemes for helping to win the war, asked how I expected to get enough containers and who would collect them?

'Old sacks will do,' I said. 'I'll cut them in half and put on string handles. As for collectors, I'll get some of the local school-children.'

The pile of old sacks, supplied by a kindly farmer, smelt of mice and stale meal, but they made adequate containers. Although without any official status, I was politely received at the cottages and houses where I called, my sacks were accepted and no one asked for my credentials. To recruit four collectors was less easy, but I finally got together a team of girls with a bossy thirteen-year-old leader. A couple of old prams served as handcarts.

The scheme worked better than I had dared to hope, at least at first. My young collectors worked in pairs, taking opposite sides of the road, which made for healthy competition. '*I've* got more than *you* have!' was the cry as they filled up the big sacks in their prams and then trundled them back to our garage. But success brings its own problems. The dustmen shook their heads when I proudly led them to the half dozen 2cwt sacks of waste paper ranged along one side of our garage.

'Can't take that lot,' said the Foreman. 'Gotter be a special collection for that sort of load.'

I asked him to arrange for a collection. He said he would, but he didn't. I telephoned the District Council Office and left a message requesting speedy collection. Nothing happened.

By the end of the first month there was hardly room for the car in the garage, nor was all the paper quite as clean as I could have wished; and I had run out of large sacks. Percy looked at the piles of paper stacked up along the wall and talked about fire risk.

'You'll either have to stop collecting or find somewhere else to store it. We can't have any more waste paper here. Someone's only got to drop a match for the whole place to be ablaze.'

With the prospect of my scheme folding I rang up the Council Offices and, refusing to be fobbed off once again I cycled into Dunmow.

The Chief Public Health Officer invited me cordially into his office. We had met once before when he had come to our house to de-infest us after bugs had emerged from a four-poster bed we had bought at an auction sale and begun taking up residence in the walls. I had been horrified; he had thought it rather a joke.

'Interesting little creatures,' he had remarked, casually picking up the tiny, beetle-like insect. 'They can remain dormant for years, you know, and then with a bit of warmth they'll come to life and start looking for a meal . . .'

'Not bugs again?' he enquired.

'No, certainly not,' I said hastily. We had quickly sent the bed back to the auction house from where we had bought it. The salvage paper had not, at least, produced that problem.

'Our garage,' I said, 'is full of paper ready and waiting to be pulped, tons of it, but you won't send anyone to collect it.'

It turned out that it was not a question of the Council's unwillingness, merely a matter of lack of communication. No one had told him about my waste paper collection.

'Sounds a splendid idea,' he said. 'I'll send a van along tomorrow and we'll make a monthly collection. I'm delighted you came to see me; couldn't have been better timed.'

Pleased and rather flattered I was about to leave when he stopped me.

'No, don't go away for a moment. I'll be right back.' He hurried out of the room and was back in a couple of minutes. Advancing on me he pinned a brooch on to my lapel, saying: 'I hereby appoint you Official Salvage Officer for Takeley. Congratulations!' then he seized my hand and shook it warmly.

'Salvage Officer? But for heaven's sake —?'

'It's all right. Just carry on what you're doing. I've been sent instructions to appoint four Salvage Officers for the area. I was wondering who on earth I could get when you walked in.'

After a while my young helpers became less enthusiastic about the job and, rather than let the scheme peter out, I did much of the collecting myself. One of my best sources of paper was from Rupert and Heather Cross. The former, being blind, subscribed to various publications in Braille. These were weighty volumes and once he had read them

Rupert had no further use for them, so they were put aside for me to collect. This led to an episode which I was never allowed to forget.

The Crosses were a sociable couple and refused to let war-time food and drink problems deter them from inviting their friends to informal parties. The party they gave that summer proved to be an especially memorable one. The invitation, by word of mouth, promised that there would be no shortage of party spirit owing to Rupert having secured the co-operation of a London friend. This turned out to be the barman of a well-known city pub who promised to come and to bring some of his special supplies of spirits to poor, blind Mr. Cross.

The tumblers, full of an unnamed brew, which were handed to arriving guests by this helpful friend, were gratefully accepted and quickly drained. For a war-time drink the stuff didn't taste too bad. Soon the party became hilarious. It was still going great guns when, around mid-night I mounted my bicycle and rather reluctantly wobbled home, Percy having sensibly preceded me on foot.

Fresh air and movement did the trick. The reckoning came quickly, my stomach rejected the barman's hooch and the next morning found us both tolerably well, Percy having mistrusted the stuff from the start and stuck to beer.

Not so our hosts, nor those of their guests who had been unable to crawl away home that night. By Sunday afternoon the last remnants of the party had taken themselves off, leaving their hostess and host still abed, asking only to be left to their misery.

It was in the course of duty as a collector of waste paper that I made my Monday morning call at the Cross's cottage.

Heather usually left the Braille books ready for me in the hall and the door unlocked. I let myself in, but this time the Braille books were not to be seen.

The house was very quiet. Then I thought I heard a cough.

'Anyone there?' I called. No answer. I raised my voice.

'I've come for the salvage. Is there any?'

Still no reply. I waited a moment or two then gave up and went away. Heather and Rupert, I learned later, still in bed and suffering, some thirty-six hours after the party, did not feel salvageable.

'There we were as sick as dogs and barely alive, and Barbara comes to the house asking if there's any salvage,' Rupert said to Percy when next they met on the train. 'All we could do was to put our heads under the bed clothes and wait for her to go away.'

August, always a dull month in the book trade, with few, if any, auction

sales, was brightened that year for Percy with the arrival of a letter from
Siegfried Sassoon, enclosing two copies of his poem, *Early Morning*,
and offering to supply more.

Percy had known Sassoon for some years and had recently been in
touch with him on behalf of a customer, a wealthy clothing manufacturer, who was collecting first editions of Sassoon's books and was
eager to add manuscripts to his collection. Sassoon had no objection to
supplying hand-written copies of some of his poems but was not
prepared to sell either the original manuscript of a published work, or
any working copies. Having learned from Percy that the customer's
name was Samuels, he thereafter always referred to him in his letters as
'the Infant'.

> I could make a fair copy of 20 poems, he wrote, either on good paper,
> quarto size, to be bound, or in an octavo book in an old red morocco
> binding, which I have by me ... I did a Ms. for St. Andrew's
> Hospital last winter and the Librarian was lyrical about it ...

He suggested £50 for a Ms. of twenty poems, ...'he (Samuels)
certainly deserves encouragement as his enthusiasm about books (apart
from the fact of his enthusiasm for mine) is admirable.'
A couple of months later Sassoon wrote:

> The infant certainly does burn with a clear gem-like flame in his
> mania for acquiring my productions! If you think it advisable we
> might try and tempt him with some piece of 'corrected Ms.',
> preferably prose. I have various odd chapters of the *Weald of Youth* in
> Ms ... for which I haven't any deep feeling, but which would make a
> very attractive Ms. if properly bound up ...

He added that he didn't need money just then as the 'W. of Y.' seems
likely to sell out its first edition (10,000 copies).
In the same letter he regretted that he had to be 'somewhat eclectic in
buying books as this house is crowded with them ...' His mother-in-
law had dumped at Heytesbury House a collection from the library of
Sir A. Scott-Gatty, Garter-King-of-Arms, of pedigree specialist-books
which Sassoon longed to replace with the 17th and 18th century folios
he loved to collect. Percy had been invited to stay, but at that stage of
the war didn't like the idea of being away from his family for more than
a day. Some time later he did go.

> It is sad that you can't get here to see them,' (his books) Sassoon
> wrote. 'The whole place is an oasis of charm and beauty, more so
> even when things are so quiet and no servants in the home. It is all

like something in a Victorian novel, and should be occupied by Lord Lufton, or some Trollope character, hum-drum and pleasant-minded; though I flatter myself that I fit in pretty well as I jog in and out of the front gate on my old horse ...'

'The Infant' was certainly a customer to be encouraged; his collecting mania was by no means confined to the books and Mss. of Siegfried Sassoon. He was building up a collection of the paintings of 20th century artists and, with some gentle guidance from Percy, had begun to buy the engravings of Stephen Gooden.

With Helen at the Bishop's Stortford High School (she had taken to school like a duck to water), I settled down to work on my third novel, a war-time love story with a happy ending as required by my publisher. I had already been warned that unhappy or undecided endings were not acceptable for their list, nor could I use any expletives stronger than 'damn'. The Lord's name was not to be taken in vain, nor my heroine 'taken in adultery'. It was permissable for her to marry the 'wrong man', but then he must either die, be killed or be the guilty party in their divorce. I chafed against these limitations, but fell in with them rather than risk not being published at all.

The combination of Percy's bibliographical journalism, my fiction writing and Elkin Mathews sales from catalogues (hardly anyone came to buy from the shelves) was bringing in a passable living. That we could not afford holidays or luxuries did not matter, for there was nowhere to go and no luxuries to be had, apart from the black market which only operated in a minor way in the village.

As the war entered its third year we had all become so accustomed to the disappearance of foods and other goods which we had once regarded as necessities, that phrases like 'in short supply', or 'sorry, we can't get it any more' were accepted with a resigned shrug. There were those who always knew where to buy on the black market but, objecting as I did to paying over the odds for something I could do without—at a pinch—I was not one of them. The war changed fashions in clothes, as war always has done, head scarves replaced hats, children wore knitted 'pixey hoods'.

'It's women like you who have ruined my business,' the owner of a London millinery shop told me reproachfully one day, eyeing the scarf on my head. His wife, I noticed, still wore a hat, although his business was closing down.

By then clothing coupon books had been introduced. Rationing of clothes was tight; if a school uniform was required sacrifices from parents were often needed. Women's organisations urged their members to 'make do and mend', and practical ladies went around demonstrating how to make door mats out of string and what to do 'when your ball-cock sticks', for plumbers were also in short supply.

In the autumn, as the leaves were falling and the wise housewife had her oil lamps ready for the power failures which were beginning to plague us, the church bells, silent since 1940, rang out jubilantly for Britain's first major military victory of the war, the Eighth Army's defeat of Rommel at El Alamein.

Winter 1942

CHAPTER TWENTY-ONE

It was towards the end of the year when Percy came home from London one evening and told me of the sad plight of a Polish Jew he had known some years before, in Berlin.

'His name is Jutrozinski,' Percy said, 'but everyone calls him Jutro. He wants to come and work for me and I must say he would be very useful. He's an experienced cataloguer and that's just what I need.'

Jutro came from a Berlin family of Polish-Jewish descent. After Hitler became Chancellor, Jutro had emigrated to Paris where he had lived amongst other literary immigrants until the fall of France, when he had managed to escape to England.

With hardly any money and almost all his possessions left in Paris, Jutro applied to join the Free French Forces but, as a German by birth, found himself instead in the Pioneers. This was a tough Labour Force made up of immigrants of various races and colours, ex-convicts and anyone else whose background was considered either too dubious for enrolment in the armed forces, or had been posted from his unit as an incorrigible hard case.

Jutro found himself in the same unit as Arthur Koestler whom he had known in Paris. This was of some comfort to him, for the Pioneer Force had all the toughest assignments, the hardest physical work. When Plymouth was blitzed, it was the Pioneers who were put on to clearing up the mess. The tributes paid to them after the war were well deserved.

A slightly built man, unused to physical work of any kind, willing but hopelessly unpractical, poor Jutro soon cracked up, and after a couple of heart attacks was discharged as unfit for further service.

Percy had not known that he was in England until a colleague mentioned that Jutro was working in a bookshop in the Charing Cross Road and by no means happy there. It was a Jewish business and the two brothers who ran it were hard taskmasters. While prepared to give employment to a fellow Jew in need, they were not above taking

161

advantage of his situation, working him long hours humping heavy boxes of books and doing all the fetching and carrying for a very small wage.

'I know he'd like nothing better than to work for you,' the colleague had told Percy. 'He's thoroughly miserable where he is, poor fellow, and afraid to leave in case he can't find another job. You'd be doing a great kindness if you would take him on.'

After hearing all this from Percy I knew we would take Jutro into our home. We would learn to live with him as we had with Kot, Dick Curle and the various other guests and lodgers who had come and gone during our married life, including an Egyptian Jew who had lived with us briefly in St. John's Wood while trying to make a living as a sculptor. And Jutro, poor fellow, would have to learn to live with *us*, unless we could find him lodgings in the village. But that, I knew, was unlikely, for a new series of air raids had brought back many of the evacuees and accommodation was in short supply.

'He's not a bad chap, you'll like him,' Percy said, by way of reassurance.

So Jutro arrived, smiling the placatory smile of the Jewish refugee, a small man with a thin, intelligent face, anxious brown eyes and brown crinkly hair growing back from a high forehead. When he wasn't working in the office he would come and talk to me in the kitchen and I enjoyed his company. In his eagerness to please he would offer to help, but I soon found that although obsessively tidy he was incapable of doing the simplest of household tasks, so that it was simpler to let him sit and chat while I got on with the work.

Almost embarrassingly grateful to have been transplanted from Charing Cross Road to Takeley, Jutro did his best to fit in and his self-deprecating presence in the household was soon taken for granted. His habit of tidying up the children's belongings scattered around the dining room was rather irritating, but resigned to the incomprehensible fads of visiting adults, they privately christened him 'Mr. Fusspot' and continued to leave their toys and books about as they always had.

Percy's satisfaction with Jutro as a cataloguer was soon tempered by the discovery that his new employee was hopelessly incompetent when required to tackle some of the routine office jobs he had hoped to hand over to him. One of these was packing parcels of books. It was not that poor Jutro wasn't more than willing to do whatever was asked, it was just that packing valuable books was a complete mystery to him. He had no idea how to begin.

'I'd better show you,' Percy said and gave Jutro a demonstration. 'It's very important to make a parcel *firm* so that the books can't move about in the packing. So you need to tie a slip knot — like this.' Having demonstrated the tying of a slip knot a couple of times he handed the books, packing material and string to Jutro and left him to get on with the job.

The next morning Jutro appeared at the breakfast table hollow-eyed. He admitted he hadn't had much sleep. I hoped he wasn't ill and my concern eventually drew from him a rueful confession; he had been up half the night practising tying slip knots.

Jutro was one of life's losers. He had once been married, but not for long. A bride had been found for him, a pretty young Jewish girl of sixteen, fresh from school. 'She was just a child,' he said with a tender smile. 'She knew nothing.' They had parted without rancour as soon as she began to grow up. She had then married a Rabbi and the three of them had remained good friends.

Jutro needed friends more than he needed a wife. Paris had suited him; there he had been one of a little group of ex-patriates; writers and artists for the most part. Not himself creative, he loved to be with people who were. His hopes were all centred on returning to the life he had led before the war, to his old apartment, his friends, the cafés where they had met and talked away the evenings. The time would come when he was able to return to Paris, but nothing would be as it was before and despair would overcome him.

For a week or two after he arrived he made a half-hearted attempt to find lodgings, but soon gave up and his occupation of our spare room was established. As far as I was concerned he had become a member of my household, probably for the duration of the war.

For Jutro, it was not so easy. His consciousness of being an employee got in the way of his relationship with Percy. Socially diffident, in England at least, if our friends invited him with us he was never quite sure whether he was really wanted. Essentially an urban man (he had been born in Berlin) he was somewhat at a loss in a country village. Like Elizabeth's cousin he had never learned to ride a bicycle and he was not much of a walker; the village inns with their local regulars and their dart matches were not for him, nor did Bishop's Stortford offer much cultural entertainment. Statistically Jutro was a displaced person; in Takeley he was also misplaced.

Freed from much of the cataloguing by Jutro's arrival, Percy had more time to spare for finding new stock — an antiquarian bookseller's perennial problem — and for writing. But soon another demand for his time cropped up which he felt he could not refuse.

Spring and Summer 1943

CHAPTER TWENTY-TWO

In March a notice went up in the village announcing that a recruiting meeting would be held in the village hall the following Sunday afternoon.

The object: 'To form a platoon of cadets in Takeley'. Lads between the ages of 14 and 17½ were invited to attend and, no doubt as an inducement to parents to encourage their sons to join, it was stated that uniforms were to be provided free of charge. The notice was issued by the 12th Battalion of the Essex Regiment.

Our local retired General, a courtly old gentleman brought up in the tradition of *Noblesse Oblige*, had been roped in to get the platoon formed. Cadets were being recruited throughout the country, the War Department having rather belatedly decided that it might be a good idea to give local lads some army training and discipline prior to conscription. Volunteers to serve as platoon and company commanders were also being sought and Percy, who had served in the London Scottish in the first world war, was asked if he would take on the Takeley Platoon.

'I thought if I didn't accept the job it would probably go to some Blimp or homosexual,' he wrote to a Harold Edwards, 'so I decided I'd better spare the time somehow.'

The chosen day for the official formation saw our General, a Staff Colonel, another officer, the Cadet Company Commander for the district and Percy gathered at the hall, awaiting a rush of volunteers.

Outside the hall a crippled boy stood shyly in the spring sunshine, wondering if he dared go inside. A fifteen-year-old friend came and joined him and presently they went in together.

Half an hour after the meeting had been due to start the General stood up and addressed his small audience apologetically:

'Well, Gentlemen, it doesn't look as if we are going to get any more volunteers this afternoon, so I think we might make a start by forming a company, even if it will be er — somewhat under strength.'

164

Percy in cadet uniform with David, 1943.

I was given an account of the proceedings when Percy came home to tea.

'So we formed a platoon as part of the Dunmow Company of Army Cadets,' he said. 'And we enrolled young John, along with his crippled friend. John is keen, at least, and he thinks some of his pals will turn up when we have our first drill. But God knows why they had to choose a Sunday afternoon for the formation, and the publicity seems to have been non-existent.'

As the news spread around the village the platoon numbers began to grow. The promised battle-dress uniforms were issued and Percy held a weekly evening drill session in the village hall with instruction in the use of small arms — much to the cadets' delight. Sunday morning exercises in Hatfield Forest were popular.

Helen was then going to Sunday school at the far end of the village, attending a class taken by a great-grandson of the famous John Spurgeon. I could usually find someone to take her there but it was Percy's job to bring her home. One morning she arrived home in high fettle, accompanied by a military escort of four. 'Daddy's cadets brought me home,' she announced in self-satisfied tones. Daddy, I gathered, was with his fellow platoon commanders at the local. The cadets had their uses not always in the handbooks.

Percy's help was needed that summer in a rather different enterprise. Women's Institutes throughout the country were being urged to make a special effort in fund raising for the Red Cross. We were all a bit tired of being asked to make special efforts for this and that, but the Takeley W.I. Committee felt they could hardly refuse to do something. A discussion rambled on as to what would be the least troublesome event to organise until I, becoming bored, asked why not a concert for a change?

This idea seemed to stun the committee. And where, asked the President, did I think I was going to find the necessary talent?

Put on my mettle I said I was sure there was some around, it only needed bringing to light. After such an incautious remark it was not surprising that I found myself landed with the job of impressario.

'Well, then we'll leave it in your hands, Mrs. Muir. If you want any help you must let us know. Now, if there is no other business ...?'

It was Percy's idea that Phyllis Calvert and Peter Murray Hill might be persuaded to perform at my concert. I wouldn't have dared to ask them to spare precious time from their busy lives for a village show, even though it was for the Red Cross, but Percy had no such inhibitions. By great good luck both were free on the appointed evening and promised us a fifteen minute sketch.

To have secured two West End stars to top the bill encouraged me to raise my sights in recruiting talent for the rest of the programme. Kingsley Martin, editor of the *New Statesman* was then living at Little Easton. As a frequent member of the B.B.C.'s very popular Brain's Trust Programme, he had become known to a much wider public than the *New Statesman* readership. Although I only knew him slightly I decided to have a Brain's Trust for the first part of the programme, with Kingsley Martin as the 'big name' in the team. He was an approachable man as regards local events and immediately promised to come. Rupert Cross was roped in to represent the Law, another of our neighbours, David Sachs, then assistant editor on the *Investor's Chronicle* represented the City and a film actor who had been drafted into the U.S.A.F. and was based at Stansted made up the team, with Percy as question master. Oddly enough it did not occur to me (nor to anyone else) that we should have had at least one woman, the so-called 'statutory woman' in our team.

For some light relief I was recommended to book a double act from the American base — Al and Cal. According to Joyce, my mother's help, they were 'ever so good', played guitars, told jokes and sang. She promised to engage them for me, and later said that they were willing to do a turn.

'You know you really ought to have one of the locals in the programme,' someone said, 'or a couple of kids to do a song and dance act, to bring along the mums and grannies. There's Ron, if you can't find anyone else. He'd play the piano as an opener. He's a popular lad ...'

Peter Murray Hill with Phyllis Calvert.

Ron was one of the cadets, a handsome young man, not lacking in confidence. His mother had taught him to play the piano and, as this was an accomplishment not possessed by most of the other boys and girls in the village, he was looked upon as something of a local prodigy. Unable to discover any budding Jessie Mathews in the village I booked Ron and hoped for the best.

The news that Phyllis Calvert was to appear in person spread through the village like wildfire. All the young girls were agog to see her and the reserved seats were sold out well before the day. I had invited Phyll and Peter to stay the night and they arrived on the morning of the show, Phyll with her wide blue eyes and auburn hair looking as pretty a box office draw as any impressario could wish for, with Peter as her tall and handsome leading man.

After lunch they rehearsed their sketch on the lawn. Percy, in a deck chair acting as prompter, was not required to help out. They had learned their parts on the train and both were word perfect. Helen and David, the audience, sitting on the grass, watched the performance spell-bound. It was a great relief to have my two stars of the show on hand hours before curtain up, and in due course everyone billed to appear was assembled back stage at the hall — except for my American double act.

'Al and Cal aren't here,' I said despairingly to Percy, who was acting as compère. I had told Joyce to ask them to telephone and confirm the booking, but they had never done so and I was beginning to doubt their existence.

Ron, the eager young pianist, was already on the stage, fingering his music. The Brains who were to follow him were chatting together in the committee room; in the kitchen Phyllis Calvert was making up the caste for the one act thriller. The curtain went up, Percy bade the audience welcome, told them of the treats to come and introduced Ron, who sat down on the piano stool and began to play his party piece, or rather party pieces, with all the confidence of a youthful Paderewski.

Presently Kingsley Martin, standing back-stage, caught my eye: 'That young man seems to be going on for rather a long time,' he remarked.

I was all too well aware of it. I had told Ron: 'Five minutes', but he had clearly forgotten. I had already tried hissing at him from the wings and he hadn't even turned his head.

Mrs. Sharp, one of the ladies who had come to help with the refreshments, had joined me and was listening critically.

'I don't know how to stop him,' I said hopelessly. 'I can't catch his eye.'

Mrs. Sharp, as those who worked with her knew, was well named.

'I'll soon stop him for you, if that's what you want,' she said and before I could ask how, she had twitched aside the curtain and stepped onto the stage. Marching across to the piano, in full view of the audience, she tapped the wretched pianist on the shoulder.

'That's enough for now, Ron,' she said firmly and audibly, and walked off.

With a couple of despondent chords Ron's performance came to an end. He got to his feet, gathered up his music, did a sketchy bow and made for the wings, to the sound of good-natured applause.

After this ludicrous opening the Brains Trust got away to a smooth start. Listening back-stage I could hear the audience chuckling as wit sparked more wit from the carefully selected questions; I almost forgot the maddening non-appearance of my American double act until the sound of a car arriving brought me to the stage door. Two lanky Yanks were unfolding themselves from a jeep; one reached back for a guitar.

'Al?' I hazarded, 'and Cal?'

"That's right, m'am.' They stood grinning down at me good humouredly.

'Guess we owe you an apology for not callin' you. But we meant to come all along.'

They were professionals as I had been told, and their number went with a swing. It was a satisfactory warm-up to Peter and Phyll's sketch which was predictably received with rapturous applause. Later I asked Phyll what they had thought of the one-act play which followed. Slightly shame-faced she confessed that they hadn't seen it.

'Neither of us can bear to watch amateurs so we slipped off to the pub after wishing them luck.'

In fact my amateurs had not been bad at all, the play had gone well and the show was voted an all-round success. At that time the usual price for reserved seats in the two front rows of the hall was two shillings and sixpence. I had charged five shillings for seats in the first six rows and sold them all. Unreserved at 1s.6d. had also been sold out. With a collection in the interval and programmes at 6d. the W.I. was able to send a satisfactory cheque to the Red Cross.

CHAPTER TWENTY-THREE

One sunny afternoon in July I was working in the vegetable garden when Isobel, the postmistress, arrived on her bicycle. She had brought a telegram, which meant bad news, for in the ordinary way telegrams and cables for the firm came through on the telephone, the confirmation arriving by post the following day. Conscientious and thoughtful as always, Isobel preferred not to break bad news on the telephone, even though it meant leaving the post-office and cycling two or three miles to deliver a dreaded telegram.

'I thought I'd better bring it,' she said. 'It's from Kenya.'

It was from my mother to say that my father had died of sub-tertian malaria.

The last time I had seen him had been in 1937 when I had waved good-bye to him on Victoria Station when he was leaving England to join my sister and her husband in Kenya. A written-out novelist with one book of a contract to complete, he was banking on a new country restoring his health, which had been poor, and his ability to work, which had been declining for several years.

Not long after his arrival in Kenya he had written home: 'It is up to me to get the tail-end of this story done somehow ... then it will be a conclusion of that for good and all. If I don't make it short it won't get done. It's only what I used to do in less than a week in the early days, after the war, and in about a month or six weeks at home last year. I've been three months on it steadily, and am re-doing the third thousand words, which ought to come right now. I doubt if I could do it much quicker anywhere; but here at this height (8,000 ft.) the mind simply doesn't work on anything intricate, you pore and pore for hours, getting nowhere ... I'm just worn out on fiction which doesn't work in my head any more, however hard I sit at it.'

Somehow he had finished the book, which had been serialised in *Answers* before publication as a hardback in 1941, titled *In Full Cry*. By then he was serving as an officer in the Kenya Royal Naval Volunteer Reserve. Officially he was 54, in reality ten years older — 'an old shell-back' as Wentworth Day had called him affectionately, in the days when he had sailed his yawl in the Blackwater at West Mersea.

The realisation that I should never talk to him again, never again find one of his welcome, descriptive letters — a writer's letters — again in my post, never ask him the questions I had always meant to ask, about his life before he became my father — that came later. At first my thoughts were with my mother. Had she been with him? How was she going to sustain his loss, for they had always been devoted to each other? What could I, a thousand miles away, do to help or give comfort?

It was after the evening meal, when the children were in bed, that sadness overcame me. It was the first death of someone dear to me that I had suffered. I felt alone in my sorrow. As Percy and Jutro sat reading in the sitting room, I slipped out into the garden and wandered about in the warm dusk thinking of my father as I believed he would have wished me to remember him, wanting my thoughts to pay tribute to his memory. I thought of him sailing his yawl, The Minion, across the Blackwater, his face ruddy with windburn, bringing her skilfully to her mooring at West Mersea on the falling tide. I remembered how we would cook the dabs we'd caught on an old oil stove in the houseboat he used as a study, where he could write his novels undisturbed. A decaying old hulk it was, stuck for good in the West Mersea mud. There, when my mother was away, he would enjoy entertaining fellow members of the Savage Club, writers mostly, who came to Mersea for the sailing. Sometimes he would invite me to a *cordon bleu* meal, refusing to let me take any hand in the cooking, and adding wine to his sauces with a lavish hand. He had taught me to fish with a fly when I was a child, showing me how to cast upstream from the grassy banks of the river Nar; he had encouraged my school-girl attempts at short stories with helpful criticism, and had been tolerant of my untidy bohemian way of life as a working girl in London. I remembered how I had always taken his affection and tolerance for granted ...

Footsteps on the path and a shadow on the lawn interrupted my thoughts; Jutro had silently joined me. He had never known my father, but he had come to give me the comfort of a sympathetic human presence.

It was some months later that I learned from my sister in Kenya that the Ministry of Pensions had tried to wriggle out of awarding my mother a naval officer's widow's pension on the grounds that my father had been some years older than his declared age, and that his death had been due as much to an old man's heart and heavy smoking as to malaria. Grudgingly relenting under pressure from my sister, my mother was eventually awarded a measly £3 a week.

One bright summer morning I looked out of the bedroom window at the back of the house and saw through the screen of wild plum trees half-circling our pond, a shimmer of misty blue. The evening before, the field behind the pond had been green; sown with a thin, wavy crop that I hadn't recognised. Now the hot sun had opened myriads of tiny bell-like blue flowers, and as the wind rippled gently through them the whole field turned blue.

I had not seen flax growing before. It was such an enchanting sight that I kept going to the edge of the field to gaze at it. But the colour was transient, needing sunshine. All too soon the flowers were gone and it was just a green field once again — and the farmer grumbled.

The crop had been an experiment and a terrible nuisance to harvest, he said. It hadn't paid him and he wouldn't grow it again.

I learned that he was short of labour for harvesting his corn. I offered to help and suggested that I would consider myself repaid if I could have a couple of sheaves of wheat for my hens. My offer was accepted and I joined the men in the big wheat field north of our house. The combine had yet to come to the farm and I was shown the art of stooking — picking up the sheaves dropped in bundles by the reaper and binder, and standing them up in little groups, wig-wam shape, to dry out. Leaning at the right angle, each supporting the other, they stayed upright, the rain running off them, the sun and air drying the ears and completing the ripening process.

Later came the job of pitching — lifting the sheaves with a pitchfork and throwing them on to the waggon that would take them to the stack-yard, one man standing on top of the growing load to fork the sheaves into position. The other pitchers would be on either side, keeping the man on top busy as the tractor, or horses, pulled the waggon along the rows of stooks. To pitch a sheaf on to the waggon when it was empty or nearly empty was not hard; to pitch it up on to the top of the load, well above one's head brought to life muscles I didn't know I possessed.

Blisters came, and so after a time did the rhythm of the work. At the end of the long, warm day, there was physical weariness with a sleepy contentment that was a reward in itself.

When the last load of corn had been carried it was the turn of the gleaners, with their baskets and sacks, to hunt the stubble for the strands missed by the reaper, or flattened under the wheels of the waggons and tractor. The gleaners were mostly women, with back-garden hens to feed. Trudging up and down the prickly stubble their eyes would constantly scan the ground, their faces serious as they stooped and gleaned, stuffing the dryly rustling ears into their baskets.

Although hens, fed on the smelly mixture of miller's sweepings known as 'balancer' or the even smellier concoction from city dustbins known as 'tottenham pudding', might never have tasted corn before, when they were thrown a handful of wheat ears their appreciation of proper food was almost instantaneous. The balancer would be left in the trough while they rushed for the corn ears and pecked or shook out the grains of wheat. So would we have pounced on a fillet of beef, had one been offered.

It was fortunate for Elkin Mathews that the printer who printed our catalogues had built up a good stock of paper. As few private customers were willing or able to make a trip to Takeley in war time, selling books by catalogue was the only way we could stay in business. Therefore, after the first emaciated little list issued from Takeley, Percy had been steadily increasing the size of our catalogue until, in 1943, we sent out a bumper one of 62 pages. It was special in more ways than one, for it offered for sale a unique set of Jane Austen's novels.

Percy had bought them from Dick Curle, before the war. Neither he nor Dick had realised what a find they were; indeed they were in such a shocking condition that Percy had been reluctant to buy them, even though he knew that they were first editions and, therefore, extremely scarce. He had made an offer which Dick had turned down. Then, failing to sell them elsewhere Dick had changed his mind and accepted Percy's offer. It was some time later, when he examined them more carefully that Percy had begun to suspect that they might be what they turned out to be, Cassandra's own copies given her by Jane after each novel was published. So the five novels, thirteen volumes altogether, were catalogued with something of a fanfare for the very reasonable sum of £650.

As catalogues went this was a prestigious one, offering books ranging over some seventeen subjects, from such feminine interests as crochet, dancing and valentines, to mathematics, medicine and science, to name only a few.

There had been another 'scoop' in the previous catalogue which had offered a copy of the 1866 (2nd) edition of *Alice in Wonderland* with a presentation inscription from Tenniel, the artist who had illustrated the book, with an inserted drawing by him of another version of the Mad Hatter. This was priced very reasonably at £65.*

Prior to the famous Lady Chatterly obscenity trial most dealers in rare books were wary of handling anything that might be deemed obscene, even though it was of literary or historical interest. The

---

* *Alice* was first published in 1865, but Dodgson, dissatisfied with the appearance of the book, had had nearly all the copies destroyed. The few that did escape his edict are so rare as to be unobtainable. The 2nd. edition was published the following year.

collection of letters that came into Percy's hands during the war could have been so described.

He brought them to me one day when I was writing, a large packet of letters written in small, fine hand-writing, very upright — a word that could not have been applied to the writer's character.

'Do you think you could type these out for me?' Percy asked me. 'I really don't think I could ask Mrs. P. to do it, but I do need them copied.'

I saw what he meant when I began to read the letters. The writer had indulged in love affairs with Venetian gondoleri which he described in considerable detail. I knew little of such goings on (unmentionable vices they were termed then) and after some initial repugnance I read the descriptive, ornate prose with interest not to say curiosity. There was much else in the letters, revealing a very curious character, a self-destructive, devious, mistrustful man who quarrelled with all who tried to help him.

The collection appeared in the catalogue under 'CORVO (Frederick William Serafino Rolfe, Baron). Autographed letters signed, written from various addresses in Venice . . . 1909-1910'. Interested purchasers were invited to write for further details. There were quite a few of these and it was not long before the collection, known as *The Venice Letters* was sold. Alas, I have no record of the price.

CHAPTER TWENTY-FOUR

The landings in Sicily had cheered us all immensely; no longer did we steel ourselves for bad news when we turned on the radio, rather we listened eagerly for more good news. Mussolini's fall from power, his internment by General Badoglio and subsequent rescue by Hitler was like something out of an espionage thriller. Soon we were to listen to reports of Allied landings on the toe of Italy.

As the tide begins to turn during a war, confidence in eventual victory breeds impatience for more action. When the progress of the war was discussed speculation inevitably turned to when we might expect what came to be known as the opening of 'The Second Front'.

Left wingers would argue vehemently that to delay opening the Second Front was to sacrifice the valiant Russians who had been bearing the brunt of the fighting for two years. 'Start the Second Front' was scrawled in white paint on the walls of bombed buildings in London and other big towns, and the Left Wing Press accused the War Cabinet of deliberate delay while Russia bled to death.

The Left Wing group in the village ran an 'Aid to the Soviet' event at the village hall, with stalls and side shows. It drew somewhat half-hearted support from the village people and despite the fact that Lady Churchill was president of The Aid to Russia fund, the local Conservatives were not to be seen throwing hoopla rings, or buying jam and home-made cakes.

My third novel had gone to the publishers at the beginning of the summer and I had just begun a new book when Joyce, my mother's help who had worked for me since she left school, told me she was leaving.

She was a big, well-developed girl and she had been stung by comments by other girls about her easy job. She had been happy enough working for me and she was devoted to David, but she thought she had better go and work in the match factory in Bishop's Stortford where several of her friends were employed.

When, in 1938, her sister Mavis had come to me, 'going into service' was the recognised work for the average young girl when she left the village school at fourteen, preferable, most parents thought, to factory work. The brightest pupils had already 'got the scholarship' at eleven and gone to the local high school to become teachers, for the most part,

175

or nurses. By 1943 it was the other way round, in no time the school leaver was absorbed into industry, or found herself working as a ward maid at the London Hospital, evacuated to Bishop's Stortford for the duration, or in Woolworth's, with her evenings free and more money in her pocket. Older sisters would have either 'registered' and gone into the Forces or the Land Army, if they hadn't dodged the column with an early marriage.

With Joyce departed to the factory (where she was soon in trouble for refusing to wear the regulation cap designed to prevent hair from catching in the machines and scalping its owner), I looked in vain for someone to replace her. To write with a three-year-old clamouring for my attention proved impossible, play groups didn't exist, and although most towns were running day-nurseries for working mothers these were usually over-subscribed and, in any case, the need to finish a novel would hardly have qualified me to join the queue.

As usual, having begun a novel I had to find some way of continuing; the story nagged at me, so did the thought of my contract and the cheque to come when I delivered the typescript. Enquiries amongst friends suggested a nursery school that had been set up four miles away by a retired governess. Highly recommended by the county family who had employed her and whose children were now away at boarding schools, her kindergarten had snob appeal and she had soon gathered a class of a dozen or so small children whom she taught, or at least, kept occupied, five mornings a week in a large room near Stansted railway station.

Middle class parents in country districts, who before the war would seldom have considered sending their children to the village school, were by this time rather resignedly doing so, at least for two or three years, before despatching them to boarding schools; but there were some of the upper crust who couldn't quite bring themselves to do this, protesting, not without some truth, that their village schools were so dreadfully sub-standard and unhygienic, with outside lavatories (more often than not with no plumbing) and cold, draughty class rooms. Neither did the alternative of using petrol for the school run into the nearest town appeal to them.

Miss G., capable, trustworthy and also knowing her place, fulfilled a need. I went to see her and found her as pleasant and sensible as described and willing to add a three-and-a-half year old to her brood for £5 a term, a sum I was happy enough to pay.

There was one obstacle in getting to Stansted; since building the Base the U.S.A.F. had done away with one road from Takeley and closed the other because the runway ended within a few yards of it, which was reasonable, but awkward for those whose work took them from one village to the other. Fortunately a compromise had been reached. The camp commander was prepared to issue permits where needs arose and the barrier across the road would be raised for the permit-holder to pass through.

I reckoned I would not be hindering the war effort if I obtained a permit and I applied for one on the truthful grounds of wishing to work in Stansted. The permit was duly granted.

There was one other problem to be solved. I had arranged for David to go to the nursery school for four mornings a week from 10 to 12 a.m., but if, having left him, I had to cycle home and then return to collect him, there would be no time left in which to write. It was therefore necessary for me to find a room in Stansted where I could work while he was at school.

The day came when I was to take David to school, strapped onto a seat on the carrier of my bicycle. My typewriter was suspended from one handlebar, a carrier bag filled with typing paper hung from the other. I still hadn't found a room, but I hadn't given up hope.

Percy came to see us off.

'What are you going to do while he's at nursery school?'

I looked up at the sky. It was clear blue, a fine September morning.

'I'll sit and write by the roadside,' I said and cycled off, before he had time to comment.

The sentry at the gates barring access to the road to Stansted glanced at my pass cursorily and waved me through. David knew he was going to school and was enjoying the ride. He had raised no objection, but it was a different story when we arrived and I led him in to meet his teacher.

'He'll settle down as soon as you're gone,' she said reassuringly, raising her voice over David's bawling. 'Come along then, David.' She took his hand firmly and led him away. By no means sure she was right, I cycled off, feeling guilty. He was a shy child and to be left with a total stranger must have been rather like being thrown into a swimming bath and left to sink or swim.

On a previous ride to Stansted I had noticed a roadside seat in a lane a little way out of the village, intended perhaps for the faithful to rest awhile on their way to and from the church. There would, I thought, be few if any passers-by to wonder (as well they might) if a mad woman had arrived in the village.

There was no one about when I propped up my cycle behind the seat, took my typewriter out of its case and settled down to work.

A seat by the roadside is not a particularly comfortable place for typing. The wind kept snatching away unsecured sheets, the seat was hard and felt damp (I regretted not having brought a cushion), bird song was distracting, a nearby pigeon wouldn't shut up and somewhere out of sight a tractor chugged up and down. Nor was the lane unfrequented. Tradesmen's vans, cyclists and private cars went by. Passers-by who would hardly have looked twice at someone sitting painting gaped rudely at a woman sitting typing by the roadside.

I stuck it out until it was time to retrieve my son from his nursery school. I had done little work, but it had been pleasant enough sitting in the sunshine. Putting my typewriter back in its case I apologised to the pigeon for cursing it. After all, it was I who was the intruder.

Further enquiries at shops in the village proved fruitless. No one seemed to want a mornings-only lodger; the one room I saw was an attic bedroom with no heating, and I was thinking of the winter ahead.

The next day was grey, threatening rain. David and I set off with less enthusiasm and once again he staged a protest at the school door, but it was, I thought, only a token one, for I had learned from Miss G. that his tears had dried as soon as my back was turned.

No sooner had I left him than the rain began coming down in earnest and I headed for the railway station. It was a dreary little branch line station, a target for the coming Beeching axe. Passenger trains were few and I thought that the waiting-room might provide a quiet little port in the storm. It was the typical small, murky waiting-room, worn sooty linoleum on the floor, slatted benches around the walls, soot engrimed windows. Under the puzzled gaze of one waiting passenger I got out my typewriter. Our eyes met, I smiled apologetically: 'I'm trying to do some work.' He nodded, baffled. I tapped away, half-heartedly, found I had written nonsense and xxx'ed it out. It was unnerving to be watched, but having started to type I felt I was expected to continue; the alternative was to explain, and that was far too complicated. Then a train came in and for a while I was left in peace.

Long before it was time to collect David I knew that I would not make the waiting-room my study a second time; nor did I fancy another morning on the roadside seat. Yet there must, I felt, be *somewhere* in the village where I could write undisturbed within four walls for a couple of hours.

'Why not try The King's Arms?' suggested Miss G. when I explained my problem. 'They're never busy before mid-day, except at the week-ends and they've got a cosy little bar parlour that I'm sure they'd let you use.' So I went across the road to the King's Arms.

The landlord had no objection. He was a matter-of-fact sort of man and uncurious as to the sort of books I might be writing. I could have the room for four shillings a week, he said, and he'd see there was a fire when the weather was colder. It was a cheerful little room with light coloured upholstered chairs, two or three tables, a tiled fireplace and one or two potted plants. The prints on the wall were unnoticeable — there was nothing to catch my eye and distract me. It was perfect for working in and within a stone's throw of Miss G.'s nursery school.

It became my writing room for the next eighteen months. The landlord had told me I wouldn't be disturbed and he was as good as his word. His wife, a devotee of the novels of Florence Barclay, never came in to talk to me (my sales, after all, were not in the Barclay class) when the telephone rang I knew it wasn't for me. With the knowledge that I had just two precious hours for work I settled down to write as soon as my typewriter was on the table. Never before, or since, have I written so quickly, or so easily. As for David, on his third morning at school he went in without a murmur of protest, and when I came to collect him he met me with a happy grin. There were no more tears.

Autumn and Winter 1943

CHAPTER TWENTY-FIVE

We were having a drink with some friends when we heard the news of Italy's surrender. I don't think any of us had expected it so soon and there was great rejoicing. Percy, never one to throw his hat into the air too quickly cautioned against over-optimism.

'Now the Germans will take over,' he said.

My thoughts were with our P.O.W.'s in the Italian camps; many had been there for more than two years, including my ex-husband. Would they now be able to reach the Allied Forces pushing up from the toe of Italy? We were to learn later that out of some 80,000 in the prisoner of war camps several thousand succeeded in doing so.

The news that Marshall Badoglio, then the Italian Head of State, had agreed to the Allies Armistice terms and that the Italian forces had surrendered, raised hopes that the war might be over the following year. There was a general expectation that the long awaited Second Front, the landing of British and American forces in France, would take place in the spring of 1944. Most people paid no attention to the campaign of the communists and 'fellow travellers' with their scrawled slogans on buildings, 'Start the second front now'. Admiration for the way the Russians were fighting was one thing; support for our home grown communists' antics was quite another. Their over-night turn-about from being anti-war to belligerency as soon as the U.S.S.R. was invaded, had lost them most of their fellow-travellers and their left-wing waverers.

As I cycled back and forth to Stansted that autumn I became aware of the steady build-up of heavy bombers, the Flying Fortresses and the Liberators, aerial juggernauts they looked, standing on the dispersal points.

The noise as they took off on bombing missions was ear-shattering. Even worse was the high decibel scream of the two-engined Marauders as their engines revved to a crescendo at take-off.

There were times when some special pleading would secure me the firm's car for the journey to Stansted, but petrol was too precious for me to ask for it except when the weather was really appalling. The slog home through the lanes on a cycle took anything from fifteen minutes to half an hour, according to whether or not the barrier at the end of the runway would be down, or the wind speeding me along or seeming wilfully to slow my progress, for there were bleak open stretches between flat ploughland.

Once home there would sometimes be visitors to be given a mid-day meal, as well as Jutro, Percy's secretary and the family, for there was no question of those who came on business getting a snack in the village. Colleagues would be invited to take 'pot luck' and seemed happy enough to do so.

On the days when I took David to his nursery school there was little enough time on my return to cook a hot meal, let alone provide a luncheon worthy of a good customer. The answer was to heat up a stew prepared beforehand — or what passed for a stew, the few bits of rationed beef or lamb bulked out by vegetables and tinned beans. The coupon-free agricultural workers' pies delivered every Wednesday were therefore a god-send when guests were coming. That these might not be acceptable to all guests never occurred to me, until the occasion of Mark Cohen's visit.

Mark was then President of the A.B.A.* and a partner in Marks & Co., of 84 Charing Cross Road, a shop to be immortalised after the war by the American writer Helen Hanff. He had come to talk about a project dear to his heart, a popular book on book collecting, designed to appeal to the book lover with a slender purse. He already had a publisher in mind and he had come to ask Percy to write the book.

It so happened that he arrived on a meat-pie day. Thankful to have a filling and tasty meal to offer (for as a family we all enjoyed the pies) I prepared some vegetables and invited Mark to the table.

He looked at his nice hot pie doubtfully, then he turned to me.

'I hope you'll forgive me for asking you, Mrs. Muir, but did you make this pie yourself?'

Innocently I said that I had not.

'They're very good, though,' I assured him. 'I think they're made mostly with mutton and potatoes'.

'Ah,' he shook his head apologetically, 'then I am afraid I must decline mine.'

He would, I suppose, have credited me with the tact not to have offered him a home-made pie containing detested pork, or with lard in

* Antiquarian Booksellers Association.

the pastry. As it was, his religious scruples were too great to allow him to take a chance; so, refusing my embarrassed offer to cook him an omelette, he made do with vegetables while the rest of us, including Jutro, enjoyed our suspect pies. Sometimes Jewish colleagues arrived with packs of sandwiches and availed themselves only of coffee, or fruit. Mostly they were content 'not to know' the ingredients of the refreshment offered, thus saving embarrassment all round.

Although sympathetic to Mark's idea for a popular book on book collecting Percy felt he couldn't take on the task of writing it. He was far too busy.* Why didn't Mark write it himself, he asked?

'No, no. I couldn't do it. But *you* could, Percy. You were the man I had in mind from the start.'

But Percy would not allow himself to be persuaded. Disappointed, nevertheless determined not to abandon his idea, Mark went back to London to look for another author.

The winter brought a renewal of air raids on London and other important towns and a fresh incursion of evacuees to the village. Amongst the original batch were a few who had found homes of their own and put down roots, cultivating gardens and taking part in village life. Takeley was near enough to London for local people to be tolerant of newcomers, unlike some of the more remote rural areas where evacuees remained 'foreigners' for years. It was depressing to hear the warblings of the sirens once again, what was more frightening was the rumour that the Nazis had developed a 'secret weapon' likely to cause more devastation than anything experienced hitherto. The German propaganda machine had been deliberately encouraging the spread of this rumour amongst their own forces, to give them fresh hopes, and amongst our own forces to cause 'alarm and despondency', as the phrase was. The Allies' slow progress in Italy generated more gloom.

We were already hearing reports of a small, but sinister device being dropped by German air-craft — the anti-personnel bomb, or 'butterfly bomb'. Rupert Cross brought back news of people picking up one of these devices and having arms blown off and of a child being killed by one. None fell in our neighbourhood, but there were warnings posted up against picking up unidentified objects, a warning I anxiously emphasised to my own children who had been coming home from rambles in Hatfield Forest with handfulls of metalled strips of paper dropped by air-craft to counteract radar. These were, in fact, harmless to those who picked them up, but suspected by many of being

---

* He was, at that time, well into a book on Beaumarchais, which was never published.

impregnated with some sinister chemical for transmitting disease — as they might well have been.

It was a bitter winter. In the book-room Percy and his staff worked in a temperature that seldom exceeded 50°F and was a good deal lower the first thing in the morning before the two electric fires were switched on. With frequent power cuts these did little more than take the worst of the chill from the air. Indoors we had sacrificed appearance to comfort and installed a slow-burning stove in the open dining room fire-place. It was a hideous contraption with a black pipe going up into the chimney. Sheets of asbestos had been wedged across the wide chimney opening to keep the warmth in, but snow, rain, and sometimes soot still found their way into the fire-place.

Visitors were apt to raise their eyebrows at this dispoilation of a splendid ingle-nook hearth, but the stove stayed in all night and was both more efficient and more economical than a wood-fire — and the cat loved it.

During the Christmas holidays a hard frost set in and the word went around the village that Hatfield lake was bearing. It was a fine lake for skating and when it was known that it was frozen people would come from miles around, the adept skaters skimming over the ice with enviable ease, as if it was the natural way to move over frozen water, while the tyros teetered ludicrously with flailing arms, in contorted efforts to stay vertical. I had first learned to skate on a London ice rink, but indoor skating, much as I had enjoyed it, was not to be compared with the joy of skating across the white, tree-fringed lake, my breath misting in the frosty air, crisp-cool on my face.

There was no one near when I fell through the ice one mid-week afternoon. I had skated over a water-fowl's fishing hole, lightly frozen during the night and it had given way beneath me as my skates struck it.

I didn't go all the way down; self-preservation operating automatically had made me throw out my arms as my body took the shock of the icy water. Instead I hung, with my elbows on the crumbling rim of the hole, the rest of my body suspended in six feet of water. It was impossible to climb out unaided; any attempt to heave myself up on to firmer ice only widened the hole. There was nothing to do but yell for help.

It seemed a very long time before I saw first one and then another skater detach themselves from the group at the other end of the lake and come speeding towards me, like rescuers in a comic strip. Luckily the first to arrive, a young medical student, knew exactly what to do. Having buckled three leather belts together he lay down flat on the ice a few feet away then slung me this life-line. I missed it the first time,

managed to grab it the second throw and held on tight with a considerable feeling of relief. A moment or two later, clutching my life-line with
both hands, I was slithering across the ice on my stomach as he reeled
me in like a fish on a line.

As soon as I reached dry land I was immediately surrounded by the
small crowd of spectators who had gathered to watch the rescue —
much to my annoyance. What I had wanted to do was to strip off my
wet trousers and don the raincoat proffered by my gallant rescuer. I
then intended to restore my circulation by trotting the 1½ miles home
through the forest. Instead a kindly elderly couple, ignoring my
protests, insisted on bundling me and the children into the back of their
car and driving me home — damp and shivering.

It was confidently predicted by everyone that I would 'catch my
death of cold', or at the very least get pneumonia. In fact I didn't even
catch a cold.

For the children, who had been sliding with their friends at the safe
end of the lake when I disappeared, it was a splendid story to be able to
relate. Percy, returning from a day in London, was hardly through the
door before they rushed to give him the news: 'Daddy, Daddy,
Mummy fell through the ice and had to be pulled out!'

I was willing enough to promise more cautious skating in future. It
was after the children had gone to bed and Jutro, Percy and I were
sitting snugly around the fire that, glancing up, I found Percy's gaze
resting on me and only then did I begin to think what it might have been
like for him if there had been no one to pull me out of the lake.

Spring and Summer 1944

CHAPTER TWENTY-SIX

One morning in March when the garden was still winter-hard I crawled out of bed with more reluctance than usual and stood dizzily peering at myself in the dressing table mirror. I had a pain in the region of my midriff, my head ached and I felt sick and feverish. The whites of my eyes were a watery yellow; dismally I diagnosed the reason and telephoned the doctor.

'Ah yes,' he said when I described my symptoms. 'Sounds like infective hepatitis, there's a lot of it about. Go back to bed and stay there until I come.'

I had no inclination to do otherwise. I felt wretched. When he arrived the doctor confirmed the diagnosis.

'You'll have to stay in bed at least a week,' he warned me 'and it will be four weeks before your liver is back to its normal size. But if you try to keep going and catch a chill on top of this jaundice you'll still be as yellow as a guinea in three months time.'

It was a salutary warning, although at that time all I wanted to do was to turn my face to the wall and sleep. The prescribed treatment was simple but boring. Stay in bed and keep warm, drink quarts of water, no alchohol, and stick to an entirely fat-free diet.

It was a disease that appeared to pick its victims without rhyme or reason, my doctor said, when I asked if the rest of the family was going to catch it. Often only one in a family would succumb; in an army camp it might be only 10%. For some reason the rest would be immune.

'If anyone else shows any early symptoms let me know,' he said as he left. 'The sooner it's treated the milder the attack.'

For the next ten days the household limped along without me. It was term time so at least Helen was at school all day. As for David, as there was no one available to take him to his nursery school, he was despatched to stay with the Pacey family for the duration of my illness, where the Pacey girls, three of whom had worked for me, delighted in spoiling him.

Our only domestic help at this time was one of my former young
pram pushers; she had grown up into a pretty, cheerful girl with a job at
a Bishop's Stortford factory and was willing to give us a couple of hours
of her free Saturday mornings. There was thus nothing for it but for
Percy and Jutro to fend for themselves.

It was a situation for which neither was equipped; Percy because it
had always been his policy to keep clear of the kitchen, apart from
giving an occasional hand drying dishes after a party, and Jutro because
he was hopelessly unpractical and barely recognised a frying pan when
he was asked to find one.

Some husbands are happy to demonstrate to their wives their culin-
ary skills. Percy had no ambitions in that direction, much as he enjoyed
good food. He held, too, that the hapless husband who allowed himself
to be pressed into kitchen duty in times of stress was likely to find
himself standing at the sink more often than he bargained for.

Nevertheless, meals were required; pubs did not serve snacks so there
could be no popping out for the evening meal, nor did Takeley boast a
fish and chip shop. There was nothing for it but to boil potatoes and
delve into my small store of tinned foods (no well-stocked freezer then)
or make do with bread eked-out with hard cheese, the ration then being
2 oz. per person per week.

For the first couple of days my housewife's conscience slept. The
thought of food repelled me, the office staff would have to make do
with sandwiches. Much dismayed, Percy and Jutro turned to the only
other female on the premises, Percy's secretary, Frances Poulter,
always called, in the formal way of the time, *Mrs.* Poulter, young
though she was. It is a truth, easily proveable that a man in need of a hot
meal can nearly always find a woman to cook one for him. With the
winter temperature in the book room seldom more than 50°, something
warmer than sandwiches was required for Percy and his staff.

Kind and helpful Frances Poulter came to the rescue, switching from
typewriter to kitchen cooker at mid-day, finding her way intuitively
around my kitchen; not only producing a mid-day meal for the two
men and herself, but bringing me vegetable broth, about the only food I
could tolerate.

After a couple of days wondering if I was going to die and half-
welcoming the prospect, my housewife's conscience stirred sufficiently
for me to offer some limited help to the two hapless males floundering
around in the kitchen. Jutro would come up to my bedroom bearing a
bowl of water, some potatoes, a waste bucket and a knife. He would
dispose of them on the bedside table and with a sheepish smile murmur:
'If you really don't mind ...?' And I would sit up and peel a saucepanful

of potatoes to accompany the cold spam or corned beef that was to be their evening meal.

There were a few other victims of the disease in Takeley, including our dedicated postmistress, Isobel who was made of sterner stuff than I. Instead of retiring to bed she stayed on duty throughout the course of the illness, presenting a brave yellow face to the post-office's customers. This, however, did not bring her universal praise, some thinking it wiser to give the post-office a wide berth and buy their stamps elsewhere.

I had been in bed a few days when a neighbour, John Robinson, rang up to enquire how I was. As I only knew him and his wife slightly I was surprised and rather touched by their solicitude.

'I've just heard you've got this bug that's going round,' he said, 'infective jaundice. Nasty, isn't it? Hope you're recovering. Anyone else in the family succumbed yet?'

'Not yet,' I said, touching wood.

'That's good. There's a lot of it about, you know. They've been going down with it like ninepins in the forces.'

I said they had my sympathy. I had just remembered that John Robinson, an 'old China hand' who had returned to England at the beginning of the war, now had some sort of a job at the hospital in Bishop's Stortford which had been taken over for the duration by the London Hospital.

'Have you got cases in the hospital?' I asked.

'We've had one or two. The problem is no one really knows how the infection is passed on. One of our medical staff here is in touch with a research team in Cambridge who are making a study of the disease and he wants to find someone in the very early stages, before they turn that nasty shade of yellow. The cases we've had here arrived when the illness was well established and apparently that doesn't help these medical chaps. So if anyone in your family, or someone working for you, does start feeling off-colour we'd be very grateful if you'd let us know. Be doing a public service and all that.'

It was the sort of request one agrees to without much thought. In any case I didn't expect the occasion to arise; Percy, Jutro and Helen were all in the best of health.

It was a week later, when I was just about on my feet again, though feeling far from lively, that my social conscience prompted me to ring up John Robinson.

'I'm keeping my promise, John. I think Helen has caught this wretched bug. I've got the doctor coming to see her today.'

'Ah, has she? Good! We'd like to have her here then.'

I didn't care for his enthusiastic reception of my news. I hadn't expected that the hospital would want the new victim admitted and I didn't at all like the idea of sending my poor ailing child away to a hospital bed, and said so.

'I'd much prefer to nurse her here. Having to go to hospital is bound to frighten her and make her think she's worse than she is. Can't one of the hospital's doctors come and see her at home and take whatever samples he needs?'

That wouldn't do at all, John Robinson said briskly. The doctor needed the patient in hospital under constant observation. There was no need for me to worry, she would get V.I.P. treatment and recover all the quicker under professional care.

'She'll be a very special patient and have a splendid time,' he went on, persuasively. 'You can visit her whenever you like, I'll guarantee that, and of course everyone will be tremendously grateful to you. This research that's being done really is very important.'

I still didn't like the idea, but I agreed to let Helen go to hospital if my doctor approved.

He arrived soon after and approved whole-heartedly.

'Far the best thing for her and for you. You're in no state to nurse a sick child, barely on your feet yourself. I'll ring up the hospital right away.'

Percy backed up the doctor and before Helen knew what was happening the ambulance had arrived and she was being whisked away in her pyjamas and dressing gown. To my relief there were no tears; jollied along by everyone, she accepted her sudden transition to hospital as rather an adventure.

Percy went along with her and after handing her over to a nurse there were the usual string of personal questions posed by a woman clerk for the admittance form, without which hospitals apparently cannot function.

'Name? Address? Occupation?'

'Antiquarian bookseller,' Percy answered to the third question.

'What?' exclaimed the clerk incredulously. 'In Takeley?'

There were no visiting hours for the children's wards at that time, the theory being that children would settle down better if parents didn't come and go, often causing tears at their departure. An exception was made only if a child was on the danger list. But I had had John Robinson's assurance that I was allowed to visit Helen and the day after her admittance I went to see her.

I had been told she would be in the isolation block. Locating the single ward where she was I walked in unannounced.

She was lying propped up against pillows, pale and speechless. From the corner of her mouth protruded a long tube leading to a basin standing on a trolley by her bedside. As I stared at her, horrified, her eyes met mine miserably and she pointed to the tube, showing that she couldn't speak to me.

I hadn't the slightest idea what was happening to her and gagged as she was she couldn't tell me. Almost at once, as I stood gazing down at her, trying to smile a greeting and some sort of reassurance a nurse bustled in, checked that the tube was in place, then turned on me crossly.

'I hope you haven't touched it. You should have telephoned before coming. In fact it would have been very much better if you hadn't come at all.'

Anxious as I was, her bossy manner was infuriating.

'How long has she had that thing in her mouth?' I demanded.

'We shall be taking it out very soon, it has to be in eight hours and it's very important that she should be kept quiet. She has been a good girl and very co-operative.' Her tone suggested that I might take a lesson from my daughter's book.

As I learned later Helen had been told that if she swallowed the tube it would take the nasty jaundice away. In fact it had no curative effect whatsoever; it's purpose was purely investigative. Helen, trustingly, had swallowed both the tube and the untruth.

I stayed with her until the tube had been removed and she was able to talk and have something to eat and drink, then I sought out the doctor in charge.

He was a tired looking man, thin faced, with a quiet manner. He invited me to sit down and said that he was glad to see me. There were some questions he would like me to answer, he said. He needed some family data.

I too had a question to put to him.

He was perfectly frank about the reason for making Helen swallow the tube. It was a way of obtaining what might be useful information.

'It does no harm, you know, and the patient soon becomes accustomed to it. It looks much more unpleasant than it actually is. Children soon forget such discomforts. Incidentally, your daughter has been very good.'

I was not mollified. When I protested that our consent should have been asked for, he replied that as no operation had been performed it had not been necessary to obtain our agreement.

'She has a very mild attack, you'll be glad to know, so we shall be sending her home soon. We're very grateful to you and your husband.'

His calm manner somewhat reduced my indignation; the effect wore off, but for a time it worked. When he picked up a long list of questions for which he needed answers, I co-operated and supplied them. There were almost as many as when, some years later, we applied for a visa to travel to the United States.

When we had gone through them and I had recalled every illness I and the rest of the family had ever had, I said I should very much like to know if Helen's and my co-operation *had* proved useful to the research being carried out into the disease. And, as a victim, I would be very interested to know how it was contracted.

'Yes, certainly,' he replied. 'If there's anything to report I'll let you know,' and I was thanked once again.

Helen made a quick recovery and was home within the week. No one else in our household or on the staff contracted infective jaundice and I never heard another word from the doctor or the hospital.

CHAPTER TWENTY-SEVEN

After three years the euphoria we had felt when Elkin Mathews had taken possession of its new premises had cooled considerably. We could congratulate ourselves that we were running a viable business, issuing catalogues regularly, bringing in much needed dollars and if not getting rich at least making a living. Since moving to Essex Percy had made some useful local contacts and was increasingly able to buy books privately. After some twenty years in the book trade he found himself, from time to time, in the mournful (if not entirely unwelcome) situation of being offered the libraries, or at least some of the books, of deceased customers.

The problem was that there just wasn't enough space for all the books we wanted, or needed to buy. Once again they were beginning to overflow into the house and what with books piling up on tables and chairs in the book room and cartons cluttering the floor, moving around, let alone dealing with the stock, was becoming a nightmare. Had a Fire Prevention Officer paid us a visit, heaven knows what he would have thought of the two unguarded electric fires and free standing paraffin heater in a wooden building full of combustible material.

To build on to the premises meant acquiring more land. The opportunity to do this came when the retired shoe manufacturer, who had bought the farm, agreed to let us buy part of the vegetable garden belonging to the bailiff's house next door. The nice old tenant farmer who had been there when we moved in, had been given the option of becoming gardener to his landlord (and moving to the gardener's cottage) or of being out of work. He had accepted demotion and the farmhouse had been let to a tenant who, the shoe manufacturer later discovered, was living with another man's wife. A sanctimonious man, he wished to spite his tenant by selling off part of his garden, hoping the man would then go.

As it turned out our neighbour, a game-keeper by trade, was a reluctant gardener and bore us no ill-will for buying his potato patch. It cost us £250, a high price in those days for a few feet of agricultural land, but the farmer knew we were desperate to buy it. Planning permission was granted without any trouble, for once again we were

191

going to settle for a 'temporary structure'. That it is still in use now is another story.

The only war-time restriction was on the use of timber and a brick building was out of the question. Sectional huts were hard to come by and anyway unlikely to be big enough, and a Nissen hut would have looked hideous and dropped condensation like an old man's nose in winter.

Once again we bought a hen house.

This time it was clean, for it had served as the prison for several hundred battery hens, and needed little adaptation. It was seventy foot long, with a low pitched roof, timber-felted, and with windows along one side. Once again we called upon our friendly neighbourhood builder, Mr. P. to erect it. With the long strip of floor laid on concrete piles it looked rather as if we were laying down a ship's deck in the garden, before the sides went up.

It was Mr. P. who put us on to buying bunks from the American base, to use as shelving. The Yanks, he said, were replacing the bunks with beds. As surplus to requirements we could buy them cheaply.

As temporary shelving those bunks served us remarkably well. They came in tiers of four with thick canvas stretched taut across a stout wooden framework. The clearance was about two foot and looking at them later, when they were filled with books, I would picture the G.I.'s lying in their bunks gazing up at the sagging canvas supporting another body a few inches above their heads.

While 'the shed', as it was always called, solved the storage space problem, as far as any bookseller does solve it, and gave us a convenient area for packing parcels, it also posed another problem. A seventy foot wooden building takes a good deal of heating if it is to be kept warm enough to work in. Central heating was out of the question in war-time and electric fires far too expensive; the solution was two second-hand greenhouse stoves.

It was possible to buy coke for business premises, although deliveries were by no means reliable, and by then we had a part-time odd-job man who agreed to come and stoke up the stoves early every morning, after he had finished his night shift as a security man guarding an electrical supply station up the road.

In cold weather these two stoves, glowing red-hot, would create a welcome, if limited, semi-tropical zone, extending to a radius of some six feet, while in the rest of the shed the temperature would barely reach 40°. It was tempting for members of the staff, on their way to collect books from the shelves or pack a parcel, to linger awhile in the comforting warm zone, toasting back and front, before returning to the less temperate regions.

It was tempting, too, for me to bring my typewriter into the shed when the children, home from school, were playing in the dining room, for fuel supplies didn't run to heating the sitting room in the day time. Leaving my 'help' to keep an eye on them I'd settle down close to one of the stoves, typewriter on my knees, and work on my current novel. Not that I was left in peace for long for, once the children had discovered my hiding place, they were likely to erupt into the shed for tears to be dried, or some problem solved. Still, some work could usually be done there.

Much later we were to add a typist's room and a lavatory to the shed but during the war the office had to rely on the house for the latter amenity, though the waste ground behind the bookstore, conveniently out of sight and shaded by wild plum trees, did save the men a trek to the house when it was not raining.

The shed filled up with books remarkably quickly. Despite the bookseller's perennial plaint 'if only I could buy some decent stock' uttered by Percy at frequent intervals, useful libraries were coming our way.

There was the occasion when Percy was invited to look at some books at a house near Bishop's Stortford and found that, apart from the books, the family possessed a trunkful of documents that had once belonged to the Duke of Wellington. The daughter of the house had been given the trunk and its contents and wished only to be rid of it.

'Don't suppose all those old papers are worth a lot', she said, as Percy, dipping into the trunk, sniffed treasure trove, 'but if they'll buy me a pig I'll be happy. Father's a dog man, you see, but I like pigs. You could call me a pig woman. What I need is a boar, a good 'un.'

Percy was happy to buy the books and the trunk. Amongst the documents was a contemporary plan of the battle of Waterloo, so the young woman got the money for her boar and a bit extra.

Grant Richards the publisher, an old friend from Percy's early bookselling days, would sometimes pay us a visit and would bring with him autographed letters and manuscripts to sell. He was a charming man, a delightful talker and always a welcome guest. His publishing activities and his own novels had brought him many friends, but unhappily less and less money until in the end he suffered the fate of the small, independent publisher who prefers to publish the authors whose works he enjoys and respects rather than meteoric money-makers who may shine brightly with golden promise and then follow each other into oblivion.

Another visitor we were always glad to see was Jim Scott. As a delicate child, Jim had become a devotee of the novels of Rider Haggard, enjoying vicariously the romantic adventures he could never hope to have. He had built up a remarkable Haggard collection at a time when there were few other collectors in the field, which meant he could indulge his fancy pretty cheaply. Percy, always glad to give up time to the diligent collector, however modest his aims, had found many books for Jim, as well as guiding his steps along the tricky paths of bibliographical compilation. Alas, the tuberculosis from which Jim had suffered much of his life was to kill him while still a young man. His bibliography of his favourite author with its portrait of Haggard, white-bearded, with high winged collar and a watch-chain across his waistcoat, staring a little quizzically from the frontispiece, was published by Elkin Mathews in 1947. The edition was limited to 500 numbered copies. Jim would be flattered to know how much it is now sought after by eager Haggard collectors no longer able to find copies of *She* or *King Solomon's Mines* for a few shillings as he once did.

A few years after poor Jim's too early death, Percy was able to buy much of Rider Haggard's personal library from his daughter, the writer Lilias Rider Haggard.

CHAPTER TWENTY-EIGHT

The morning of June the sixth was fine and breezy. After breakfast I strapped David into his wooden seat on the back of my bicycle and set off as usual to take him to his nursery school in Stansted. The B.B.C. News had, that morning, told us of the Allied Landings in Normandy. My first reaction had been relief. It had happened at last! Even though we had all been expecting it for weeks it was tremendous news.

I didn't doubt that the Allies would succeed in establishing a bridgehead and that the eventual outcome would be the rolling back of the German armies and the final defeat of Hitler. But no one expected a quick victory and I couldn't shut from my mind the thought of the heavy casualties we had been warned to expect, that were probably already taking place as I was riding safely and peacefully in the quiet of a country lane.

Not that it was altogether quiet, for I could hear ahead the thrum-thrum of aircraft engines warming up, a noise that was increasing in volume as I neared the control point, where the flight path crossed the road leading to Stansted village. The warning lights were flashing as I came to the gates which were closed, as they always were when aircraft were taking off.

I got off and waited, putting my hands over my ears as a Liberator took off a couple of hundred yards down the runway and roared overhead. Then the sentry let me through.

Half a mile down the road there was a dispersal point close to a sharp bend, where aircraft would sometimes be standing. As I neared the bend the roar of engines became deafening. In a moment I could see why; three heavy bombers were standing on the concrete apron, one of them only a few feet from the road; the noise was hellish and the wind force they were creating rushed at us like a typhoon as we came round the corner. It was impossible to ride, not easy even to stay upright. I lifted David from his seat, his eyes popping with terror, his mouth open wide. I knew he was yelling at the top of his voice (which was lusty enough when he was making a protest) but in that ear-shattering volume of noise I couldn't even hear him.

It didn't occur to me to turn back. To get past the dispersal point

195

meant walking only fifty yards, but the struggle took our breath away. With one hand I pushed the bike, with the other I dragged David along, edging round the bend on the far side of the road, almost blown into the ditch. The slip-stream from the bombers was like an invisible enemy intent on keeping us back.

Then we were through; it was as if a storm had suddenly abated. I lifted David back into his seat, subdued but no longer crying, and we rode on until the noise was only a distant humming and our half-stunned ears could pick up normal sounds again.

David had been scared, but he was quick to recover and pleased to have such an adventure to talk about at school. After leaving him I settled down in my room at the pub and did my usual stint of writing, disciplined by then to make the best use of my two hours freedom from domestic ties. When it was time to take David home I started off with some anxiety. I needn't have worried. There were no bombers on the dispersal point; presumably they had all taken off for Normandy; the lane was peaceful again, the only sound the hiss of my tyres on the macadam and the whisper of the wind in the wayside trees. At the control point the gate was open and the sentry gave me a cheery wave.

While I was tapping away at my typewriter, trying to finish my fourth novel before the summer holidays made consistent work near impossible, Percy was working on the book that he had said he hadn't the time to write.

When, some months before, he had told Mark Cohen that, sympathetic as he was to Mark's cherished idea that a popular book on book collecting was needed and should be written by a member of the trade, he was not the man to write it, Mark, refusing to be discouraged, had found someone else to take on the job, and had managed to find an interested publisher. But it had not worked out. The publisher had set a deadline, the book must appear in the autumn of 1944, or the deal was off. This was a deadline the author felt he could not meet, so back Mark came to Percy. Here, he said, was a willing, even eager publisher for the book, with enough paper for a sizeable paper-back edition; such a chance might well not come again, and it was a book he knew Percy could write.

That was true. Busy though he was, Percy was loathe to disappoint Mark and time was running out. He agreed, and began the book straight away. Within six weeks the completed typescript was on its way to the printers, comfortably within the deadline. Under the title, *Book Collecting as a Hobby*, it was written in the form of a series of *Letters to Everyman* and was full of basic, practical information on how and what to collect within a modest income limit. There were four pages of illustrations, ninety-eight pages of text, plus an index and it was to be published at three shillings and sixpence.

The publisher, Gramol, was an off-shoot of the National Magazine Company, the American owners of *Good Housekeeping* and *Harper's Bazaar*. In his dedication of the book to Mark Cohen, then President of the Antiquarian Booksellers Association, Percy concluded: 'And so this typically English book, suggested by a Jew, written by a Scot and published by an Irishman, goes forth.'

The Irishman was a man called McPeake who had been given the job of expanding the National Magazine Company's U.K. interests. Book publishing, under the Gramol imprint, was a part of this expansion.

We were to see a good deal of McPeake during the next few years, as Percy became involved in the publishing venture, both as an author and as an editorial advisor for the Gramol List.

He was an ambitious man, smooth talking and with considerable personal charm. A 'go-getter' in the American sense of the term, he had energy and drive and he and Percy were soon on excellent terms, working together on various publishing projects. Later came some disillusionment, for Celtic charm sometimes conceals less appealing qualities. For Percy, once disillusionment set in, there could be no putting the clock back — it was always final.

With his task completed Percy proposed a family holiday. We could, he rightly said, do with a break and a change of scene. Simon Nowell-Smith was then living in the village of Benson, in the Thames Valley. His children, one of whom was Percy's god-son, were in the same age group as ours so at his suggestion we booked rooms at the Castle Hotel, a comfortable, old-fashioned pub which at that time was being run by two enterprising young women. With an American air base nearby they were doing good business; what was more to the point, as far as we were concerned, they contrived to provide a very good table.

The holiday was booked when one morning a small lump appeared on one side of David's neck. It had popped up overnight without any noticeable sign of illness, although he had complained the day before of a sore throat.

'A T.B. gland,' said the doctor. 'Unmistakeable. Where do you get your milk, because that is almost certainly the cause?'

Milk distributors were not obliged to pasteurize milk at that time, although there was a vociferous lobby to make them do so. Nor was tuberculin testing obligatory. Luckily Helen had resisted the infection but there were other cases in the locality, one a three-year-old girl who lived down the road from us who had reacted as David had done. Curiously, she was the only one to be infected in a family of five. Both children had a slight initial fever and then seemed perfectly well, although the lump in their necks, the size of a small bird's egg, remained.

'Does it really matter?' I asked our family doctor. 'Yes, I'm afraid it does,' he said, and advised surgery, which would also mean a tonsilectomy. There was no hurry for this, in his opinion, but it would be unwise to postpone the operation too long in the hope that the lump would disappear of its own accord, because that was most unlikely. As for our proposed holiday, there was no reason at all why we shouldn't go. It would do the child good.

So we set off for Benson, crammed into our ancient Ford Anglia, leaving Jutro and Mrs. P. 'to mind the shop'. All seemed quiet on the home front; the news that Hitler's secret weapon was already operational from launching sites along the Pas de Calais was still being kept out of the newspapers.

The change of air had no effect on David's T.B. gland. The little lump on the side of his neck grew no bigger, neither did it fade away. The holiday was enjoyable, the two families foregathered and there were punts to hire and pleasure launches going as far as Oxford. On one of these David knocked my handbag from my lap so that the wallet inside containing my money and clothing coupon books shot across the deck and into the river.

The man at the helm was unmoved by my pleas to pull into the bank so that I could dive in and recover it. In a couple of minutes we had rounded a bend and the spot where it had hit the water was out of sight.

I was still mourning my loss some hours later back at the hotel when, from the window of the lounge, I spotted a man going by on a bicycle whom I recognised as the owner of a small boat station, where we had hired punts the previous day. At once the conviction seized me that he had found my wallet and was on his way to the Police station to hand it in.

When I said as much there was general disbelief. Nevertheless I ran after him and found that I was right. A couple of lovers lying clasped in one of his punts had spotted the floating wallet and rescued it. The ration books, thick wads of paper, had kept it afloat. They had dried out the contents, handed it over to the boat station owner and waived any idea of a reward.

Intimations of the flying bomb menace came to us while we were still at Benson. None had fallen in Essex, but on our return we heard stories of casualties south of the Thames and it was not long before it was common knowledge that pilotless planes carrying an explosive charge were being sent across the channel in large numbers. It was known that so long as one could hear them all was well. It was when the engine cut out that one needed to dive for cover, for within seconds the explosion would follow as the flying bomb nose-dived to the ground. Many people found the 'doodle bugs', or 'buzz-bombs' as they were variously called by the newspapers, more unnerving than the conventional bombers, especially as it was believed, at first, that we had no real defence against them. But it was not long before we were heartened to learn that the defensive belt, quickly deployed to frustrate the new threat, was having considerable success. This consisted of fighters operating along the coast a few miles out to sea, anti-aircraft guns along the coastline firing out to sea, and behind these an inland fighter belt. With the use of improved radar, the guns took an increasing toll and the fighters learned how to intercept and send the pilotless planes plunging to the ground in open country.

Nevertheless, more than 2,000 did get through to explode in built-up areas and cause a great many casualties. Although there was no general panic a good many evacuees who had returned to London had second thoughts so that there was a new exodus to the country, especially when the Germans began launching the even more terrifying V2s. This rocket, with a one-ton warhead, travelled too fast and too high to be seen, so that a devastating explosion was the first one knew of its arrival — if one survived.

Once the battle for Normandy was over we waited eagerly for the liberation of Paris, hoping against hope that it would be spared destruction. Patton was not one of the British Press's favourite generals, all the same it was exciting to hear of his spectacular advance and then of our own pursuit of the Germans to Rouen and of Eisenhower's arrival at Le Mans. Then came the great news on August 25th that Paris was surrounded and the garrison had surrendered.

The British Movietone newsreels of the liberation of Paris and of General de Gaulle's triumphant march on foot, at the head of his Free French troops, down the Champs Elysées to the Place de la Concorde were pictures that never faded from my memory.

For a while after our return from our holiday we postponed a decision on an operation for David's T.B. gland. I shrank from the prospect of subjecting my four-year-old (a mummy-clinging child if there ever was one) not only to an unpleasant operation, but also to letting him suffer the experience of finding himself in a strange environment, amongst unfamiliar faces, not knowing when (or if) he would see me again. To tell a young child that Mummy will visit him on Sunday, or in two days' time, can be little or no consolation as the hours he cannot count go by and still she is not at his bedside.

CWK–N

The policy of discouraging parents from visiting their sick children was strictly maintained at the hospital where David would go. It was said that because children became upset and cried when visiting time was over that it was better that the parents shouldn't come at all. A hospital sister with whom I once argued the point said, frankly, that parents were a nuisance in a hospital. To allow a mother to see her sick child every day, or to let her stay in the hospital if need be, was dismissed as quite impossible. A change of attitude amongst nurses was slow to come. It needed much pressure from women's groups, including the Women's Institutes.

Before agreeing to the operation I discussed it with Winifred de Kok, A.E. Coppard's wife, who was a paediatrician and gave radio talks on the care of children. The Coppards had come to live at Duton Hill, near Dunmow, and Percy, who had known Coppard some years before at a time when he was living a Thoreau-like life in a wood, quickly renewed the friendship. There was, as was apt to happen when a bookseller and an author get together, a spin-off helpful to both from this renewed contact in the form of editions of the author's works to be bought and later catalogued by Percy. Coppard had been a collected author for some years; his first book of short stories, *Adam and Eve and Pinch Me* was the first book to be published by the Golden Cockerel Press. The handsome limited edition bound in white buckram was much sought by collectors — and still is.

He was at that time in his late sixties, but looked younger; with a zest for life and talk. Duton Hill suited him, his wife Winifred told me. He liked the village people (later he served on the Parish Council) and found it was a place where he could work. While he talked I always had the feeling that he was very much aware of his surroundings, that invisible antennae were collecting impressions of everything and everyone around him, storing them up to be put to use later in one of his short stories.

Winifred was a splendid partner for him, a big-built woman, practical, competent, protective of his creative talent, ensuring that he could write in peace and quiet. At that time their clever daughter was attending the same school as Helen and used to keep an eye on her on the school bus.

Winifred was much against the removal of the tonsils and adenoids of young children and shook her head when I told her that we had been advised that David should have his T.B. gland removed.

'That means he will have his tonsils and adenoids removed as well,' she said. 'And they will grow again, and cause more trouble.' As long as David seemed well she advised waiting for two or three years at least.

My instinct was to take her advice, but when the Consultant at the hospital insisted that the operation was necessary and our doctor, a personal friend, urged us to have it done before the winter, we reluctantly agreed. In September David was driven to hospital 'a little victim, all unconscious of his fate', clutching the cot pillow he cuddled when he went to bed.

'He'll want to keep this,' I told the ward sister, when, with considerable misgivings I handed him over. 'He won't sleep without it.'

She took it, rather sniffily I thought. Admittedly it was a scruffy little pillow, with stains that I had been unable to wash out. What they did with it I never found out. It was eventually returned to me, but David had had to learn to sleep without it.

It was a week before he had the operation; yet we were barred from visiting him on the grounds that 'it would only upset him'. I was tempted to insist on my rights as a parent, but was deterred from making a fuss lest I should antagonise those concerned and embarrass our doctor.

The operation duly took place and, according to our doctor, our son was making a good recovery. As well as the T.B. gland his tonsils and adenoids *had* been removed 'as a matter of routine' we were told. They did, in fact, grow again, as Winifred de Kok had said, and were to cause problems with ear-ache and catarrhal deafness.

I worried about the effect of hospitalisation on a small child and rang up the ward to ask when he could come home.

'Yes, he has quite recovered,' said the ward sister. 'There's no reason why he shouldn't go home, as far as I can see, but he must be seen by the surgeon before he can be discharged. I expect it will be all right for you to collect him tomorrow, but you had better ring up in the morning first.'

The next morning I rang again. It was a Saturday.

'Can we come and collect our little boy?'

'I'm very sorry,' the sister's voice was apologetic. 'I'm afraid Mr. W. didn't see him after all yesterday and unfortunately he won't be here again until Tuesday.'

'Does that mean David will have to stay in hospital another three days?'

'Yes, I'm afraid it does. He can't be discharged until Mr. W. has seen him'.

'I see. But suppose my husband and I come to the hospital and say we want to take him away today, even though Mr. W. hasn't seen him?'

There was a moment's silence, then I heard sister's voice, and it was not unfriendly.

'If that is what you *wish* to do we have no right to prevent you.'

I thought it over for a while, then I went to talk to Percy. He was alone in the bookroom, sitting at his desk, writing. The staff did not work on Saturdays and Jutro had gone to London for the weekend.

I told him what the sister had said.

'Shall we go and fetch him? He must be thinking we've left him there for good.'

We agreed that we should and I telephoned to say that we would collect David that afternoon. After lunch we drove to the hospital and walked along the concrete passage way between the long huts that had been tacked on to what had once been the old infirmary, until we came to the children's ward. It was a moment or two before I saw David, then there was the small, disconsolate little figure standing beside one of the cots. When I called him he stood where he was, as if he didn't believe we were real. I picked him up and he clung to me.

The Sister was friendly and put no obstacles in our way.

'I'll go and get the book for you to sign,' she said. We waited while the other little patients stared at us and David put his toys together. It was quite a while before she came back with a board-covered book. She hadn't been able to find it at first, she said, because no one had known where it was, or could remember when last anyone had signed themselves, or their child out.

'He *has* been very quiet,' said the nurse who gave me his belongings. Quiet was not a word we would have used to describe David before he went to hospital. There was a small puckered scar on one side of his neck; he was pale, subdued and snuffly. During the drive home he said little and when he did speak it was almost in a whisper. He was a very different little boy from the one I had taken to hospital two weeks before.

Happily the change was only temporary. Within a few days he was as talkative and lively as he had been before.

Autumn and Winter 1944

CHAPTER TWENTY-NINE

As the summer came to an end we heard, once again, the dismal warbling note of the Dunmow air-raid siren. For months it had been silent, now with the V1 launching sites on the Pas de Calais in Allied hands, the Germans had begun using a site somewhere near the Hague. London, or at least Greater London, was still the target, but now Essex was in the line of fire.

It was usually in the early evening that the warning would come. At the first wail from the siren I would run out into the garden, staring into the dark sky, ears strained for the first distant note of the jet engine. Usually there was nothing to hear and it was only the following day that we learned where one or more had fallen.

One night, when we had gone to bed earlier than usual, I was lying awake when I heard the angry buzz of an approaching V1. Jumping out of bed I ran to the window in time to see what looked like a very small aeroplane with a red glow spewing from its tail speeding low over the fields behind the house, so low that I could see it clearly as it roared past, heading west towards Stansted.

It sounded as if it was going strongly but I waited, listening tensely lest the engine should cut out before it passed the Sachs' family cottage a couple of miles down the road. When I could no longer hear it I got back into bed, still keyed up from having seen the thing and, inexplicably, glad that I *had* seen it.

'It's gone,' I said unnecessarily to Percy, who had stayed where he was. 'It looked like something straight from hell.' We heard the next day that it had come down in a field and there had been no casualties.

By then Herbert Morrison, the Home Secretary, had announced in the House of Commons that 'the battle of London is won.' The cost in lives from the V1's was heavy, more than six thousand civilians killed and many more seriously injured. But for our defences against it, it could have been far, far worse.

The V2 rocket bombs were even more frightening. Because of their high speed and height they were invisible until the final second when they plunged to earth; so once they had been launched there was no defence against them and no way of knowing where they would land. Most of them were launched from The Hague and they began coming over early in September, some five hundred reaching the London area.

'If your number's on one there's nothing you can do about it,' said those who liked to appear nonchalant about this new menace. I was not one of them, although it was calculated that the chance of being killed by a V2, at least for anyone living in the country, was no greater than the chance of being struck by lightning.

The sight of the V1 passing so close to our house, reminded us that we were on one of the routes that both V1s and V2s had been programmed to take them to Greater London. No announcement had been made about the latter, but we knew that some had fallen in London, causing horrific casualties. There were always the bad news-mongers who liked to tell one about such horrors.

We certainly weren't thinking about bombs that Saturday as we sat around the breakfast table. It was a fine autumn morning, a day to go blackberrying. The crump-crump that made the house quiver, the crockery crash to the floor, brought us all to our feet. Our first thought was that an aircraft must have crashed very near. I ran upstairs to look out of the bedroom window from where I could see almost to Stansted airfield. Smoke was rising from a great tangle of metal lying on the stubble two fields away, smaller pieces were spread around.

The children had to be restrained from rushing to the wreckage to collect souvenirs. They were not at all frightened; but two labourers who had been cycling to work along the A120 had had the fright of their lives when a great grey cylinder had suddenly appeared out of the blue above their heads, diving steeply to earth. Jumping from their cycles they had thrown themselves under the shelter of a hedge and a split second later there had been a double explosion. One, they main-tained, just before it hit the ground, the other on impact.

The shake-up our house had suffered cracked the plaster on one side from the gable to the ground, but all the leaded windows withstood the explosion with the exception of one where the pane had been loose anyway. Although the V2 had fallen only two fields from us, that was the only damage we suffered.

Our shoe manufacturer farmer was indignant when he arrived to inspect the mess in his field, regarding the incident as a personal attack on his property.

'I shall ring up the A.R.P. people,' he said. 'I shall tell them they must do something about all this wreckage littering my land. They must send someone to take it away.'

He was even crosser when a voice from A.R.P. headquarters told him: 'Very sorry Sir, but I'm afraid we can't help you.'

'But what am I going to do with it?'

'That's your problem. We don't want it.'

It was a problem not easy to solve, but in the end the mass of twisted blackened metal was collected and taken away by a scrap merchant, after souvenir hunters had taken their pickings. There was no bomb crater like those in many fields and in the forest, for the V2s exploded as they touched the ground, thus causing far more devastation~~than~~ if they came down in a built-up area.

Percy had been in London on business when the doodle-bug menace was at its worst. He was lunching with a friend in a restaurant in Baker Street when the unmistakeable high pitched buzz could be heard approaching.

'It was an uncanny experience,' he told me later. 'At one moment everyone was talking, and waitresses were hurrying about with trays, then, suddenly there was dead silence, except for the increasing noise as the doodle-bug came nearer. No one moved. We sat listening and waiting. It roared overhead, the noise began to recede and everyone began talking again and eating their lunch.'

There was great excitement on September the sixteenth when people living in and around Dunmow saw a fleet of aircraft with gliders in tow. They had taken off from the glider base at Easton Lodge, a couple of miles from Dunmow en route for Arnhem. Not all got away according to plan. One glider, coming adrift from its tow, glided down to land safely on one of Yda Cory-Wright's fields. Inside, Yda told me later, was one jeep and four men, 'all very disconsolate.'

The publication of Percy's *Book Collecting as a Hobby* in October caused no great stir, not that Percy had expected it would. He had never shared Mark Cohen's rather touching belief that the man in the street, the 'Everyman' to whom the book was addressed, had been eagerly waiting for such a book. Although he had taken on the job reluctantly, once he got down to it he had rather enjoyed writing it. The initial royalty payment certainly didn't come amiss, but he had no expectation of further payments.

Reynolds Stone, who had designed our letter heading, had been commissioned, at Percy's request, to design the cover, which he did very stylishly with white lettering on a dark brown background and a central design of books and scrolls. This, as well as the contents, was to make this modest paperback something of a collector's item in years to come. As there were four pages of half-tone illustrations the price, three shillings and sixpence, was not dear.

Our early autumn catalogue carried a gentlemanly announcement:

> 'This book is intended mainly for the novice,' Percy wrote, 'but it is hoped that older hands will find it not unprofitable and that they will also further its intended purpose by recommending it to those who aspire to become collectors, but who are uncertain as to how to set about it ...'

The advertisement on the verso of the page was, in contrast, aimed at the top end of the market. It was for Elkin Mathews' own publication, the first since Percy had had control of the company and very much a collector's item; *An Iconography of the Engravings of Stephen Gooden*. Campbell Dodgson, an expert on Gooden's work, was the compiler and Sam Samuels, 'The Infant Samuel', the sponsor. The edition de luxe, limited to 160 copies and signed by the artist, was to cost seven guineas, the unlimited edition three guineas.

Percy had known Stephen Gooden since the 1920s when he had bought from him a set of the proofs of the beautiful engravings for the Nonesuch Bible. Mona, Stephen's wife, was a poet and I soon found I shared with her and Stephen (not, to my regret, with Percy) a delight in cats, for she had published an anthology titled *The Poet's Cat*, a charming little book with Stephen's engraving of their cat on the title page.

The Goodens had, at one time, lived in Bishop's Stortford, but were then living near Amersham. During the months when the *Iconography* was in preparation we saw a good deal of them — which was a pleasure. They were a devoted couple and seemed to me completely in tune with one another.

With Stephen one was conscious of the gifted craftsman's underlying strength of purpose. He was the descendant of a well-known 19th century engraver, Henry Linton and, according to Campbell Dodgson, he was the first young 20th-century engraver to use the burin for his own imaginative compositions. Alas, neither he nor Mona were destined for a long life; both died of cancer, Stephen in 1955 and Mona a few years later.

Through the Goodens we came to know another gifted artist, Geoffrey Rhoades, who with wife Joan was living near Dunmow during the war years. Geoffrey, who later taught art at Ruskin College, was an imaginative and individualistic book illustrator and was to do the illustrations for Percy's book of fairy stories, which *Good*

Housekeeping brought out just after the end of the war. This was another wartime friendship which we both valued.

Some six weeks after the publication of *Book Collecting as a Hobby* when the rather mild initial interest in the book had apparently faded away, a rave review of it appeared in James Agate's *Daily Express* column.

'This book is brilliant,' he wrote and urged all book collectors and would-be collectors to buy it.

Such was Agate's influence that sales shot up immediately. The first printing was sold out by the end of the year and a second impression was put in train, which meant a welcome cheque for the gratified author.

Gramol had already planned a collecting series, which Percy was to edit. Stamp collecting was an obvious choice for the next book in the series and Percy did not have far to look for the author. Our old friend and ex-evacuee, Dick Curle included philately amongst his multifarious interests and agreed to take on the task.

McPeake believed in doing things in style, so when Percy was invited to attend editorial conferences the venue would be a suite at the Dorchester and a working lunch. At first I was rather envious, imagining Percy enjoying all sorts of delectable dishes while we at home were putting up with scrag end of mutton and little enough of that. Food was so constantly in our minds that when he came home from the first of these conferences one of my first questions was. 'What did you have for lunch?'

'Porc a l'American.'

'What's that?'

'Grilled spam.'

I used to serve spam when the meat ration ran out. Perhaps the Dorchester had put it on the menu fot the same reason. It was not, as Percy remarked, quite what one expected of them.

One way and another things were looking up for us at last. We were not making a fortune by any means, but the business was prospering and thanks to Percy's ever active pen we were no longer having to count every penny. My own contribution to the family income had improved, for I had a new contract with Hurst and Blackett which meant a larger advance royalty.

The failure of the Arnhem operation and the heavy loss of life after a courageous stand at Nijmegen cast down everyone's spirits. But Brussels had been liberated, maps in the newspapers showed the allied armies steadily advancing towards the German borders and the Russians surging towards Berlin from the east. By November most of

the V1 and V2 launching sites had been over-run and the evacuees who
had fled their houses at the onslaught of Hitler's new 'terror weapons'
took leave of their hostesses, in some cases for the third time. For a few
weeks we had a widow from the East End to stay, a quiet little body
who promised to visit us and kept that promise.

As Christmas drew near, and with the usual hunt for a few small
luxuries for the table, war weariness made tempers edgy and good
manners became a war-time casualty.

Toys were scarce and usually of poor quality; children's books were
a better buy, but my family were never short of these. Often, returning
from buying a library, Percy would dump a carton full of children's
books on the dining room table, telling Helen and David to help
themselves; thus they soon had their own library of favourite authors,
E. Nesbit, A. A. Milne and the Doctor Dolittle books were special
favourites. They grew up, too, with Percy's own collection of toys —
the automata he had been collecting since the beginning of the war.
There was the monkey-faced magician who sat at a table making
coloured balls and dice appear and disappear to the tinkling strains of a
hidden musical box; there were the two clowns in a music-hall set,
balancing revolving plates on sticks; there was the tight-rope walker,
stepping gingerly along a wire while two attendants below him clashed
cymbals and, cleverest of all, two gallant troubadours in brocade
waistcoats, white breeches and wearing wide-brimmed hats playing
guitars, nimble fingers moving up and down the strings, while their
toes tapped to the musical-boxes tunes. Glass domes enclosed all these
treasures; miraculously, although children's parties were held in the
room where they were displayed, none was ever broken.

One evening Percy came home from a buying trip with a pair of
peasant automata from Switzerland. In each was a different scene; in
one a troupe of performing cats turned somersaults; in the other an old
man, bent double was working a bellows as big as himself, which blew
round the sails of a windmill, whilst every other minute a villainous
employer popped out of the mill and threatened him with a stick.

For a time we enjoyed the company of a white mouse which, at the
touch of a button, would spring from a red plush Easter Egg, violin in
hand and play a sprightly tune, disappearing as suddenly as he had
appeared. Even the cat took no exception to this creature. We were all
upset when a customer, who was not to be denied, insisted on buying it.

The unexpected German offensive in the Ardennes cast a shadow
over Christmas. Once again we joined forces with the Sachs family,
pooling our saved-up Christmas goodies, many of them from generous
friends in the U.S.A.

Percy with some of his automata.

As usual, the radio was dutifully turned on for the King's traditional Christmas Broadcast. My own feeling about this not very inspiring ritual was that since tradition obliged the Monarch to address us at three o'clock on Christmas Day, when he would no doubt have preferred to relax in peace and quiet, the least we could do was to listen, even though he would never know whether we did or did not.

1945

CHAPTER THIRTY

A collector we should have loved to have known was F.R. Bussell. He was a Lloyds Underwriter who lived in a fine old house in Kent. Adjacent was a large barn which he had adapted to house his collection of books and bygones. Unfortunately, we were never privileged to meet him, but some while after his death Percy did visit his home, romantically named 'Black Charles', and saw where the children's book collection had been displayed, on shelves specially made on a scale to suit their size.

After Bussell's death the collection went to Sotheby's and one January morning — a red-letter day in Percy's life — he found the catalogue for the sale amongst his mail. It was announced as 'an important collection of Children's Books, Primers, Battledores, Games, Telescopic Views, Toy Books, Harlequinades etc. Unusually, it was to be offered as one lot (no doubt that was what Mr. Bussell had wanted) but if the reserve price was not realised each lot was to be sold separately.

Before he had read to the end of the catalogue Percy knew that this was a sale not to be missed. Such a collection, built up over the years at a time when children's books and juvenilia were little collected, might not come up again in his lifetime and it was absolutely up his street.

When the time came to view it he took Jutro with him and the two of them spent the whole of two days, the second a Sunday (with Sotheby making a special concession), carefully examining and estimating the value of each of the several hundred lots. When they had finished Percy was confirmed in his belief that it was a collection of unique importance. Not given to superlatives, he nevertheless had to describe it as 'fabulous'.

He longed to buy it for himself but the reserve price was well out of our range, nor could the firm put up so large a sum at that time. The alternative was to interest a collector. Fortunately we did not have to look far. The National Magazine Company were impressed by Percy's estimate of the books' value and had faith in his judgement. They saw that there was useful publicity and prestige to be had in acquiring such a collection and in allowing it to be exhibited both in London and New York. They agreed that Percy should bid on their behalf.

My diary for February 5th, 1945 recorded: Today Percy bought a £2,000 collection of children's books, toys and games at Sotheby's . . .

I didn't record Percy's joy in his successful bid, great though it was, perhaps because I had just gone down with 'flu. An epidemic was sweeping through the country and both the children had been victims. Two days later Percy also succumbed, the bug having luckily spared him until after the auction — or maybe he had kept it at bay from necessity. It might have been worse; we were all soon on our feet again.

Impelled by his eagerness to get his haul back to Takeley and begin the enjoyable job of cataloguing it, Percy was back at work in two days.

There they were, the nursery rhymes and pictures we had all loved as

Percy with Queen Mary at the National Book League
Children's Book Exhibition, 1946.

children and read to our own children, many of them in the form in which our great, great grandparents had read them. There was *The Comic Adventures of Old Mother Hubbard and her Dog*, dated 1805-1806, in three little books. There was *The House that Jack Built* (circa 1820), *Stories from Mother Goose* translated from the original French version, in 1741 by Robert Samber, first editions of such classics as *The Diverting History of John Gilpin* and *Swiss Family Robinson* and so on, not to mention all the boxes of educational games and other juvenilia.

The National Magazine Company became the owners of the books, the major part of the collection, while Percy kept the toys, games, peepshows and other amusements for himself. The following year the collection was to be on show in the elegant Georgian premises of the National Book League at No. 7, Albemarle Street, once the home of Fanny Burney. The N.B.L. had risen like a phoenix from the ashes of the old National Book Council, with Maurice Marston, a good friend of Percy's who had valiantly kept the N.B.C. in existence against all odds, becoming its first Director. Percy was to arrange the first exhibition, *Children's Books of Yesterday*, John Masefield, Poet Laureate, would open it and Queen Mary would not only visit it (it was to be Percy's rather daunting task to escort her round the exhibition) but present it with some books from the Royal nurseries, and the little pink catalogue of the exhibits which included many items from Percy's own collection, was to become a collector's item.

My diary for January 1945 recorded: 'A dreary month, more than 20 days of frost.' The biting cold made cycling to Stansted, with David astride the back wheel, something of an ordeal. The north wind blowing over the flat, frosted fields around the airfield was an enemy nipping at my fingers and David's toes and doing its best to slow my progress to my cosy little room at the King's Arms. Sometimes, if the weather was worse than usual and the car available, a concession would be made and I would be allowed to use it. It was still a cold journey (no car heaters in those days) but a considerable improvement on cycling.

Our old Ford Anglia, bought from Peter Murray Hill early in the war, had served us well, but after our much loved Lancia it was an uninteresting little car and aroused no affection. Its redeeming feature was that, given the petrol, it nearly always got us to our destination. I had taken it one wet morning and was driving home with David from his nursery school, my thoughts still revolving around the novel I had been working on at the King's Arms, when they were interrupted by a loud and ominous sound from the engine, short and sharp as if someone had hit it with a hammer.

I thought it as well to stop and investigate, but bearing in mind that we were still two miles from home I took the precaution of leaving the engine running. When I opened up the bonnet the reason for the change of engine note was all too obvious, there was a long, gaping crack right across the top of the cylinder block. It was, I was pretty sure, mortally wounded, yet it was still going, if noisily. Would it take us home? Might it explode, catch fire, or just stop?

It did none of these things. I closed down the bonnet, got back into the driving seat and we were off, rattling down the road in low gear, arriving home safely, when the engine was allowed to expire.

New Anglias were not to be had, nor could we have afforded one. Instead our garage found us another engine at a cost of £25. After this transplant our car served us for another two years.

With London no longer subjected to air raids Jutro was drawn back to city life, his natural milieu. My attempts to find him rooms somewhere in the neighbourhood had come to nothing and he himself had made little effort to find accommodation, perhaps because he had come to us for sanctuary and a respite, and that need was now over. He had the offer of work in an art gallery in London, a job that apparently suited him, and he left us in the spring. We saw him from time to time when we went to London; it seemed, then, that all was going well for him. Nevertheless, he must still have yearned to be back in Paris for soon after the war ended he returned. Did he believe it would be possible to pick up the strands of his old, pre-war life there?

It was not long after the end of the war that we were saddened by the news that he had committed suicide, turning on the gas in his room in Paris.

'He had not been happy', said the friend who brought us the news, 'I think, perhaps, he was lonely.'

Spring took us by surprise in mid-February; suddenly it was as warm as May, birds sang, almond blossom was pink against a blue sky, primroses demurely showed themselves beneath the tall privet hedge that now hid the garden from the road. The hens brightened up and, deceived into the belief that they were continuing their species, gave me eggs and to spare. We now owned half a pig, the other half being owned by the odd-job man who lit and stoked the stoves in the shed and whose daughter spared me two hours on Saturday mornings, for a high-speed clean through of the house. This was the only domestic help I could get at that time.

To be an amateur (or back garden) pig-keeper one needed feed coupons for barleymeal to mix with the swill — inevitably pretty thin stuff since the pig owner's family left little of much food value for the pig bucket. The coupons were grudgingly given, but rather less so if they came through a pig club. I was willing enough to join any club that could provide extra rations and was disappointed to find that there was not one in the village.

Through the grapevine I learned of other pig keepers in Takeley all of whom, as I did, bewailed the lack of a club.

'If we were to form a club I'd be willing to be secretary,' Haddon Spurgeon offered. So I added the chairmanship of the Takeley Pig Club to a few other community jobs and up went the barleymeal ration.

As the days lengthened and the radio each day brought us news of further allied advances along the whole Western Front we waited eagerly to hear that the Rhine had been crossed.

At that stage of the war we were taking it for granted that it was a question not of 'if' but of 'when'. The good news, when it came over the radio and was spread across the front pages of the newspapers, gave further impetus to the endless speculations as to what Hitler would do when faced with defeat.

Almost immediately after the news of the successful bridgehead across the Rhine (which Churchill, as we learned later, had witnessed from nearby high ground) there came the ghastly revelations of the Nazi concentration camps. That such camps existed was common knowledge, but few had any conception of the scale of suffering; it needed the visual evidence of the photographs in the press and the eyewitness stories from reporters to bring home to the public the full horror of Auschwitz, Dachau and the rest. Even then the almost unbelievable inhumanity of Hitler's 'final solution' was not fully known.

That the Nazis were capable of organised inhumanity was no great surprise to either Percy or me. We had seen and heard enough of the behaviour of 'Brown Shirts' and 'Black Shirts' on our pre-war visits to Germany. I had argued with pacifist friends when they refused to accept that peace could not be bought at Hitler's price. After the liberation of the concentration camps did they, I wondered, still maintain that the price of fighting fascism by force of arms was too high?

Jutro had barely departed for London when Eddie Meyerstein invited himself for the Easter holiday. He was living in his flat in Greys Inn once again, thankful to be back amongst his books and away from what he liked to describe as 'academic malignity'. Although he preferred to live in London he enjoyed visits to the countryside, especially in spring. Like the minstrel of olden times a poet, he felt, should expect to be welcomed, especially in a literary household.

A fine Easter Saturday gave him the opportunity to combine a country walk with a captive audience. Canfield Church was suggested as a suitable objective and the three of us set off. Percy enjoyed a walk as much as Eddie and the two men kept up a good pace until Eddie, spotting a straw stack, suggested a rest and having seen us settled down in relative comfort whipped his latest narrative poem out of his pocket and proceeded to declaim.

It was a long poem, the straw was tickling and the wind was nippy. My thoughts strayed, but murmurs of appreciation were all that were required; the reading ended and we were allowed to continue our walk.

He had also brought with him his latest literary discovery, a manuscript he had bought in an antiquarian bookshop and was painstakingly editing for publication by the Oxford University Press. It was the journal of Edward Coxere, a 17th century merchant seaman, a colourful character who survived imprisonment by both the Turks and the Spaniards, not to mention a spell in the gaol in Yarmouth, after he had become a Quaker.

Eddie was in high fettle over his discovery and the following year we received a copy of *Adventures by Sea of Edward Coxere*, as a bread and butter present.

'Not a first edition', Percy commented, glancing at the verso of the title page. Presumably Eddie had decided that our hospitality didn't rate higher than a 'second issue'. We had, by then, a shelf-full of his writings, some with rhyming inscriptions. All, up to then, first editions. The Coxere book was to be the last we received for, after his spring visit to us the year following its publication, we were clearly considered undeserving of further inscribed copies. We had on that occasion committed the unforgivable sin of failing to show sufficient appreciation of the miracle play he had brought to read to us, and to the friends we had invited to meet him. I had done my best, but Percy, who disliked miracle plays in general, had not taken part in the rather muted murmurs of praise after the reading.

The letter we received following this visit was an unhappy mixture of malice and self-pity. Like a child whose pride has been wounded, he meant to inflict hurt in return.

I am sure, he wrote, you did *everything* you could, and of course it is interesting for me, as a comparatively unknown man, to watch big business at close quarters ... and when I saw you (Percy) greeting the miracle play with that dignified absence of comment that I have learnt to associate with Oxford and Cambridge intelligentsia, I saw exactly how things would be. Well, one has to live, and as long as one lives for oneself one must, I suppose, try to combine the bray of the

poet and the song of the rentier ... don't think me bitter ... for I have
no happiness except in lonely creative struggles (though thank God
there are no wife and brats clamouring for the results of *work that pays
in the offing*) ...

After a dig at me ...

casual ruthlessness combined with absence of mind are grand assets
for the battle of life ...

he concluded that

it is probably very good for me to pay such visits once a year. It will
be long before I forget standing on the Takeley Rd., outside your
gate in the night air, invited to listen to 'our nightingales'.

The letter finished with:

Always with genuine wonderment,
Yours, E.H.W. Meyerstein.

After we had digested this curious 'Collins' we decided that such
visits were not really very good for us, even if they were for Eddie.
Alas, many of Eddie's friendships had ended in this way.

Through our introduction he had sometimes contributed to *The
Music Review* and he did come once more to Takeley, this time to stay
with the Sharps. On that occasion he walked up the road to pay us an
afternoon call. We invited him to stay for tea; he did so and was on his
best behaviour. When he bade us good-bye there was, I thought, a
gleam of malice in his eyes as he bowed with exaggerated courtesy and
thanked me for 'my kind hospitality'. It was the last time I saw him
although Percy, subsequently, bought some books from him at his flat
in Grey's Inn.

The literary success that had eluded him for so long came shortly
before his death in 1952 with the acclaim for his novel *Robin Wastraw*,
followed by *Tom Tallion*, published the year of his death, when some
critics compared him with Dickens and others with Defoe.

After Jutro's departure it was, admittedly, pleasant to have the home
to ourselves, our spare room free for guests of our own choice. I used to
worry that those who shared our home, temporarily, during the war
years, might sometimes feel that we wished them elsewhere — as from
time to time we did. But they, poor things, were in the same boat; they
were stuck with us. I tried — most of the time — to be a good hostess,

but war-time life with the Muirs was a far cry from gracious living. A hotel rating might perhaps have given us one star, rather grudgingly, allowing that the meals weren't bad, considering. But many points would have been lost on account of draughts, beams for bumping heads on, children and cats underfoot, cold bedrooms, a single loo for the whole household, unpredictable plumbing and periodical outbursts of matrimonial discord which came, like a summer storm and, though as quickly forgotten by the protagonists, could be trying for an unwilling onlooker. These, and occasional absent-mindedness on the part of the hostess when in the throes of literary creation were some of the disadvantages of staying with the Muirs.

For Percy, the sharing of our domestic life with a third party had been harder than it had been for me. He was not gregarious by nature, pubs and clubs had little appeal for him. Happy though he would be to spend an evening with friends of his own choice, he was just as happy to spend it beside his own hearth, reading or listening to the radio, preferably with the children tucked up safely in bed.

In the post-war years Elkin Mathews would call on our spare room again when Percy's cousin, Laurie Deval, stayed with us during his apprenticeship to the firm, and there would be a couple of young Frenchmen aspiring to be antiquarian booksellers, one of whom, reluctant to learn English, greatly improved my French. Laurie, in due course, became a partner. The young Frenchmen failed to stay the course.

CHAPTER THIRTY-ONE

As the Allied forces swept on through Germany and the Russians neared Berlin, there was endless speculation as to what Hitler might or might not do. Would he retreat to the Bavarian Alps and carry on a resistance movement from his redoubt at Berchtesgarten? Would he escape with other Nazi leaders to some already planned sanctuary in South America? Was he, perhaps, already on his way there in a submarine, leaving a double posing as the Führer in Berlin? It was all uninformed conjecture and profitless, but the subject was irresistible.

We had seen the grim pictures of Mussolini's undignified end, his body strung upside down from a gibbet, beside his mistress's, like a carcase of meat at a slaughter house, an execution carried out by his own people — pictures I have never been able to forget. When Hitler's end came I was glad that there was nothing for the cameras to film.

It was on May Day that we heard the news that he had died by his own hand, with Eva Braun beside him, in his Berlin bunker. At first after the discovery of the charred bodies there had been rumours that the body, supposed to be Hitler's, was really that of his double. Then came a statement that the body was undoubtedly his.

My own feeling was one of intense relief. I did not care how he had died. It was enough that he was dead, along with the equally fanatical Geobbels, who after administering poison to his six children had, by his own orders, been shot, with his wife, by an S.S. guard. I was thankful that the world had been spared the spectacle of Hitler and his Propaganda Minister posturing at the war criminal trials, still able to disseminate evil and perhaps even then succeeding in influencing the young and credulous with their repulsive beliefs.

A week later I recorded briefly in my diary: 'End of war in Europe announced soon after 7 p.m. ...' We had been awaiting this official announcement throughout the week-end, since the news had come of the German armies' surrender on May 4th. I had put the children to bed and Percy and I were sitting quietly in the sitting room contemplating the future, as people do after a life-threatening operation when they are told that their recovery is assured.

The B.B.C. had just announced that the next two days, Tuesday and Wednesday would be official holidays and known as V.E.1 and

218

V.E.2 — V.E. standing for Victory in Europe, to remind us that this was only a part-peace, that the war against Japan was still to be won and might continue for a long time yet.

Left on our own Percy and I would probably have stayed quietly at home that first evening of peace in Europe, had not our neighbours Fran and Margaret Kent arrived in high spirits, eager to begin celebrating without delay.

'We're going to drive up to London,' they said. 'We're going right away. Why not come with us? It's a historic occasion, after all, we can't just stick around here in the village'.

I looked at Percy. Rather to my surprise he was in favour of the idea, for he was not given to parties on the impulse of the moment. But the Kents had infected us both with their enthusiasm. I ran across the road to ask our handyman and his wife to sit in for me and the four of us set off.

It was a fine spring evening; with double summer time it was light until nearly ten o'clock and London was only an hour's drive at that time of day.

As we drove through the blossoming countryside, passing green cornfields and lush meadows dotted with grazing cattle, an aircraft, silvered in the sunshine, drew a long fluffy vapour trail acros the sky. No need to wonder any more where it came from. We had been fortunate, the countryside was much as it had been in 1939; the few small scars, the bomb craters, had been covered and healed by nature. The army Nissen huts would go. As for the airfield at Stansted, we supposed then that it would go too, the fields return to farming.

All was quiet in the villages as we headed for the A.11. Here and there a Union Jack hung from a window, but few people were about. There was little traffic on the roads; the evening sunshine warmed the mellow old houses along Epping's long high street, as deserted as the villages. Sunshine filtered through the freshly green leaves of the beech trees in the forest; then we were through Woodford Green, and coming into the drab, war-scarred East End with its boarded up houses, crumbling, weed-sprouting half-houses, factories, litter-strewn bomb sites, grey-brick Victorian Gothic schools and grubby little corner shops doggedly surviving. Here and there bunting was going up, and youths were piling rubbish on bomb sites for the next day's celebratory bonfires. After all it had been a working day and a Monday at that. The East End worked long hours, but with the next day a holiday, the pubs would soon be filling up.

We were making, inevitably, for the West End. We were on a pilgrimage of sorts, with Piccadilly Circus as our Mecca. The traffic thickened as we came into Regent Street; we parked in Golden Square, then joined the flow of people heading for the Circus, linking arms to keep together as the pressure carried us along the pavement until we reached an unoccupied shop doorway on the corner of Windmill Street. There, having eased ourselves out of the stream, we paused to view the scene. The crowds flowed past us through the Circus, young and not so young, a few in uniform, mostly civilians, laughing good-humouredly like a bank holiday crowd. Sometimes the flow would check and coagulate as ever more streams of people converged from a different direction; some, like us, dropped out to pause and let the rest go by.

There were no excited revellers, no strangers embracing (that may have come later) no obvious drunks, just a lot of people moving around or across the Circus, smiling amiably, feeling, perhaps, as we did that it was enough just to be there on that first night of peace in Europe after five and a half years of war.

As we stood there I saw a couple of American airmen emerge from the Underground in front of Swan and Edgars. Tall, uniformed figures they paused for a moment surveying the scene, broad smiles on their faces, then they swung round the corner into Piccadilly and out of sight.

Daylight had faded, the lights were on; once again the Circus was brightly lit. There against the darkening sky were the familiar outlines of the encompassing buildings, survivors of the Blitz, the London Fire Insurance building, the London Pavilion, the Criterion. Eros, absent since 1939 for safety's sake, would soon return. The Circus had become shabby, like the rest of us, but it could still exercise its old magnetic pull.

From the Circus we moved on to Trafalgar Square. There were the same good-humoured crowds, savouring the first hours of peace amongst the lions and the hungry pigeons; children ran around and hawkers, quick off the mark, were selling flags. We considered going to Buckingham Palace, or maybe Downing Street, but I had promised my obliging 'sitters-in' that we wouldn't be very late and I had plans for a Victory party the next day. So we set off for home, happy and still stone cold sober.

There were, in the village, families who had a son or a husband in a Japanese prisoner of war camp; for those, and for other families who had been bereaved, the general rejoicing must have rung hollow. In Takeley Street one son would return home from a Japanese camp, one husband would not. While rejoicing, no one could forget that we were still at war.

Nevertheless V.E.1 and V.E.2 were days of celebration with bands playing, bonfires blazing and the pubs full. Drink hoarded for the occasion was brought out of cupboards for celebrating at home and food was pooled.

Determined to have my own party, I hastily collected all our friends within range, dipped into my reserves of tinned food and bundled the children off to bed before the evening revelry began, with a promise of a picnic with some of their own friends on V.E.2 and permission to stay up for our street bonfire afterwards. This time, with no bathtub hooch to poison us, there were no casualties on the morrow.

As a family we had been fortunate, we had come through the war years unscarred, our home hardly damaged. The years ahead would be full ones for us both. Earlier in 1945 Elkin Mathews had acquired a show room in Cambridge over Gray's book-bindery where one day our son would learn the craft of book-binding. Soon Percy would take over the lease of a book-shop in Bishop's Stortford and for three years we would sell new books from there, which would mean a seven-day working week. But three years was quite enough of that.

Nineteen forty-six would see Percy elected President of the Antiquarian Booksellers' Association. While in office he would ensure that the Association backed the founding of an international association — the I.L.A.B. of which he would become the second President.

The years ahead would not be tranquil ones. There would be lecture tours, much travelling and too much committee work — for both of us. Only on book buying trips abroad when we were able to snatch a few days holiday in Salzburg, or by the sea in some little French town where the sun shone and the wine was good and cheap, would there be time to 'stand and stare' — or, rather more in our line, to potter around in old churches and eat and drink with friends.

Could I have had a pre-view of our life together during those busy years I doubt if I would have wished it otherwise.

Index

Note

Where fictitious names have
been used these do not appear in
the index.

200Tmk